FIRST AMONG EQUALS

For Bron

FIRST AMONG EQUALS

Prime Ministers in
Westminster Systems

PATRICK WELLER

GEORGE ALLEN & UNWIN
Sydney London Boston

© Patrick Weller 1985
This book is copyright under the Berne Convention. No reproduction
without permission. All rights reserved.

First published in 1985
George Allen & Unwin Australia Pty Ltd
8 Napier Street, North Sydney NSW 2060

George Allen & Unwin (Publishers) Ltd
18 Park Lane, Hemel Hempstead, Herts HP2 4TE England

Allen & Unwin Inc.
Fifty Cross Street, Winchester, Mass 01890 USA

National Library of Australia
Cataloguing-in-Publication entry:

Weller, Patrick, 1944– .
    First among equals.

    Bibliography.
    Includes index.
    ISBN 0 86861 500 5.
    ISBN 0 86861 508 0 (pbk.).

    1. Prime ministers—Australia. 2. Prime ministers—
    Canada. 3. Prime ministers—New Zealand. 4. Prime
    ministers—Great Britain. 5. Legislative bodies—
    Australia. 6. Legislative bodies—Canada.
    7. Legislative bodies—New Zealand. 8. Legislative
    bodies—Great Britain. I. Title.

324.2'2

Set in 10/11.5 Bembo by Asco Trade Typesetting Ltd, Hong Kong
Printed by Bright Sun (Shenzhen) Printing Co. Ltd, China

Contents

Tables

Abbreviations

ALP	Australian Labor Party
CEC	Cabinet Economic Committee (New Zealand)
CHOGM	Commonwealth Heads of Government Meeting
CP	Country Party (Australia)
CPRS	Central Policy Review Staff (UK)
EEC	European Economic Community
FPRO	Federal-Provincial Relations Office (Canada)
ILP	Independent Labour Party (UK)
IMF	International Monetary Fund
MoD	Ministry of Defence (UK)
NCP	National Country Party (Australia)
NEC	National Executive Committee (Labour, UK)
NZBC	New Zealand Broadcasting Corporation
P&P	Priorities and Planning (Cabinet committee, Canada)
PC	Progressive Conservative (Party, Canada)
PCO	Privy Council Office (Canada)
PLP	Parliamentary Labour Party (UK)
PMC	(Department of) Prime Minister and Cabinet (Australia)
PMO	Prime Minister's Office (Australia and Canada)
PRS	Priorities Review Staff (Australia)

Acknowledgements

Writing a comparative study of prime ministers in four parliamentary systems has inevitably incurred widespread debts. I have consistently relied on the advice and assistance of people who know the details of their own system far better than I ever could; they have provided me with background information, allowed me to try out my ideas and tentative conclusions, corrected my more blatant errors and helped guide this book along its somewhat rocky road.

Of all those from whom I received that assistance and advice, I would like to thank in particular David Butler, Peter Self, Lord Crowther-Hunt, George Jones, Tony King and William Plowden in Britain; Bruce Doern, J.R. Mallory and Richard Simeon in Canada; Peter Aimer and Keith Jackson in New Zealand. I was a visiting professor in the department of public administration at Carleton University in 1980 and that gave me the great advantage of contacts in Ottawa.

On my visits I stayed with Jim Mallory, Richard Simeon, Keith Jackson and Peter Aimer; Trish Donelley and Tony Haas took in a stranger and made my stay in Wellington most enjoyable. I would like to thank all for their hospitality.

An earlier version of Chapter 3 was published as 'The Vulnerability of Prime Ministers: A Comparative Perspective' in *Parliamentary Affairs* 36(1), Winter 1983; an earlier version of Chapter 6 was published as 'Do Prime Ministers' Departments Really Create Problems?' in *Public Administration*, 61, Spring 1983. They are reprinted here with permission.

In Canberra Nancy Sever, Ellen Ruffles and Kerry Nixon deciphered, typed and retyped drafts of the book with considerable skill. Susan Fraser, Virginia Cook and Stephen Hunter were at different times most conscientious research assistants. Robert Parker, Keith Jackson, Peter Loveday, David Adams and Glyn Davis read parts of the book in draft form and provided comments that have both reduced the errors and improved what remains. It is not their fault if I will not listen to good advice. I am grateful to them all for their help in the production of the book.

My greatest debt must be to those who remain unnamed. The prime ministers, ministers, civil servants and participants (both past and present) in the four countries who gave readily of their time and their views. The unattributable nature of their contribution should not be taken to undervalue its importance. Without it, the book would have been almost impossible to write.

Patrick Weller
Canberra
June 1984

1

Prime Ministers and Power

'The influence of the crown has increased, is increasing and ought to be diminished': this famous motion. by Dunning was passed in the House of Commons in 1780. Two hundred years later similar comments are made about the power of prime ministers. Their influence is said to have increased to a level at which it cannot be checked; their control over government activities is regarded as excessive, and their accountability as far too limited. Observers complain that the system has changed from cabinet government to prime ministerial government, or that the office of prime minister has been 'presidentialised'. As a result the prime ministership has been the subject of proposals designed to limit its power. These views have been expressed most frequently in Britain, where debate on the subject has continued for twenty years, but similar feelings are noticeable in other parliamentary democracies like Canada, Australia and New Zealand.

Obviously the power wielded by prime ministers is substantial. They hold the key position at the 'apex of power' in democratic governments. Government are as often known by the names of the leader as by his or her party; the Trudeau, Thatcher, Hawke and Muldoon governments are terms as common as the Liberal, Conservative, Labor or National governments. The media concentrate their attention on what prime ministers say and do. Prime ministers represent their countries overseas. Therefore knowledge of what they do, how they relate to other parts of the political system, what options are available to them, is essential to an understanding of the way we are governed.

How powerful are they? The question is of fundamental importance. In a parliamentary democracy the language of government is collective. We speak of collective ministerial responsibility and of party control of parliament. The main decision-making body is said to be cabinet; its decisions are authoritative. Prime ministers are not presidents, that is individuals at the top of the pile; they are the leaders of teams. The processes of government have been developed on the assumption that these constitutional doctrines are accurate. Ministers sit at the head of departments which they must run and for which they, not the prime minister, are constitutionally responsible. If this assumption is mistaken—and that has still to be proved—then the impact on government will be considerable. For instance, some senior public servants in Australia believe that a move towards a 'presidential' style has deepened the gap between ministers and their departments because lines of accountability are blurred. Ministers, they argue, are too concerned with the prime minister's demands to act effectively as head of departments. The change in the prime minister's power has overstrained a structure still nominally directed to service the processes of a collective government. The misfit creates serious functional problems: procedures designed to serve cabinet are not well-suited to an individual's decision-making. That claim of prime ministerial power may be exaggerated, but the necessity of fitting form with function remains. At the same time, if a new set of arrangements is introduced to reflect accurately the distribution of power, those changes might undermine consitutional myths that are in themselves useful as a means of making the process easier to defend in public and in parliament.

It is necessary to understand the scope that prime ministers may have for wielding authority, if only to explore the reality that exists behind those myths. Realistic approaches to structural or procedural reform are likely to occur only if we know what it is that needs change. Does the prime minister need greater bureaucratic support? To make any assessment of that we need to know what is currently available, how well it works and what problems need to be solved. In a sense this is repeating Anthony King's (1969: ix) plea that we need to describe the prime minister's job so that we can understand it better. Yet research on prime ministerial power has been as indecisive as the debate. In part that may be due to the nature of the subject. Obviously it is difficult to predict precisely how prime ministers will react in any given situation, and discussion will always be surrounded by caveats; 'if' and 'maybe' are common riders.

Despite these problems, royal commissions, parliamentary committees, disappointed practitioners and academic observers have presented a series of proposals designed to alter the prime ministers' position. Some want to increase their power, to introduce greater authority at the centre as a means of establishing more cohesive and purposive government (e.g. Blondel 1982; Dell 1980; Hoskyns 1983; Berrill 1980). Others want to decrease or limit this power in order to balance the authority of prime ministers with that of the party or the parliament (Benn 1981; Sedgemore 1980). The proposals pose interesting questions. For instance, what would be the impact of a prime minister's department in Britain; or the consequence of an elected ministry? Many of the suggested reforms pay little attention to experiments tried elsewhere and to what extent these have succeeded. They are often limited and culture-bound, and based on guesswork when they need not be, for there is a plethora of experience on which to draw if observers chose to look further afield.

This book is an attempt to take the debate on prime ministerial power a few stages further. By comparing the position of the prime ministers in four parliamentary or 'Westminister' systems, it will:

1 Seek to identify the factors that assist or constrain prime ministers in the exercise of their power. The comparative approach will allow factors often taken for granted in studies of single countries to be seen in a clearer light. It therefore attempts to understand the environment in which prime ministers must work, the impact that environment has on their actions and the ability that they have to influence government decisions.

2 Use the empirical evidence drawn from the four countries to examine some of the proposals for bureaucratic or political change that have been suggested as a means of changing the prime ministers' position one way or another. Many of these are system-bound or culture-bound and the comparative material can give some indication of what *might* happen if they were introduced.

3 Ask whether there is, can be, or ought to be, a job description for prime ministers. Many observers approach their studies of prime ministers with implicit normative views of what prime ministers *ought* to do. This study asks how valuable and how accurate those approaches are. If prime ministers effectively make their own rules within the limits of the institutions they operate, is there any point in trying to be prescriptive?

This is an institutional study, not a particular study of how any one prime minister works or how prime ministers work in any one country. It intends to explore the nature of the job, the institutional frameworks within which prime ministers live and the constraints which they must accept. It is intended as an argument, rather than a full account of everything prime ministers do. Description is therefore provided only as far as it is needed for the argument, and secondary sources are used wherever available. Indeed the literature of memoirs and analysis is excellent for a study of the British prime minister; it is adequate for Canada too. In Australia it is almost non-existent, despite the prevalence of many legends, and much basic work is still required. In New Zealand there is little contemporary literature. The secondary sources are supported by a series of interviews undertaken in Britain in 1979–80, in Canada in 1976 and 1980, in New Zealand in 1983, and at

various times in Australia between 1976 and 1983. Material derived from those sources is always unattributable. However this analysis is less concerned with uncovering new facts than with trying to make sense of the ones we know.

THE DEBATE ON PRIME MINISTERIAL OR CABINET GOVERNMENT

The view that prime ministers have become pre-eminent was first expounded in detail by John Mackintosh in his study of the British cabinet (1962, 1968, 1977). It was then popularised—and at times in Mackintosh's opinion (1977: 629) extended to an unwarranted degree—by Richard Crossman's introduction (1963) to Walter Bagehot's *The English Consitution*. Crossman restated his views, with the benefit of six years of ministerial experience, in the Godkin Lectures presented at Harvard in 1970 and later published as *Inside View* (1972). He then provided massive (if at times contradictory) evidence in his three volumes of *The Diaries of a Cabinet Minister* (1975, 1976, 1977). Mackintosh answered critics of his argument in a series of books and articles (1974, 1977a), although in the third edition of *The British Cabinet* he did not tackle them directly because he believed that 'events since [1962: the date of his first edition] have done so much to confirm the general case argued in this book' (1977: 631).

Reduced to simplified form, the argument of Crossman and Mackintosh is that the prime ministers' powers were exerted through their control over several important levers. The first two are traditional:

1 The right to select and dismiss ministers. All ministers are chosen by prime ministers and depend on them for their jobs. Even though some ministers may be chosen because of their position in the party, prime ministers can keep out those whom they do not want.
2 The right to control cabinet's structure and proceedings. Prime ministers control access to cabinet through the agenda, chair the meetings, summarise the decisions, decide the composition and subject matter of cabinet committees and may limit decisions to meetings of inner or partial cabinets.

These two levers have existed for over 150 years, although their value has been extended by the increase in the workload of cabinet and in the size of ministries. To these have been added four other factors:

3 The development of disciplined parties, which support prime ministers and try to guarantee that they can maintain a parliamentary majority.

4 The increased direct influences of the media. Since the media concentrate on the figure at the top, prime ministers can use that attention for their own purposes. The immediacy of access to the general public provided by the electronic media and the development of a mass, and manipulable, press have provided great opportunities for prime ministers to get their message across.

5 The increase in the levels of prime ministerial patronage. — support

6 The development of the new processes of co-ordination have provided sources of intelligence and manipulation which allow prime ministers to control the large bureaucratic machines of which they are the head.

The general argument can be summarised by two passages. Mackintosh's original proposition, re-affirmed fourteen years later, stated:

> The country is governed by the Prime Minister who leads, coordinates and maintains a series of Ministers, all of whom are advised and backed by the Civil Service. Some decisions are taken by the Prime Minister alone, some in consultation between him and the Senior Ministers, while others are left to the heads of departments, the Cabinet, Cabinet Committees, or the permanent officials... There is no single catch-phrase that can describe this form of government, but it may be pictured as a cone. The Prime Minister stands at the apex, supported by and giving power to a widening series of rings of senior ministers, the Cabinet, its Committees, non-Cabinet Ministers, and departments. Of these rings, the only one above the level of the Civil Service that has formal existence and acts as a court of appeal for the lower tiers is the Cabinet. (1962: 451–2; 1977: 541–2; for the reaffirmation, see 1977a: 6–7)

Crossman's formulation was slightly different. He relegated cabinet to join the other dignified, if unimportant, parts of the constitution and argued that the prime minister was 'now the apex not only of a highly centralised political machine, but also of an equally centralised and vastly more powerful administrative machine' (1965: 51). Then, adjusting Bagehot's view of cabinet to his own purposes, he wrote: 'The post-war epoch has seen the final transformation of Cabinet Government into Prime Ministerial Government. Under this system "the hyphen which joins, the buckle which fastens", the legislative part of the state to the executive has become one man' (1965: 51).

These two passages indicate the degree to which Crossman extended Mackintosh's argument. Yet there is considerable similarity between the two in the predominance given to the prime minister as the centre of most action. Neither argues that prime ministers make *all* the decisions or that they can ignore their ministerial colleagues; but they do suggest that prime ministers have few limitations on their power, that they decide where decisions will be taken and often what they will be.

Critics of Crossman and Mackintosh argue that the picture they paint exaggerates prime ministerial power. George Jones has consistently argued that they underestimate the power of ministers who can have an independent influence; the prime minister is only as powerful as his or her colleagues allow; they are restricted in their choice of ministers and in their treatment of cabinet (Jones 1969). Jones provides an epigrammatic summary of his counterview: 'The British system of government cannot really be called prime ministerial government, nor cabinet government. The right term is ministerial government' (1979: 1). Patrick Gordon Walker, like Crossman writing with the benefit of considerable ministerial experience, is concerned with one basic question and its answer: 'Where does political authority lie? Where can the great political decisions be made? I hope to have shown that the answer in Britain is in the Cabinet and in the Cabinet alone' (Gordon Walker 1972: 162). He argues that, despite obvious shortcomings as an efficient decision-making body—a function for which it was not designed—cabinet is never the creature of the prime minister. Ronald Butt (1969) has argued that parliament too is more influential than Mackintosh and Crossman suggest and that it cannot be taken for granted by the prime minister. Ian Gilmour (1969) suggests that the power of the great departments of state is such that they can act as a counterweight and that British government is thus self-limiting. In turn, these writers have tried to reinstate the power of ministers, cabinet, parliament and the civil service against the claims of prime ministerial power.

Prime ministers too have denied that they hold the excessive power attributed to them by Mackintosh and Crossman. Macmillan (Evans 1981: 289) and Heath (*Listener*, 22 April 1976) both declared that they would not take important decisions without consulting cabinet. (They did not indicate whether they felt certain of carrying cabinet with them when they did consult.) Wilson declared that the

> predominantly academic verdict of overriding prime ministerial power is wrong. It ignores the system of democratic checks and balances, in Parliament, in the Cabinet, and not least in the party machine and the party in the country... Cabinet is a democracy, not an autocracy; each member of it, including the prime minister, seeks to convince his colleagues as to the course to follow. The Cabinet bears his stamp, it is true, on each and every policy issue, but it is the Cabinet, not the prime minister, who decides. (1976: 20, 21)

Of the people interviewed for this study, those closest to a prime

minister were always most conscious of the limitations on prime ministerial power.
It is easy to overstate either side of the case (see Mackintosh 1977a: 15).
By extracting general propositions stated in absolute terms, and then testing them against empirical evidence and individual events, it is fairly easy to disprove any notion as broad and vague as prime ministerial dominance.
An argument that prime ministers will always dominate their cabinet can be discredited by finding examples where they have been overruled, but a few instances do not disprove a general tendency concerned with the distribution of power.
Obviously propositions about absolute authority serve little use: prime ministers are part of political systems, interaction is continuous, calculations of advantage and position are consistently re-evaluated.
To present an argument on the grounds that one side will always win is too crude.
In 1975 Tony King was critical of the literature on both sides:

> Unfortunately, neither side has ever specified in any detail what is takes the term 'prime ministerial government' to mean and therefore what its empirical referents are; both sides, instead of analyzing the available evidence systematically, have resorted to proof by illustration... As a result most of the debate has been conducted at the level of a barroom brawl. Some good points have been made, just as at least a few good punches are landed in most barroom brawls. But remarkably little new evidence has been forthcoming and the terms of the debate in the 1970s are almost exactly what they were in the early 1960s. (1975: 232–3)

Little has changed; there has been no effort to define the terms, in part, perhaps, because of the inherent difficulty of doing so within the confines of a single country.

The argument has been contested most fervently in Britain, but it has been joined on similar lines in other countries with parliamentary systems of government. In Canada the long terms that many prime ministers have served may have helped the case; Trudeau, after all, was prime minister for fifteen years, with only one break of nine months; Mackenzie King held office for twenty years, thirteen of them unbroken. Following the development of the British argument, in 1969 Denis Smith argued that Trudeau was clearly trying to presidentialise the system and spoke of his 'unerring presidential instincts' (1977: 322): he concluded that Canada has 'created ... a presidential system without its congressional advantages'. His summary is worthy of inclusion alongside those of Mackintosh and Crossman:

> Before the accession of Pierre Trudeau, our presidential system, however, was diffuse and ill-organized. But Pierre Trudeau is extraordinarily clear-headed and realistic about the sources of political power in Canada. On the

one hand, he has recognized the immense power of initiative and guidance that exists in the federal bureaucracy; and he has seen that this great instrument of power lacked effective centralized political leadership. He has created that coordinated leadership by organizing around him a presidential office, and by bringing order and discipline to the Cabinet's operations. He has made brilliant use of the public opportunities of a party leader, in convention, in the general election, and in his continuing encounters outside Parliament. He has recognized that the public responds first to personalities, not to issues, and so he campaigns for the most generalised mandate. And now, finally, he has successfully altered the procedures of the House of Commons so that it may serve the legislative purpose of an efficient presidential administration. (1977: 323)

Others have emphasised Trudeau's dominant, if changing, role (Campbell 1980). Yet this has also been challenged by arguments similar to those espoused in Britain (see the contributions to Hockin 1977; Punnett 1977; Matheson 1976). One senior official commented that the presidential image was a 'figment of the non-accountable media's imagination, nurtured to the point of a vendetta'. He argued that Canadian prime ministers, and particularly Trudeau, were usually powerful but patient.

In New Zealand, writers in the late 1960s and early 1970s were careful to point out that their country had *not* followed British trends and they deliberately repudiated the idea of prime ministerial government. Austin Mitchell wrote that, even if the prime minister is more than the first among equals, Mackintosh's views are 'clearly [too sweeping] for New Zealand. Powerful as the Prime Minister is, he remains the leader of a team rather than conductor of an orchestra' (1966: 30). Keith Jackson concluded that 'the controversy about prime ministerial (or presidential-type) politics which has aroused great interest in British political circles hardly applies in New Zealand... New Zealand Cabinets work far more as a team than their British counterpart' (1973: 161). These observations pre-dated the accession of the pugnacious Rob Muldoon to the prime ministership.

In Australia there is less academic literature on the question. Several journalists emphasise the central role of prime ministers, particularly of Menzies, Whitlam and Fraser (for Fraser, see Schneider 1980), and attribute to them considerable power. While the discussion is seldom systematic, belief in over-powerful prime ministers has become orthodox. Some challenges in works tangentially concerned with the subject have been made (see Hawker *et al.* 1979; Weller and Grattan 1981).

In all four countries the argument has two interrelated parts: the first is that the power of the prime minister has *increased*; the second tries to identify how much power a modern prime minister *actually has*. Both issues have been debated at some length, but more recently debate has concentrated on the second—which raises questions of more immediate importance.

The argument for the increase in power is that when changes in the party and media are coupled with the existing controls over cabinet and patronage, the prime ministers' powers must be enlarged. Whether that growth has been gradual or spasmodic is disputed (see Brown 1969), and there are problems of comparisons of historical material. Given that the scope of government has increased dramatically, that modern economic management has extended the government's tentacles and public expectations, and that many of the processes have altered, it is questionable how realistic historical comparisons are. It might be possible to argue that Sir Robert Peel had greater control over his ministers than Douglas Home, while still being able to argue that his national influence over the people was much less. But that would be as much a comment on the impact of government as on the power of the prime minister. Some of the political conventions and institutions may have remained, but the environment in which politicians work has become very different. Comparing the actions of prime ministers across a century (e.g. Punnett 1977) understates the pressures of modern society. For that reason, the analysis in this work will concentrate on politics since 1945—a period of Keynesian and post-Keynesian economics, high expectations, mass media, international interdependence, and other modern political problems. Obviously at the time each problem appears to be unique, but in general terms the functions of government have not changed as dramatically in these post-war years as they did in the preceding equivalent period.

The second theme in the debate concerns the power of modern prime ministers. What capacity do they have to get their own way? The immediate problem that confronts such a debate is one of personality. The important factor, it is argued, is not institutions but individuals. Modern prime ministers are uncommon creatures. In the 1945–82 period there were nine prime ministers in Britain, six in Canada, eight in New Zealand and nine in Australia. Those small numbers make classifications difficult and allow considerable scope for differing explanations on the basis of style.

Obviously personality and style do make a difference. As Rose (1980: 43) comments, 'In the most trivial sense there *is* a difference in personality and style between Prime Ministers. Clement Attlee was not Winston Churchill, nor was Edward Heath the same sort of politician as Harold Wilson'. The influence of particular individuals also changes over time: electoral success, public prestige and a high professional reputation give prime ministers authority that can easily be diminished when those temporary advantages disappear. The Attlee of 1945, fresh from a great victory and surrounded by powerful lieutenants, was in a different position from the tired man of 1951. So too the Trudeau of 1968 from the withdrawn leader of 1975, or Holyoake in 1960 and 1971. Political circumstances and individual energies lead to variations in prime ministerial power that are perhaps as great as changes of people. Of course the final policy outcomes would be different if the prime ministers were to be changed; no-one would seriously argue that prime ministers have no influence. Yet systematically relating personality to patterns of outcome is probably impossible.

Research on prime ministerial power can be concerned with identifying the framework and processes which *do* limit or assist the influence of personalities and which shape those outcomes. Rose (1980: 44) argues that prime ministers are inevitably constrained by traditional expectations.

> There are certain roles that all Prime Ministers must undertake. While individual Prime Ministers may respond differently to the demands of office, the imperatives tend to remain constant.
>
> The high degree of institutionalization in British government— encompassing informal Whitehall norms even more than formal organizations—is the most powerful determinant of what a Prime Minister can or can not do. Personal style influences how a Prime Minister carries out the demands of office, but it does not determine what is to be done. The first priority of a Prime Minister is to do what is expected of him or her.

To examine institutions rather than personalities is not to deny the importance of the latter, but rather to concentrate on the framework within which they must work.

Institutional arrangements make demand on prime ministers, who have a limited amount of time. If they first do what they must, that is if they first obey the institutional and normative imperatives of office, only then do they have the scope to make choices of what to do with the remaining time. Imperatives may be created by the demands of the job or by the expectations of their colleagues and the wider public. It is important therefore to understand these norms and imperatives, to be aware of what the expectations are and how they work. A systematic study of prime ministerial power must be concerned with the institutional and conventional sources of authority, within which personalities can operate. An understanding of those structures provides initial insights; an awareness of how they can be or have been changed can show what opportunities also exist for prime ministers to extend their positions. Norms can be challenged or examined, their strength analysed and the alternative options sketched out.

Yet even such an apparently obvious process has its problems. The first is concerned with the identification of prime ministerial influence. Cabinet government is collective government. Some decisions may be made individually by prime ministers; many more are formally made, or at least endorsed, by cabinet. It is often difficult to identify the impact of prime ministers, or to discover who makes the important decisions. In a presidential system the issue is more straightforward. The question is not whether the president has the constitutional power, but how that power can be used. Richard Neustadt's most celebrated finding—that the presidents' power is the power to persuade—was important in that it emphasised the limitations of presidential power and the means that have to be adopted to get things done. His interpretation of 'persuade' was broad; its usefulness was to show how limited was the presidents' power to command, though some of their tools of persuasion would be hard to resist. That conclusion was within the context of a system where, at least formally, the president is assumed to have the power to command. In a prime ministerial system such a distinction tells us little. Prime ministers *only* have the power to 'persuade'. Statutory responsibility is usually vested elsewhere, with departmental ministers. Prime ministers generally act through their colleagues—at least nominally.

To agree that prime ministers only have the power to persuade is not a very useful conclusion, though it is useful as a general reminder. We also need to know *how* prime ministers persuade. If they are dominant, what levers of power can they use? Why do ministers often accept directions, if they are not constitutionally required to?

This question goes to the basis of the prime ministerial position. To adopt the term used by Burns (1978), it is *transactional* leadership. Prime ministers are party leaders; they hold the former position only as long as they hold the latter. They have been chosen or elected in order to deliver political success, ideological satisfaction or party unity—or combinations of these and other aims. They survive as long as they lead their party and maintain a parliamentary majority. Of course their position is more powerful than that of a party leader—the resources available to a national leader are both material and psychological—but their position is still based on that original transaction with the party. What is more, the troops in the army need to be led; the prime minister needs to understand what they want and how they feel. One Australian senator once criticised Malcolm Fraser's style: 'You confuse leadership with command' (Schneider 1980: 6).

Prime ministers cannot act purely as dictators. They may get away with what they can; but they cannot habitually ignore their supporters and expect to survive. It is therefore crucial to discover how extensive that freedom to act is and in what circumstances it can be used.

These problems of studying the power of prime ministers are increased by the difficulty of examining political figures who play many roles at once—as party leader, public figure, cabinet chairman and so on. In his book on *Presidential Power* Neustadt (1970) criticises studies that examine the president separately in each of his various hats; he is more concerned to describe how the president protects his power stakes. Obviously he has an important point: to discuss in isolation the role of a prime minister as chairman of cabinet and the powers that that position might give is essentially artificial. Prime ministers play all their roles at once; they are aware in cabinet of public image and of party pressures. Yet for the observer to approach prime ministers as integrated individuals also limits the analysis. Obviously prime ministerial influence may be ubiquitous. Obviously prime ministers are concerned to protect their power stakes (to use Neustadt's term). Obviously power is a limited resource to be husbanded, to be used sparingly at the most apposite moments. Prime ministers will fight hard for some policies, not for others. What is required is an understanding of how, on those occasions they choose to fight, they can win, what factors or patterns of behaviour assist them and why the make *those* choices. Power suggests a relationship. Prime ministers have the power to get others to do what they want. Relationships will change from institution to institution as the resources are different in each case, but resources and relationships must be at the centre of any discussion of prime ministerial power.

These factors become particularly important when the decision *not* to use power that might exist is made, when restraint is exercised. Is that an indication of actual limitations on prime ministerial power or merely a tactical means of gaining a consensus? Crossman (1972: 8) has argued for the second explanation. A decision of a prime minister not to exert full authority is a conscious refusal 'to make use of the powers which now constitutionally belong to his office', even though Crossman did agree that the decision might be 'of his own volition or by force of circumstances'. Rose has argued that 'Prime Ministers accept without hesitation the self-restraint of cooperative government. It is part of the job description' (1980a: 340). Yet if that self-restraint is exercised by 'force of circumstance' or as 'part of the job description', one wonders how much it is indeed *self*-restraint. Presumably it is not simply a decision to be less powerful that day but a calculation about costs and values. To say that a prime minister does not have the political will (an over-used catch-all phrase) to impose his or her view might be to suggest that other political factors make the costs too high. The prime minister's political will is shaped by the influence of those other factors. These, then, are constraints that need to be understood. It is not that prime ministers, often hungry for power, choose to limit themselves; rather the position they are in requires limitation.

It is therefore necessary to be conscious of the different ways in which prime ministers can influence decisions. They can *initiate* or *respond*; that is, the ideas may come from the prime minister and be fed to the minister, or the prime minister may react to other people's proposals. They can be *positive* or *negative*; that is, they can support or stop the proposals that other people are presenting. Prime ministerial support is often seen as important, if not crucial, to the success of a . minister's project. Influence can also be *direct* or *indirect*. A prime minister's power does not have to be used directly in order to exist; people may decide not to act because they anticipate prime ministerial opposition.

If precision is impossible (there are too many variables to predict how a particular individual will react in a given situation), to discuss capacity is not. We can understand what factors/institutions/traditions will assist prime ministers. A basic test can be applied: what is a prime minister's capacity, faced with a problem of any sort, to take *independent* action or, by whatever means, to *influence* or *direct* outcomes. The emphasis is then on intention and capacity. If we can discover the impact of the relationship between prime ministers and various parts of the political systems, the opportunities that they provide or the problems they create, then it may be possible to understand better the prime ministerial job.

It is necessary to add one rider. In this concern to establish who has power, we are concerned to determine who is influential *within* the political system, who decides what the government will try to do. We judge prime ministerial success by its impact on colleagues and the system of government, not on its capacity to make government policy work in society. The latter would bring into play a whole range of questions about the effectiveness of governments in the modern state. In that discussion, the individual influence of prime ministers becomes impossible to isolate (see Mackintosh 1974: 35 for discussion).

Yet power must be relative; one person or institution has power over another. How then can it be identified? When considering the best way to identify the influence of prime ministers, three strategies can be adopted: to compare the power of prime ministers with that of other parts of the political system; to compare the impact of different prime ministers in the same political system; and to compare prime ministers in different political systems. Each has its own problems.

First, it is difficult to compare the power of different institutions. The questions only have to be posed to indicate the problems. Are prime ministers more powerful than cabinet; can they control cabinet? To what degree does the executive dominate parliament? Analyses of these questions in a parliamentary system seldom lead to clear conclusions. The prime minister is part of cabinet, the executive part of parliament. This inconclusiveness of such debate is perhaps inevitable when institutions that derive their power from different sources are compared. It is better to compare like with like; if prime ministers are to be analysed, then surely it is preferable to consider the roles of different prime ministers.

A similar point can be made about advancing the argument within the constraints of a single system. As Rose argued, every prime minister is limited by institutional arrangements and normative expectations. Often these are created by historical traditions or constitutional conventions which are taken for granted as part of the political framework within which actors must work. They are regarded so much as part of the political environment that their political influence is underestimated.

Yet there is nothing sacred about historical traditions; in different countries the parliamentary machinery has developed susbstantially different traditions, leading to a wide range of practices that are all legitimate. There is nothing inherently rigid in any of the systems that need prevent one adopting the procedures of another. Nor is there anything binding about conventions. A convention is a generally accepted practice that helps make a system work smoothly. Once that general acceptance declines, so that its maintenance is no longer of benefit to all practitioners, its lifespan is limited. If the benefits to be gained from breaking conventions outweigh the costs incurred by the condemnation for ignoring them, conventions will be of little value. Besides, prime ministers will often regard such limitations as liable to amendment. They will often try to adjust the rules in mid-stream, to their own advantage. We need therefore to be conscious of the implications and importance of traditions and conventions, of the way they limit and shape our thinking about practical problems, and of their capacity for change. That is difficult to achieve in looking at the one system where, so far, particular conventions are regarded as binding.

A second problem is that, in stable constitutional systems, changes are likely to be marginal and often reversible. Yet because they are the *only* changes, they are credited with great significance, perhaps deservedly, as long as it is realised that they occur *within* the established framework.

Difficulties that occur when that perspective is not maintained can be illustrated by British and Canadian examples. In Britain 'the most significant, though as yet relatively small, institutional change in the political direction of government . . . since 1945 has been the introduction of political advisers into Whitehall offices, including 10 Downing Street' (Rose 1980: 45). Though significant for Britain because of its traditions, this change is not new or unusual for a parliamentary system or a prime minister (see Weller 1983). Institutional assumptions make what may be seen as marginal from other perspectives into a major change within a single system.

For Canada, Denis Smith gives as an indication of presidential tendencies the new rules on the guillotine introduced in 1970: 'the provision meant that if necessary a determined Government could guide a piece of controversial legislation through the House in a minimum of four days of debate over a period of ten sitting days against the protests of the minority' (1977: 322). That change may have appeared to be a dictatorial limitation of parliamentary freedom to debate in Canada, but other parliamentary oppositions would be delighted to be granted so much time to discuss important legislation.

How then can the strengths and weaknesses of prime ministerial positions be more effectively estimated? A third strategy is to compare like with like. King has argued:

> There are two reasons for studying institutions comparatively which, taken singly or together, strongly suggest that single-instance studies are almost bound to be defective. The first is that observing several instances almost invariably leads one to ask questions of each single instance that one would not have asked otherwise... The second reason ... is that unless one does, one has no 'control' in the scientific sense. One does not know what is peculiar to a specific country, what general to a number of countries; one has no means of discovering which correlation among phenomena are accidental or spurious, which are genuinely causal. (1975: 248)

It is of course necessary to compare systems that are sufficiently similar for the impact of established factors to become more obvious. By looking at four similar systems, we can throw the differences that exist into greater relief and assess their importance.

Comparative studies also have their difficulties. The most obvious one might be termed 'trial by anecdote'. Those who have a detailed knowledge of one system can indicate instances where a broad generalisation does not hold and argue that the situation in the country can only be properly understood by reference to the unique features of political tradition and personality. They have a point, perhaps, if explaining the outcome of particular events is the objective. Different historical and social backgrounds have of course led to different practices, expectations and traditions. They matter in determining how the political system has developed and how it works; in the relevant places they can be explored. Superficially identical institutions may work differently in practice—but that is the point of comparison: to establish the different positions of prime ministers and their different strengths and weaknesses. To look at patterns of behaviour is to try to understand what happens most of the time. Only by doing that can we extract from the evidence useful comments about political practice. That is not the same as arguing that the broad patterns can ever be prescriptive; it is saying only that it usually appears to happen this way and that it can be usefully compared with regular practices in other similar polities.

The four parliamentary systems studied in this book—those of Australia, Britain, Canada and New Zealand—developed from the nineteenth-century British parliamentary model. They have all—including that of Britain—developed away from that model in their own way. Yet each has a similar political heritage, similar constitutional assumptions, and similar terminology. In each, cabinet means the same thing and the roles of the prime minister are similar, although by no means identical. As a result, the more subtle differences are easier to identify and their impact is easier to assess.

Consider first the similarities. In all four parliamentary systems prime ministers are heads of political parties whose tenure of office depends on maintaining a majority in parliament. Cabinet contains only parliamentarians. Collective and ministerial responsibility is still regarded as the corner-stone of the constitutional system, even if there is some doubt about how it is to be applied. The bureaucracy is largely anonymous, non-partisan and career-oriented. The constitution—whether or not in written form—leaves a large amount to convention. There are no formal rules prescribing how prime ministers acquire or lose their office (for contrast, see comments on later Westminster-style constitutions in Fry 1983). The prime minister and cabinet may have no formal legal existence; they exist by virtue of tradition and convention. Elections are regular and free. Governments for the past 30 years have been formed from a single party or by the very tight coalition between the Liberal and National (formerly Country) parties in Australia (there was never any serious question of them not combining); more flexible coalition governments are unknown. Many of the symbols and practices are thus the same. To remove any of these common factors would make the process of comparison far more difficult.

The differences are also substantial. Australia and Canada are federations; Britain and New Zealand have unitary systems. Britain and

Canada have powerless upper houses; Australia has an immensely powerful Senate; New Zealand has neither. Australian, New Zealand and British parties are class-based and national in coverage; Canadian parties are not. All four countries differ in the methods they use for choosing prime ministers. The size of each population ranges from 3 million to 60 million. And so on.

The point is not that one model is somehow 'correct' and that others should be judged against it. It is as valid and as useful to talk of the Canberra model (Butler 1973) or the Ottawa model (Campbell 1980) as it is to refer to the Westminster model. It is also valid to assume that there is no one proper way of making systems of parliamentary government work. It would be incorrect to argue that the way the British prime minister works is the way prime ministers *should* operate. The Westminster system has always been sufficiently flexible to allow multiple interpretations of what is proper. There is no theoretical model to be adopted. Rather the four systems have sufficient factors in common to allow them to be used to compare and contrast their procedures in such a way as to emphasize the importance of the structural and traditional as well as the changing balance of power. A comparative study thus allows us to get away from normative ideas of how prime ministers ought to behave.

Systematic and comparative study of the prime ministers in four similar but not identical systems may therefore throw some light on the relationships that prime ministers have with different parts of the political system, on the importance of institutional and traditional forces in forming those relationships and thence on the capacity of prime ministers to use their powers. The test of prime ministerial power must be related to capacity and intent. Even if that test may be impossible to apply rigidly, it provides pointers for discussion.

Each of the following chapters examines one of the important factors that help shape a prime minister's capacities—methods of election and dismissal, links with the party, use of patronage, organisation and running of cabinet, bureaucratic machinery providing policy support to prime ministers, relationship with parliament and impact of the prime minister as public figure. In some areas the distinctions are more marked than others, but each will provide some insights into the different opportunities that prime ministers have and the different problems that they must overcome. The approach in the chapters varies. Some provide brief country-by-country analysis with a comparative conclusion; others are comparative throughout. The strategies are determined by the need to draw out the lessons in the most effective way.

2

Prime Ministers and Party Influence

In the parliamentary systems of Britain, Canada, Australia and New Zealand, parties are the foundations on which prime ministers must build. There the transactional link is most obvious. Prime ministers hold their position because they lead the elected majority in the popular chamber. That majority is maintained by party discipline. As long as prime ministers retain the party's support they *may* continue in office, but as soon as they lose the leadership they lose their job, unless they can exchange the support of one majority for that provided by a different party or coalition of parties. In exchange party members have their own expectations of the leader; these may include electoral success, party unity, ideological direction or combinations of them.

In all four countries the parliamentary parties are, to a greater or lesser extent, coherent, disciplined and ideologically united—at least by contrast to American parties. The leader and the party stand or fall together (the only exceptions when prime ministers switched parties and retained the leadership of the government are Hughes in 1917 in Australia and MacDonald in 1931 in Britain.) The party's success is in the leader's interest; the leader's success is in the party's interest. Co-operation and interdependence are necessary. There may be times of national crisis in which a party does agree to be led without question, but they are rare. Far more often it has to be persuaded that, for its individual and collective benefit, a line of action is desirable. The relationship between the party and the prime minister is continuous. Prime ministers must interact with various parts of the party organisation on a regular basis. Support has to be husbanded and maintained; it can not be taken for granted.

The weapons of persuasion available to a prime minister are in part the subject of this book. But the members of parties have some weapons too. The most basic is the party's choice of leadership. The party decides who will be prime minister. That support may at times be withdrawn.

The impact of parties on the prime minister's powers permeates everything. Discussions of parliament, patronage and cabinet in subsequent chapters take for granted the existence of strong and disciplined parties, but first, the relationship between leaders and followers needs to be discussed. Two aspects are particularly important: the election and dismissal of leaders, and the day-to-day interaction between the party organisation and the prime minister. The former, considered in Chapter 3, concerns what implications the procedure for electing and dismissing leaders and/or prime ministers may have for the degree of answerability that prime ministers have to their party; it therefore concentrates on the spectacular and the unusual and asks what impact these have on the day-to-day exercises of power. The latter covers more routine questions: what influence is wielded by meetings of parliamentary parties or by the external organisation and the mass membership? And, more generally, how large does the party's influence loom in executive government?

Prime ministers are regarded as the head of their party, but it is important to ask what that means. If to be head means anything more than being a mere spokesperson, then there must be means by which prime ministers can influence the actions and thinking of part, or all, of the party. To put it another way, are prime ministers accepted as the principal source of ideas and orthodoxy for organisation and policy? To what extent are those functions shared with, for instance, independent party presidents?

The same point can be approached from a different angle. If the party–prime minister relationship is essentially transactional, then a set of relationships has to be maintained. How many people or organisations have to be kept on-side; how many party relationships have to be nurtured? The more time that a prime minister must spend on party affairs, the less is available for the other functions of governing. It is necessary to distinguish between the extra-parliamentary party and the caucus within parliament; the two are distinct areas which supply different needs and require different resources.

PARTY ORGANISATION OUTSIDE PARLIAMENT

The structure of the party outside parliament determines the number of independent centres of power that exist within the party and therefore the number of bodies with whom the prime minister may need to maintain a direct relationship. Smiley (1980: 121–2) has distinguished two types of party model in federal systems. In the 'integrated' model the national and state/provincial parties draw on the same groups for electoral allegiance, use the same organisational machinery for all activities, maintain a common ideology and compete at both levels. In a 'confederal' system, there is no party symmetry at provincial and national levels; the ideology of parties at each level is often distinct; the parties rely on different groups for support and maintain autonomous orgainsations, even though the name of the party may be the same. According to these models, the Australian party system is integrated, the Canadian system tends towards the confederal. In the unitary systems of Britain and New Zealand, a third model of centralised, ideologically coherent parties can be found.

Each of these models has implications for the role of prime ministers. Where the organisation is confederal, the independence of the national party from internal state pressures will give it greater authority within that party. Where the party is unitary, the opportunity for prime ministers to control the party machinery may be enhanced. The situation may best be understood by asking how many legitimate centres of power exist. In a centralised unitary structure there will be probably only one or two in a party. In an integrated federal system each party will have numerous centres of power, each with its own interests and its own legitimacy, yet all needing to co-operate within the same party structure. The more centres of power that exist, the more different, yet legitimate, interests that they represent, the less easy it may be for a prime minister to act without consulting other people within the ruling party.

In Australia both major parties, Liberal and Labor (ALP), are integrated federal parties. They consist of six state branches, each of which is in effect a semi-independent fiefdom with considerable autonomy in its own sphere. Each has a network of local branches, permanently employed officials and elected state executives, and an annual conference. The state branches collect the bulk of the funds. In the ALP trade unions are affiliated to the state branches, electing directly over half the delegates to state conferences. Members of the state executives meet regularly, are geographically concentrated in the state capitals and control most of the party's resources. Candidates for both federal and state parliaments are chosen by state branches; the methods adopted for this process are entirely within their control.

By contrast the national organisations are small and their influence, such as it is, only recent. The national conferences are federal in structure, made up of delegates from the state branches. Their sessions are infrequent; the ALP's national conference meets once every two years for five days. Before 1982 the conference consisted of an equal number of delegates from each state, despite the massive differences in population and party membership. It was made more representative in 1981, but still retains a partly federal structure. Labor's national executive, which is still based on the principle of equal representation for each state, meets only three or four times a year. The national secretariats of both major parties have developed their influence only in the last decade. The Liberal secretariat did little during the 23 years of Liberal rule from 1949 to 1972; the advice of the public service was both better and more extensive. Only when the party fell into opposition did the need for external support became apparent. Gradually the secretariat hired people with the capacity to provide support to opposition spokesmen in their development of policies. When the Liberals returned to office in 1975, the director of the party, Tony Eggleton, developed a close working relationship with Fraser and earned the reputation of being the best campaign organiser in the country. Apart from being primarily responsible for the structure of Fraser's three winning election campaigns, he became the constant day-to-day adviser of the prime minister and, when parliament was sitting, was involved in the daily preparation for question-time. It was however a personal relationship; it was Eggleton, not the Liberal party's national secretariat *per se*, who developed the links with the prime minister. When Fraser resigned in 1983, Eggleton had to establish new links with the leader of the opposition, Andrew Peacock.

In the ALP too, the importance of the national secretariat depends largely on the personal ties at the centre. Apart from a brief unsuccessful appointment in the mid-1960s, Labor did not have a full-time federal secretary until 1974. The secretariat now has a permanent media and research staff but exerts influence mainly through the federally structured national executive. The executive has the authority to intervene in the internal affairs of state branches to protect the general welfare of the movement, but even then it can only do what a majority of the delegates from the state branches want it to do. So while the decisions of the national conferences, and between conference the decisions of the executive, are binding, the federal institutions do not have an existence independent of the state branches. Their decisions are in practice those taken by assemblies of state delegates and, despite the recent growth of the national secretariat, those state branches still control the majority of the available resources.

State and national parties are both fully integrated. Federal campaigns are run by a national committee, with the state branches providing local support. Prime ministers often participate in state election campaigns (although they are not always welcomed and have occasionally been told bluntly to keep out). State election results are, however unfairly, assessed in terms of what they suggest about the popularity of the federal government. For instance, the return of the Queensland National government in the 1983 state election was interpreted at the time as the first set-back for Hawke; Queensland and its National premier, it was argued, would be the springboard from which to start the defeat of the Hawke government. State and national politics are inextricably intertwined. Party members are committed notionally to the same principles and are all bound by the federal platform. Federal parliamentarians often hold key positions on the state executives; state branch officials invariably fill several positions on the national executives.

This integrated, federal structure has several important implications for any discussion of the power of an Australian prime minister. First, every state branch has a dual purpose—to achieve office at both federal and state levels. Resources have to be husbanded and applied where they may bring the greatest return. If a party is in government at both state and federal level—a situation that is very common—and the two are in dispute over policy, tactics or resources, it is by no means certain that the state executive will support the prime minister's line. Indeed the state premier is likely to have closer working relations with the state branch, in which he has an exclusive interest, than the prime minister; often indeed state premiers have dominated their branches. In 1982, for instance, the Western Australian branch of the Liberal party openly attacked Fraser's enthusiastic policy of introducing retrospective penalties for tax avoidance, while the Queensland branch (the junior partner in the state coalition) was critical of Fraser's cosy relationship with the National party premier. State branch leaders will readily dissociate themselves from a prime minister if they think it will help their own electoral prospects. In 1975 the Labor premier of South Australia claimed he was being slandered by being associated with the federal Labor government, while in 1983 the Western Australian premier bluntly argued that Fraser's presence in the state election would be a liability. Such attacks from within their own party do not make the prime ministers' position any easier to maintain.

Second, the presence of state political leaders, and often of state premiers, from the same party increases the number of spokesmen who can legitimately speak for the party and claim public attention in their own right. State leaders are always concerned to maximise their chances of electoral success. If they are also state premiers, their own government's interests may require frequent 'Canberra-bashing', that is blaming the federal government for all their problems. If the prime minister comes from the other major party, that may add spice to the task, but coming from the same party does not stop the fights. There is much truth in the comment that two state premiers, one Liberal and the other Labor, have far more in common than two Liberals, the one a state premier and the other a prime minister. Where other legitimate party spokesmen with different interests but the same organisational base exist, a prime minister must always take their likely reactions into account or, preferably, consult them before taking any decision that affects their interests. To be publicly brawling with state premiers from the same party can help undermine a prime minister's position. One of the reasons for the removal of John Gorton as prime minister was the opposition of state premiers, Robin Askin of New South Wales and Henry Bolte of Victoria; they accused him of being centralist in approach and of failing to consult them adequately, although it was as much his style as his policies that upset them. Working through the state branches, they boosted the growing dissatisfaction with Gorton in the federal party and thus affected the outcome of the vote that brought him down.

State branches can never be taken for granted, even when the prime minister needs their support in federal matters. When Andrew Peacock was challenging Fraser in April 1982, the prime minister tried to persuade a meeting of state presidents to endorse his leadership publicly. The Queensland president declined to be involved and the proposal was dropped.

Pressure also springs from a third factor created by the federal structure. Members of federal parliament are selected as party candidates by the state branch. Since, according to party rules, all members of all parties may be challenged for party selection before every election, their political future depends on maintaining support in the state branch and at local constituency level. It is true that a Liberal prime minister is responsible for promotion to the ministry, but where the state branches are out of sympathy with the prime minister a member may feel competing pressures. Several leading rebels in the Liberal party are sustained by branch support; this is particularly true of Liberal senators from Tasmania, Queensland and Western Australia because senators are chosen by the state party executive.

In the ALP, where factions are so well-organised within some state branches that they run their own newspapers, party preselection depends almost totally on factional alignment. Those factional links will determine the future of members, their continued hold on the seat and their access to the ministry rather more than the prime minister.

Prime ministers have almost no direct influence on party preselection. They may wish to get better qualified candidates into parliament from whom ministers can be chosen, but the safe seats are not in their gift. There are of course power-brokers in all state branches who can deliver seats, but prime ministers can only work through them. They are unlikely to be able to ignore them, and would usually be too smart to try. Indeed, when prime ministers become unpopular, their support may be counterproductive. In 1981 Fraser wanted one of his more promising cabinet ministers in the Senate to receive the preselection for a by-election for a safe seat in the lower house. The minister lost, in part because the local branches did not want a candidate imposed on them. In general prime ministers accept as party colleagues whoever survives the process of branch selection.

A fourth factor is that the timing of all decisions has to take into account the electoral interests of state branches. Between 1969 and 1972 the Liberal party held office federally and, either alone or in coalition, in every state. When there are seven governments, each with three-year parliamentary terms (in two cases that has now been extended to four), elections are always around the corner, even if every parliament lasts its full term (which by no means all of them do). Elections have to be synchronised to maximise the party's advantage, although that does not always happen. In 1983, when Fraser was determined to call an election quickly, the fact that the federal campaign would swamp the Western Australian state campaign that had already been opened was ignored. That was most unusual. Policy announcements have to be made to benefit different sections of the party; a new federal housing policy was announced rapidly in March 1982 to benefit a beleaguered state government in Victoria (which lost anyway). Promises to deliver federal goods are often given by prime ministers campaigning in state elections. Federal promises to act, or the delaying of embarrassing statements, are regular and regarded as necessary.

Consider therefore the restrictions that the party structure places on an Australian prime minister: state branches and federal parliamentarians suffer from divided loyalty; elections have to be synchronised; the timing and content of decisions have to take into account the interests of state governments; there may be up to six state premiers from the same party, each of whom can speak authoritatively as a government leader on behalf of the party. Yet the party must remain unified enough to appeal to the electorate because all state branches are part of the same organisation and it has been traditionally assumed that the picture of a party in disarray harms the prospects of government at both levels. In party terms therefore the interests of party supporters are not necessarily those of the prime minister. The latter has to cultivate a set of relationships with state leaders, each of whom has an independent base. This is time-consuming, has to be done by persuasion, not dictation. On occasion when those state interests have been ignored, the resulting furore has generally been to the prime minister's disadvantage.

In Canada the parties are confederal rather than integrated. First the parties have a national coverage only in the most nominal sense. In 1980 the governing federal Liberal party won only two seats in Manitoba and none at all in any of the three western provinces. Nor has it won any representation in the three western provincial parliaments recently. Historically it has dominated federal politics because of its almost total control in Quebec and its majorities in Ontario and to a lesser extent the Maritime provinces. In the past it was assumed that a successful federal party needed to build on success at provincial level (Wearing 1981: 13), but that no longer applies. There is little connection between voting habits in federal and provincial elections. Liberal federal success has not been mirrored by equivalent success at provincial level. In 1980 the Liberal party did not hold office in *any* of the provinces. The traditional two-party model applied in the Maritimes, but nowhere else. In Ontario the Liberals were the third party and in Quebec they were the main opposition to the Parti Quebecois. Elsewhere the party was not in the race. In contrast the Conservative party had almost no presence in Quebec.

Second, it is widely accepted that, since provincial and federal parties have different interests, they should also have different organisations. If they do not, the interests of the more successful level may predominate. For a time during the Liberal revival in Quebec in the early 1960s, there was a single Liberal organisation. That survived while the party remained in opposition at both levels, but when Liberal governments were formed in Ottawa and Quebec it was perceived as more useful to create two separate bodies—the Liberal Party of Canada (Quebec) and the Quebec Liberal party. Ontario followed this example in the late 1970s. At the higher levels of the party, the personnel are now distinct. Each maintains its own party office and employs its own personnel. Even if at the riding level there is an overlap of office-holders, the division is effectively complete; discussions of whether a similar break should occur where the provincial Liberal party is even less successful in the west are fairly common (Wearing 1981: ch. 4).

Third, Canadian parties are not programmatic organisations; they are essentially electoral machines (Meisel 1981: 43). This factor has created internal tensions in the Liberal party between those who believe there ought to be massive participation from the membership and those who see the party's main function as winning elections; the former want decentralisation, the latter see the advantages of centralisation (Wearing 1981: 70). At times the party machine in some provinces has degenerated into rival cliques, grouped around ministers and competing for control of patronage. On other occasions, particularly in Quebec, participation has been extensive; that trend reached its height around 1970. Since then the advisory machinery in the Liberal party has atrophied and the party has become more centralised around the office of the prime minister (Clarkson 1981: 160). The Liberal party has at local level been concerned with the selection of candidates and at national level with running campaigns.

The organisation of the federal party emphasises these points. The National Office in Ottawa has always been small; its access to government depends on the links of the party president with the prime minister. Trudeau's relationship with Senator Gil Molgat was always more distant than that with Jim Davey, the long-term electoral expert. When the National Office did not appear to be delivering sound advice, the centre of power shifted to advisers within the Prime Minister's Office (PMO). Attempts to allow the National Office participation in patronage delivery, and hence to give it greater political clout, soon failed (Wearing 1981: 14–45). When Trudeau's principal private secretary failed to win a by-election, he was made chairman of the party's planning committee (*Globe and Mail* 13 January 1982). The close links with the prime minister were retained.

At provincial level the existence of an organisation designed entirely for federal purposes naturally gave greater say to federal leaders. The most efficient Liberal machine was in Quebec; it was generally run by the prime minister's Quebec lieutenant. Trudeau delegated much of that responsibility to Jean Marchand and Marc Lalonde who became involved in many of the details of campaigning. Where federal and provincial organisations were not divided, there were problems; there were consistent battles between Otto Lang, the senior federal minister for Saskatchewan, and the Liberal leaders there. The provincial leader, Ross Thatcher, was more conservative than the federal leaders, but more importantly he wanted to maintain full control of the delivery of patronage. Within the federal party therefore the centre was dominant; it became responsible for the revitalisation of the party at election times, depending heavily on the impact of federal ministers, to whom some influence was delegated, and the close circle of prime ministerial advisers.

One reaction to these developments in party organisation was scathing. A former national director of the party, Blair Williams, described it as an 'election-orientated, leader-dominated, media-manipulated marketing machine' (*Globe and Mail* 4 July 1980). He wanted branch members to be continuously active, both in policy discussions and as a means of counterbalancing the bureaucratic state. Yet reform is likely to occur only with the consent of the centre and another leading Liberal argued that there had been no reform because of the 'prime minister's iron-fisted control' (*Globe and Mail* 1 March 1983). The Liberal party appears to be an electoral machine, in which the prime minister's (or leader's) influence is extensive.

In the Progressive Conservation (PC) party, the party structure is more unified because the concentration is on provincial politics where the party has been far more successful. Strong provincial premiers, undoubted masters of the party in their own areas and with long records of electoral success, face an unsuccessful federal party. For men like Lougheed of Alberta and Davis of Ontario, the question that dominates intra-party discussion is the impact of federal politics on their own electoral prospects. They regard strong regional governments as the only real check on any federal prime minister with a parliamentary majority. The degree of support given to Joe Clark, both during the election campaign of 1979 (when he was viewed with some suspicion) and while he was prime minister, was by no means complete. Davis and Lougheed did not appear to throw the full resources of the provincial parties into the 1980 campaign (Troyer 1980). Certainly the leader maintains full control over allocation of funds for the national headquarters and for determining what should be done; yet since the party is essentially federal in structure, those resources are limited. No doubt, had the Clark government remained in power, with Progressive Conservatives in office in seven of the provinces, relations within the party might have developed on the lines of the Australian model; but alternatively tensions within the party might have led to a division of the party on Liberal lines. However the government did not survive, and that relationship is one that the new leader will have to mould, particularly if he wins the next federal election.

Referring mainly to Canadian *Liberal* prime ministers, it is possible to draw some conclusions about the impact of a confederal party on their influence. First, they can act as the sole spokesperson for their party. Not only have they been elected by delegates drawn from the whole country and therefore have a national mandate of a sort, but there are no provincial premiers with the same party label—and there are unlikely in the foreseeable future to be more than one or two. Even then these will be formally the head of a different organisation. A Liberal prime minister is less concerned to consult provincial colleagues about the impact of federal policies on provincial electoral prospects because they are anyway perceived to be poor. The national party can be more exclusively concerned with its own organisational interests. Reports that Trudeau wanted to complete the patriation of the constitution before the (incorrectly) anticipated win of the Liberal party in the Quebec provincial election (*Globe and Mail* 2 October 1980) indicated that he may have anticipated greater problems dealing with his own party, because it would require consultation rather than more brusque treatment. The scheduling of elections, made easier by five-year terms, does not require them to take account of provincial premiers' plans.

Second, the separation of party organisations does not divide the loyalties of participants. Officials of the national parties are concerned with national campaigns; the relationships are clear-cut, or at least appear so. In practice the separations in Quebec (in 1963) and Ontario (in 1976) were undertaken because the provincial branches saw disadvantages in being tarred by the federal brush. The result has been to centralise much more of the federal organisation in Ottawa and, because the federal office is comparatively weak, in the hands of the prime minister and his advisers in the PMO. The prime minister appoints the directors of the campaign and is in control of the determination of strategy. The changes in strategy between 1972 and 1974, and between 1979 and 1980, can be explained in part by the different personnel in PMO to whom attention was being paid. Such a process gave considerable authority to the prime minister, who had fewer interests to consult.

Third, the spasmodic existence of provincial parties may make party candidate selection easier for the centre to manipulate. It is true that the selection of candidates is now the responsibility of local riding associations. It was not always so. For over twenty years Joey Smallwood, the premier of Newfoundland, chose all provincial and federal candidates himself. The Quebec party was notoriously undemocratic in the 1950s and early 1960s. It was comparatively easier to attract good candidates by effectively guaranteeing their selection for winnable seats, as with the introduction of the three wise men—Marchand, Pelletier and Trudeau—to parliament in 1965. Mackenzie King, St Laurent and Pearson (the latter two distinguished men recruited directly into cabinet) could thus draw into parliament candidates of ministerial calibre. Indeed they positively sought and persuaded leading citizens to run and then rewarded them with an immediate ministry.

However, the development of the belief in participation made this practice more difficult. It is still possible, by the rules of some sections of the party, for candidates to be imposed on a riding. In Quebec the powerful Electoral Commission of the party, which in effect meant the Quebec lieutenant Marchand, effectively chose Monique Begin and discarded the sitting MP (Wearing 1981: 103). On other occasions a party organiser in Ontario might be provided to assist the convention campaign of the favoured candidate, usually successfully. The choice is nominally local, but often, not surprisingly, the choice of the central office is selected. Pierre Juneau, chairman of the Broadcasting Commission, was appointed minister of communications and then given the party nomination for a Quebec seat just vacated by another minister. Jim Coutts, head of the PMO, was parachuted into an Ontario by-election nomination in 1981 after its incumbent had been promoted to the Senate to create a vacancy, although like Juneau he then failed to win the seat. The federal Liberal party always encouraged leading citizens to seek nomination; the fact that the Liberal party was *only* successful at federal level meant that there were no alternative arenas in which to satisfy ambitions. Therefore notables either ran for the national parliament or not at all. But there was little central control most of the time.

The PC leader did have a power of veto. Any selected candidate had to be endorsed. Stanfield once denied a candidate endorsement and his decision was accepted. He also encouraged many talented people to stand. Yet it seems that the leader's involvement in selection has declined in both parties. Trudeau was more inclined to accept those who emerged from the local process (Wearing 1981: 235) than his predecessors were.

In comparative perspective, the Canadian prime minister is far less constrained by intra-party relations than an Australian leader. A confederal party—and particularly one which is unsuccessful at provincial level—allows greater centralisation of control in the leader's hand and requires less consultation with provincial colleagues. The leader is much freer in actions and in campaign timing, structure and tactics.

British party leaders are secure from the problems created by federal structures. The parties are centralised and unified; there is only one Central Office and no provincial or state body. In the Conservative party it is accepted that the leader is totally in charge of the Central Office. The chairman of the party is the leader's appointee, so are the leading officers in the central organisation. Thatcher dismissed Heath's choices and replaced them with her own. She dispatched her own choice as chairman, Lord Thorneycroft, in September 1971 and appointed Parkinson instead. It was accepted during the 1975–76 leadership challenge that the Central Office was the leader's office and it fought vigorously on Heath's behalf. There are limits to the choice; the chairman has to be a person of stature in the party, because the prime minister cannot be involved in daily administration (Norton and Aughey 1981: 224). Thatcher, indeed, has chosen to reduce the role of Conservative research department to a secretariat; she relies for policy ideas far more on the Centre of Policy Studies which she co-founded in 1974 (*Economist* 21 January 1984). But it can be assumed that the central organisation will always have the leader's interests in mind and, equally importantly, will never be found to be working against her. At constituency level the party is decentralised, with branches being run by local notables. Powerful in their own area, they are no threat to the dominance of the prime minister within the party. Nor in return can prime ministers impose their candidates on local branches; indeed Douglas Hurd (1979: 138) regarded working at No. 10 as a disadvantage when he was seeking party endorsement. The Central Office maintains a list of acceptable candidates—to which other names can be added—but does little more. Of course in Britain local connections are not regarded as essential for MPs, so leading party members can seek seats throughout the country. There is only one legitimate spokesman for the Conservative party as a whole—the party leader.

In the New Zealand National party a similar situation exists. There is only one party, divided into five regional divisions. The organisation is the responsibility of the party president, who is elected by the party conference. The prime minister, in the capacity as party leader, plays a continuous and active role in organisational matters. He is an ex-officio member of the biannual Dominion Council and the Dominion Executive which meets every second month; Muldoon seldom misses meetings of either if in New Zealand at the time they are held. The prime minister is also an ex-officio member of all party committees; Muldoon frequently attends meetings of the finance committee, and often goes to regional meetings. He approves all the material produced by the Publicity Committee, even though he does not attend its meetings. The relationship between leader and party is very close, and always has been. Holyoake too was punctilious in maintaining contacts with all levels of the party.

In part this is a function of size, but it goes further. The National party has a large nominal membership; it has claimed to have had 200 000 members which means that about a third of those who regularly vote National in general elections are also party members (Levine 1980: 15). Even though 'membership' is a nominal status—there are no set annual fees and those who join simply get receipts—the ratio of party members to voters is far greater than any larger democracy can hope to achieve. Keeping the members happy in a small democracy where access to leaders is taken for granted becomes a high priority. All National prime ministers, particularly Muldoon, have spent time meeting and addressing the party, occasionally pandering to its prejudices in small things to keep its support in larger ones. Muldoon, according to both his supporters and his critics, is

skilled in judging the mood of the party and appealing to the Archie
Bunkers (an American Alf Garnett) in the party and the electorate.

However local autonomy is protected in party selections, carried
out by a conference of local delegates, with one person representing
each twenty local members. The numbers of those involved may vary
from 50 to 250. A local panel reduces the number of candidates to four
or five and there is a provision for the Emergency Committee of
Council (of which the leader is a member) to exclude unsuitable candidates or declare that the quality of the pool is not adequate. This is
seldom done and there is no provision for names to be *added* to the lists
by central dictat. At the final selection meeting the candidates have to
answer among other things two written questions, one sent by the
president, one by the party leader. Some candidates consider they
have been helped by a question that the leader knew they could answer
effectively; Marilyn Waring, then a 22-year-old research officer and
later a parliamentary rebel, considers that she was assisted by Muldoon's choice of housing as the topic for his question as he knew she
knew the subject well (Aitken 1980: 203). But assistance from the
leader has to be carefully delivered. Further, when Muldoon
threatened to have the selection of one backbench MP withdrawn, the
local party quickly objected; no change was made.

However, the National leader is the sole spokesperson on policy
matters of a party dedicated to winning national elections. The
National party does not run candidates for local elections and is an
electoral machine, effectively organised, with a large membership.
The prime minister can directly influence everything in the party except the selection of candidates.

In the British Labour party the lines of authority are more in doubt.
The National Executive Committee (NEC) is elected by annual conference, with delegates selected by the large unions and the constituency parties. The parliamentary leader and his deputy are ex-officio
members of the NEC. The NEC claims to be the principal spokesman
of the party; so of course does the parliamentary party. There has
been, according to Dennis Kavanagh, a 'traditional neglect of what
representation means in the Labour party. The questions "who speaks
for the party?" and "when the party speaks, who does it speak for?"
are important and have been neglected' (1982a: 204).

Parliamentary leaders, and particularly prime ministers, have always stated that they are independent of the NEC. For a long time,
without defining their constitutional position formally, the parliamentary and extra-parliamentary sections of the party managed to co-exist
without too much difficulty. When a chairman of the party, Harold
Laski, attempted to set himself up as the official spokesman, he was

put down by Attlee with withering contempt. However since the NEC has drifted to the left, it has increasingly become less sympathetic to government policy and confrontations have developed. When MPs, even ministers, are members of the NEC, they are usually there because they have been elected as constituency representatives—a section always to the left of the party—not as MPs. This can set up a problem of divided loyalties. In what capacity do they sit there? 'Labour ministers who are also elected members of the NEC are particularly vulnerable to competing loyalties. As ministers they are bound by the convention of collective cabinet responsibility, yet as elected NEC members they are also responsible to conference' (Kavanagh 1982a: 209). When the two bodies became rival centres of power, problems emerged. In 1969 Callaghan used his position on the NEC to lead resistance to *In Place of Strife*; a White Paper introduced by the Wilson government to restructure the industrial relations system. In 1974 other ministers openly dissented from government policy there.

Prime ministers can attempt to assert their authority. Wilson circulated a memorandum requiring that the principle of collective responsibility be applied as much to the NEC as the other bodies (1976: 232), but political sensitivities probably made the use of sanctions against a minister who breached the convention in the NEC impossible.

Further the Labour prime minister has no control over the staffing of central office. The Labour Party Research Department is responsible to the NEC, not the parliamentary leadership. At times indeed it has become its rival, developing alternative policies to those being adopted by a Labour government; the director of the department was quite prepared to take on the prime minister in discussion of its 'proper' role (Finer 1980: 95–7). In the central organisaton prime ministers have little control over personnel and their rights as the main spokesman of the party, as opposed to the government, may be occasionally challenged.

In the New Zealand Labour party the potential for division exists, even if it has broken into the public arena only recently. The party conference and executive are responsible for organisation but, in the two decades before 1979, the party president was *generally* also an MP. Since MPs had free internal travel, it saved the small party expenses. It also ensured that the interests of the parliamentary party were well-represented. In the late 1960s, for instance, Bill Rowling was party president and a leading shadow spokesman. From 1979 a non-MP, Jim Anderton (who was later selected for a safe seat), was elected and at times in 1983 there were public brawls between Anderton and Lange before the two decided that there should be clear areas to which each should restrict himself. It is now widely accepted in the party that presidents ought *not* to be MPs—provided that they restrict themselves to organisational matters when speaking for the party. To that extent the party accepts the need for both to have their spheres of influence.

One of the president's spheres of influence is the selection of candidates. Labour candidates are chosen by a panel consisting of three central representatives (including the president) and two or three local people; these may include a vote from a poll of local members. The prime minister or party leader is not involved—which was one of the bones of contention between Lange and Anderton when sitting members were being rejected. In the past leaders have occasionally become involved, even if their influence was indirect. Rowling successfully discouraged alternative candidates for a seat in 1978 when the executive wanted to find a seat for a member whose constituency had been abolished in a redistribution (Jackson 1980: 111), but failed to persuade the panel to choose his preferred candidate for a by-election in 1976. Most of the time leaders realise that their influence can only be indirect, and has to be used carefully in organisational matters.

However in neither Britain nor New Zealand are the party leaders faced with challenges at different levels of government. The national leaders of the British Labour party, indeed, have shown little interest in local government (Sharpe 1982). Crossman's famous mistake in announcing increases in social service charges in the first week of local government elections (Wilson 1971: 814) could never have happened in a federal country. Despite the fact that the population of the Greater London Council is almost equivalent to the population of the whole of Australia, no state election there would be of such small moment to allow such a mistake. In Britain it appears that swings against national government in local elections are perceived as normal.

In all these unified parties the selection of candidates is undertaken at local level. The capacity of the prime minister to get leading people selected is low; indeed the support of the prime minister may actually be a disadvantage as the difficulty met by Callaghan's press secretary in finding a seat illustrates. In New Zealand prime ministers are involved in organisational details because of the small size of the country. For everything except candidate selection, both British and New Zealand parties are highly centralised. That removes from their prime ministers many of the problems that the party structure creates elsewhere.

PARTY CONTROL OVER POLICY

In his discussion of the distribution of power in the British Labour party, Robert McKenzie asked 'Why has the Labour party, like many other parties of the left, and so many political theorists concerned with the role of parties in democracy, found it so difficult to grasp the relationship between intra-*party* democracy and the formal democratic institutions of the polity' (1982: 194). McKenzie's own view is that 'Intra-*party* democracy, strictly interpreted, is incompatible with democratic government' (1982: 195).

In this view he has been eminently consistent. In his classic work on British political parties, he described the idea that the parliamentary party should be the servant of the outside movement as an 'old naive view' and criticised the Independent Labour Party (ILP) because it '*refused to conform to British parliamentary practice in the way the Labour party itself had already done*. The ILP had refused to acknowledge the autonomy of its parliamentary party and insisted that its parliamentarians should be subject to the direction of the party organisation outside Parliament' (1963: 445—original emphasis).

McKenzie's assertions reflect a generally accepted view in Britian, although this has come increasingly under challenge in the British Labour party. The implications for prime ministers are of course extensive. If the external organisation can to any extent determine party policy, this creates a set of relationships that has to be maintained; choices about confrontation or manipulation have to be made; challenges to government policy may have to be met or avoided. The assumptions about the degree of party involvement are therefore basic. However they are not as clear-cut or simple as McKenzie makes out, for there are processes by which the intra-party democracy and democratic government can be seen to be compatible.

In discussions of such assumptions, two categories of party can be identified: those that follow the belief that the external party organisation should have no more than an advisory role and those that believe that the organisation has some rights to determine policy. The former category includes all the non-labour parties in Britain, Canada and Australia; the latter includes the ALP and New Zealand Labour party. How the British Labour party should be classified would be a matter of dispute within the party.

The policy impact of the extra-parliamentary organisations of the non-Labor parties can easily be described, for it is minimal. There have been occasions in Canada when the participation of party members in policy discussion has been sought, at least partly to encourage a feeling of involvement. It is part of the permanent tension between the contrasting principles of participation and centralisation. The belief in participation in the Liberal party reached its zenith around 1970 when a four-stage process was devised. First, a 'thinker's conference' considered areas of policy and discussion papers. Then their recommendations were discussed, initially by the riding associations and then by a special policy convention. Finally the policies that emerged were to be drafted into an election platform. It was grandiose proposal that largely did not work. The proposals that emerged out of the thinker's conference were not well-digested, the ridings associations often gave little or no attention to the ideas and the policy conventions passed resolutions that contradicted one another. More important, it became immediately evident that, whatever policy statements had emerged from the convention, they were not going to be binding on the party leaders in cabinet or on the prime minister. The day after the convention dispersed, Trudeau publicly repudiated some of the more important resolutions (for details, see Clarkson 1979). This action followed precedents set by earlier leaders. Policy was to remain the prerogative of the prime minister and cabinet. Since 1970 it seems to have been accepted that effective policy conventions are a thing of the past (Wearing 1981: 206).

Similar roles are envisaged for the party conferences in Britain and Australia of the Conservative and Liberal parties respectively. Their resolutions are advisory—and their role is readily accepted as such by participants. The appearances of leaders—and particularly prime ministers—are occasions for applause rather than debate. Obviously the resolutions do have some importance. They indicate the general state of thinking in the party, the views of rank and file or, in Australia, of branch officials. The occasion allows some expressions of differences from government policy. In Australia changes to the Liberal party platform—a rare event, since the 1982 re-drafting was only the second change since the 1940s—may not have an immediate policy impact, but they are a good indication of the mood of the party (Sawer 1983). Perhaps Fraser showed how important he believed the conference was by going overseas in the middle of the 1982 meeting. However he and all prime ministers are too shrewd not to take account of the views expressed there.

The New Zealand National party has a policy committee, composed of three MPs, the party president and two members elected by the Dominion Council, of which the parliamentary leader is chairman. Its decisions are consolidated into a large party policy document which is released to the public. Obviously everything included has the full endorsement of the prime minister; even when his critics have been elected to the committee, the final choices are clearly his. However it does allow the extra-parliamentary wing participation, however nominal, in the process of discussion.

Labour parties have different attitudes, primarily because they grew out of the trade union movement and accepted early the principle of

solidarity and the notion that elected members were delegates of the
party. In the ALP these ideas have never been challenged. The ALP's
national conference makes decisions that are binding on all members,
including a prime minister. The conference meets every two years for
five days (although there is a provision for special conferences). It
debates changes to the platform in the form of reports from policy
committees; some of these reports are carefully prepared, others are
primarily the work of the minister or shadow minister. Decisions are
taken by vote and, however small the majority, are binding. The right
of the conference to dictate policy is not challenged, by Labor leaders
or by anybody else.

However different rules have led to different politics. Rather than
confront the conference or try to assert their independence, Labor
leaders have sought to use the conference to bolster their own position. Between 1967 and the election win of 1972 Whitlam persuaded
the three national conferences to write into the platform the core of his
schemes for reform. Then, when they were brought to cabinet, he
could use the fact that they were 'in the platform' or 'in the policy
speech' (soon dubbed the Old Testament and the New Testament respectively) as a means of overcoming opposition. Since the platform
was binding, arguments for rejection or delay, particularly from the
Treasury, could be overcome. When a conference was held when the
Labor party was in office, it could be used to amend policies or even to
settle finally inter-ministerial disputes. ALP prime ministers are so
rare that it is unlikely they will often fail to carry conference.

Further, the nature of the Labor party's platform is changing.
Many delegates at the conference, particularly those who are parliamentarians or even ministers (and they usually make up about a third
of the delegates), have increasingly sought to write the platform in
such general terms that a future government has considerable room to
manoeuvre, depending on the political and economic circumstances.
On those few areas of policy which are symbolically important, such
as the party's attitude towards a capital gains tax or uranium mining in
1982, the wording may be precise. More often the final document is a
compromise which ministers either endorse or are prepared to live
with. The leader's policy speech emphasises the important sections;
the cabinet decides what will be implemented and when.

The existence of an externally determined binding platform mainly
creates a set of constraints for ALP prime ministers. It would be difficult for them to adopt a policy that is directly contradictory to a
plank in the party platform—difficult but not impossible, for if they
can carry the parliamentary caucus there are no easy means by which
the *conference* can bring sanctions to bear. In practice, since Labor

prime ministers will probably have written many of their ideas into the platform, or can get the platform changed (even retrospectively) to endorse their actions, the possibilities of a confrontation between prime minister and platform are probably exaggerated—though that prospect can sometimes be used to curb ambitious ministers who want to go beyond its proposals. Nevertheless the existence of the platform and the need to live within it or change it are ever-present facts of life for an ALP prime minister.

Hawke's behaviour in his first six months in office illustrates the point. In two areas he wanted to ignore party policies: on the exporting of uranium and on the recognition of Indonesia's right to control East Timor. On the latter he declared that circumstances had changed since the party conference and the policy was therefore no longer operative; on the former he tried to persuade the party to accept his interpretation of what the policy meant. He gained the support of the parliamentary caucus with a narrow majority. Neither tactic was well-received; both needed consistent follow-up by Hawke and his supporters. The examples are instructive not only because they illustrate how a prime minister can avoid binding policy but also because they showed how much effort is required to take the party along.

In New Zealand Labour policy is also binding. It is officially put together by a Policy Council consisting of five parliamentarians (who will include the leader and deputy leader), five members elected by conference and some regional representatives. The Policy Council considers the resolutions passed by conference but is not obliged to accept them all. Rowling, for instance, persuaded the Policy Council to tone down some of the conference's more anti-American motions. The resulting policy is thus an amalgamation of the generalities to which conference is increasingly limited and the view of what can be sold to the electorate that members of caucus bring to the council. Thereafter it is meant to be binding; to Kirk, as to Whitlam in Australia, that meant that what was promised had to be implemented. The platform therefore supported the influence of a programmatic prime minister.

In Britain the left of the Labour party is now challenging the accepted wisdom that McKenzie has described. At one time Attlee did argue that the conference 'lays down the policy of the party and issues instructions' (quoted in McKenzie 1982: 192), but that was when he was in opposition. In government he and his successors as prime minister denied that conference had any more than an advisory role. When a conference criticised the policy adopted by the Wilson government, he retorted: 'Conference does not dictate to the government' (Finer 1980: 93).

Two points are involved. First is the political one: prime ministers have clearly indicated that, if conferences choose to adopt resolutions that contradict government policy, there will still be no change. As heads of government they do not intend to give up their independence of action. Nor have they. When conference, dominated by the big unions, rejected Callaghan's wages policy, it made no difference to that policy, even if it may have incidentally made it more difficult to apply.

The second point is constitutional: should conference be allowed to dictate policy? McKenzie argued that, once in office, a cabinet received advice from a variety of sources; it is also faced with the hard facts. In making decisions the party ideology, the electoral programme and party pressures will be factors, but not the only ones. If the prime minister and his colleagues were responsible to the extra-parliamentary bodies, then the party would supplant the legislature and executive as the ultimate decision-making body (1982: 195–6). Herbert Morrison (1964) consistently espoused the sovereignty and independence of parliament and the parliamentary party.

Yet it is precisely because some parts of the extra-parliamentary party want to limit the independence of the prime minister that demands for a binding platform are being presented (see e.g. Benn 1981). In policy terms this includes demands for the policy speech to be composed jointly by the NEC and the parliamentary leader, thus avoiding a repetition of the events of 1974 when Wilson could ignore or play down the more radical parts of the manifesto. In practice on the main occasion when consultation did take place, in 1979, Callaghan showed how a prime minister could bulldoze his way through at a time when he was indispensable to the party; he threatened to resign if certain planks were included. He won his point.

Whether the left will succeed in evolving a practice of creating a binding policy is doubtful. Traditions die hard, particularly where there is great value in their maintenance, as there is for Labour leaders and prime ministers. Conventions and constitutional principles are of course politically flexible. However if they do change—and if the Australian example is any guide—the new rules may force a Labour prime minister to follow new tactics that to an extent neutralise the changes.

Even while conference decisions are not binding on a Labour prime minister, time and resources are still required for consultations to ensure that a satisfactory result can be achieved. Rebuffs to a prime minister can be politically embarrassing. Opposition within the extra-parliamentary party can lead to policy change. In conference prime ministers win where they can and live with defeats where they can not.

Yet, whether or not party policy is binding, it does provide a context in which prime ministers must live. The party activists provide links to the grass roots. Even if Attlee argued that he was no more limited by the conference than a Conservative leader, it was doubtful whether, given the growing militancy of the extra-parliamentary bodies, that view could be maintained. Party conferences and executives, if they have a regular existence, need to be consulted; however they do not meet often enough, and their ideas are seldom precise enough, to limit the independence of prime ministers by much, even if they have theoretical authority to do so.

THE MEETINGS OF PARLIAMENTARY PARTIES

The relationship between the prime minister and the party's backbenchers is continuous. Support of backbenchers on a day-to-day basis is essential if a government's legislative programme is to pass. How that ongoing relationship is maintained depends largely on the structure of the party in parliament.

The importance of party meetings can depend on two factors: the access that they provide to leaders, and the authority that they can wield. In formal terms, therefore, the party meetings that have the least authority are those of the Conservative party in Britain. The 1922 Committee meets weekly when the party is in office and it elects its own chairman and executive committee. It consists exclusively of backbenchers; ministers attend only when invited. On two or three occasions a year the prime minister may be invited to speak to meetings. No votes are taken and the chairman is responsible for informing the prime minister about the views there. The 1922 Committee thus has no *direct* authority. At the same time the chief whip also acts as a channel of communication of the views of individual members and the opinions expressed in the range of party subject committees and opinion-groups like the Bow Group or the Monday Club (Norton 1981).

Lack of formal access does not mean that the prime minister need be isolated from party opinion. Messages are constantly relayed through party channels. Ministers meet with the party committees and may actively discuss policies with them; their views may affect the proposals that come to cabinet. How close the relationship is has varied from one Conservative prime minister to another. In the 1970–74 parliament much of the dissatisfaction with Heath related to his failure to consult with, or listen to, his backbenchers (Norton 1978). That reluctance led to his downfall. Thatcher was always been conscious of the need to maintain close links with the backbench. 'During her first four years in government she met with all the officers of Conservative back-bench committees at least once a year and with the 1922 Executive on a more regular basis' (Burch 1983: 409). She was accessible and often maintained personal lines of contact, a growing necessity in a party whose backbenchers had been becoming more independent and powerful since 1970.

Yet even if contacts are more frequent, it remains true that there is no mechanism apart from informal pressures by which prime ministers can be forced to back down by the party meeting. Possibly one result is that in Britain government members cross the floor far more frequently than they do in Canada or Australia. Even if this cross-voting is unlikely to bring a government down—since party members will vote solidly when a question of confidence is before the house—it can be embarrassing on particular items, such as the new immigration rules in 1982. Further, as politicians become increasingly career-oriented and professional politicians more numerous, they expect their contribution, even as backbenchers, to be attributed more weight (King 1979).

In the other non-labour parties, meetings of the parliamentary party are more regular and with full parliamentary membership. In Canada Trudeau attended the regular weekly party meetings. There he and his ministers answered questions about policies, or discussed forthcoming legislation. All bills were considered by the relevant party committee before being introduced to parliament (Trudeau 1977), and Trudeau was likely to be the last speaker at each meeting. Lester Pearson (1977: 257–8) argued that

> leadership in the party has to be established first with party members; and in the parliamentary caucus. I used to take caucus meetings seriously and I was always available to members of caucus for discussion ... I used to subject myself to every kind of examination. I used to encourage the frankest kind of question, however critical.

Though the prime minister is not bound to take that advice, the opportunity for debate is there and occasionally cabinet will change direction because of demands made in the party room (Clarkson 1981: 163). Several backbenchers argued that their involvement is much greater—and more important—than the media and public believe.

A similar situation can be found when the Liberal-National party coalition is in power in Australia. The parties have weekly joint meetings when parliament is sitting. Ministers attend and answer questions; backbenchers can criticise government actions in private. Before any legislation is introduced into parliament, it is considered in detail by the relevant party committee and changes in the detail of the proposals are often made. Indeed so established is the belief that the party backbenchers should be consulted that in early 1983 a backbencher could argue that a cabinet decision was not brought to the party room and 'without such discussion in the party room no party member, in theory, is bound by that decision' (*Canberra Times* 8 January 1983). Frequent consultation is thus seen as extending the principle of collective responsibility to the party room. Certainly defections on the floor of the House of Representatives are very rare.

In New Zealand the meetings of the National parliamentary party are credited with even greater influence. They are the forum in which ministers announce and explain what they are doing, answer questions and discuss policies (Alley 1978). At times they are drawn into decision-making and are regarded in New Zealand as an important factor in policy-making. After each election, prime ministers have asked members of caucus to provide a secret straw vote, to indicate who should be chosen for which ministerial jobs. The caucus is often consulted on appointments; although this process usually entails bringing a name to caucus for endorsement, there have been occasions when another name has been substituted. Caucus committees examine all legislation and liaise with the relevant minister. At times, in areas where governments have made no decisions, demands from members of caucus may lead to action. The decisions to end the cotton mill contracts in 1962 and the moves to deregulate the transport industry in 1983 were both examples of caucus pressure leading to policies not initially favoured by the prime minister. Caucus could be used to 'ginger' cabinet. On other occasions, issues might be taken to caucus before a decision was made. Holyoake, it was argued, was a genius at knowing at what level decisions ought to be taken in order to ensure party cohesion. In recent years there has been an increasing role for caucus committees in reviewing legislation.

However, while the influence of caucus can be constant and occasionally constructive, it should not be exaggerated. One New Zealand MP commented that caucus was only allowed to take decisions when cabinet did not mind what the decision was and that caucus was influential when the hierarchy chose to ask its opinion. Another said that the review of legislation was often rushed and superficial because backbenchers (having no research assistance except a government research unit) did not have the time or the facilities to consider it in adequate detail. Often members of caucus learnt of important decisions by reading about them in the press. One concluded: 'Despite the prevalent public conception of the powerful position of the MP, for the non-Cabinet MP it is largely a myth' (Waring 1978: 94). Besides, the prime minister chaired caucus (unlike most parliamentary parties outside New Zealand). He only called on ministers who agreed with him to speak (the others were anyway bound by collective solidarity if cabinet had made a decision), could amend the agenda to suit the mood, and occasionally had controversial topics he could throw to caucus like a bone to allow the squabbling dogs to fight over. His resources in caucus remained considerable.

Caucus's influence in the New Zealand National party is therefore constrained, but it is probably greater than those of the other non-labour parliamentary parties. Access to the prime minister has been regular, particularly after 1981 when the government for a time had a bare majority of one. In a small party of 46 members, personal relations are crucial. Further, the ability to have one's say in caucus, even to move there for a change in government policies, is perhaps sufficient for members who do not thereafter feel obliged to oppose the party in parliament as a means of proving their bona fides.

In Australia, Canada and New Zealand, access for backbenchers is simply easier than in Britain. The prime ministers have their main offices in the parliament building; particularly in Australia, backbenchers can usually get to see the prime minister within a reasonable time.

In Labour parties the ambivalence of the belief in intra-party democracy means that the system is more blurred. In Britain the Parliamentary Labour party (PLP) also meets regularly; its meetings include ministers and the prime minister; at times it has insisted on voting on major items, although it is accepted that if all the ministers attend and vote—as they are expected to do when cabinet has made a decision—the payroll vote will probably guarantee a majority for the prime minister. But there has never been any question that cabinet is expected to clear its proposals with the PLP or gain approval for legislation. Morrison (1964: 135) has argued that 'if the parliamentary party of the government, in formal meeting assembled, could control the government in detail and determine its policies before they were announced to parliament, certainly the most undesirable situations could arise'. That formal position has not changed.

There have been occasions where the meetings have led to strong clashes between the party leaders and dissident backbenchers. Wilson used his famous analogy with dog licences and argued that 'every dog is allowed one bite, but then the licence may be withdrawn'. Sedgemore (1980: 66) recalls Callaghan brutally telling the party meeting that, like it or not, he intended to follow his selected course, and also ensuring that enough ministers turned up to win the ensuing vote. Yet the frequent cross-voting that occurred in the 1974–79 parliament perhaps indicates the powerlessness of the party meetings. Some changes in legislation might be achieved from opposition within the party meeting, and the prime minister frequently met delegations from members of his party (Wilson 1976), but where they were not successful some were prepared to take the fight elsewhere, often into the public arena.

The federal caucus of the ALP has considerable formal powers. It can vote on any issue and the decision of the majority of those present is binding on those eligible to vote, including the prime minister. Caucus meets weekly during parliamentary sessions. It has a formal agenda, drawn up by the chairman who, since 1972, has not been the leader. All legislation has to be discussed by the relevant party committee before coming to full caucus for approval. Caucus can overturn cabinet decisions, and on occasion has; it can direct cabinet to act. Within the constraints of the party platform, caucus has supreme authority. At times it has considered budget strategy in debate with the Treasurer (Hawker et al 1979: Ch. 9). This means that Labor prime ministers must spend some time ensuring that the numbers are there to support their proposals. In practice they usually are.

The formal powers of the ALP caucus are difficult to assert. Caucus meets only when parliament is sitting; it has little research support and spends much of its time reacting to government initiatives; there are likely to be a number of backbenchers who will generally support the leader; and if a government measure is implementing the platform it is difficult to stop anyway. The doctrine of collective responsibility is in a sense extended to caucus. Cabinet decisions may not be final until its endorsement is received. During the Whitlam government, ministers who disagreed with a cabinet decision could raise the proposal in caucus and try to get it revised there. The Hawke cabinet decided very early in its term that cabinet members would be as bound by collective responsibility in caucus as they were in public. Prime ministers may still have strong opposition in caucus, particularly if they are trying to bypass or amend formal party policy. All the same, during the 1972–75 government, there were probably not more than four or five occasions when caucus reversed cabinet decisions; the press attention given to those instances was out of all proportion to their frequency.

In New Zealand the Labour caucus has similar formal authority to that of the ALP. Also like its National counterpart caucus reviews legislation and appointments. However the evidence suggests that caucus has been used by prime ministers in New Zealand as often as it has restricted them. Kirk dominated the caucus. When opposed to rises in government charges (see Chapter 5), for instance, he lost in cabinet's priorities and planning committee and in full cabinet. He then took the item to caucus and, with the support of members from marginal electorates, reversed the earlier decisions. On other occasions he post-poned decisions in cabinet for discussion in caucus because he was more likely to get his way in the larger, less informed body. Its au-thority was undoubted, but given the small size of the polity and the rarity of Labour premiers, that authority scarcely acts as a restriction on the leader. However it could, if leaders do not maintain close links.

What is important is not the number of times that cabinet decisions can be overturned, but the potential that caucus has. The prime minis-ter therefore adopts means to circumvent the system of caucus approval (a difficult but possible strategy) or more often takes into account the likely reaction of backbenchers. The fact that changes are seldom made is an indication of the prior consultations that take place, not the lack of power or an unwillingness to use it. The formal right of caucus to be involved has an important impact on what Labour prime ministers can do.

In party meetings the greater the authority and the more frequent the access, the more limited the prime minister may appear to be. In cases this is true: an Australian Labor prime minister may face being overruled. Yet often the process strengthens the leader's hand by keeping party opposition within the comparative privacy of the party room. If legislation is discussed in advance and members can have their say and perhaps influence the decision there, they will be less liable to continue on the floor of the house. If they do not have an opportunity, or feel it has been negated by an over-vigorous use of the pay-roll vote, cross-voting in the house may follow. This means that the party room debate to some extent pre-empts, and even stifles, parliamentary debate. For a prime minister who wants to maintain a united party, and for whom the views of his own backbenchers are far more important than the ritualistic noises of the opposition, that may be a positive advantage. Perhaps the more disciplined parties in New Zealand, Australia and Canada are an indication of the greater oppor-tunities for debate in the party room. In that case the freely given rights of the party room, and the apparent answerability on individual items that has emerged, particularly in Australia and to a degree in Canada, may actually strengthen the prime minister by institutionalis-ing the process of consultation. Bringing the party formally into the process of legislation—and thereby perhaps keeping it working and out of other areas—may be a successful process of ensuring coherence.

3

Incumbency and Vulnerability

Changes of party leaders or prime ministers are rare and treated as of great significance. Properly so. The electoral process may favour some types of candidate, backgrounds and strategies. It creates a variety of political debts. But the analysis must go further. If the relationship between leaders and followers is transactional, then leaders may lead only as long as they deliver. When they fail—when they do not fulfil their part of the bargain, be it electoral success or party unity—they go. Or do they? Leaders have considerable political resources that can bolster their position. To remove them is not easy. But the degree of security they feel is likely to be important in determining how they will lead their party and, in office, the government. It is therefore necessary to explore the ways in which prime ministers and party leaders are elected, whether they can be removed and the impact of those processes on the way that prime ministers must work.

Churchill said: 'The loyalties which centre upon number one are enormous. If he trips he must be sustained. If he makes mistakes he must be covered. If he sleeps he must not be wantonly disturbed. If he is no good, he must be pole-axed' (quoted in Norton and Aughey 1981: 241). But is there any mechanism by which prime ministers can be sacked by dissatisfied supporters?

This chapter talks about *incumbency*, that is how prime ministers' gain and lose the job, and the implications of this for their power in relation to the other elements of government. In all the four systems prime ministers hold their job by virtue of their lower house majority. In most cases that majority consists of loyal members of one or two parties and the prime ministers are the leaders of those majority parties (or of the larger of the two).

Of course incumbency depends on other factors too. The majority is the result of a general election or, very occasionally, of some realignment of loyalties in the lower house. Prime ministers are actually appointed by the Queen or governor-general. They can lose

45

the job by an adverse vote in house, by electoral defeat or even, in quite exceptional circumstances, by dismissal by the governor-general. This chapter, however, is concerned only with those factors connected with the prime ministers' leadership of parties with majorities in the lower house. It will examine how people become party leaders, what factors help or hinder leaders *who are prime minister at the time* in holding on to their position, what forces may persuade them to give the position up voluntarily and what provisions (if any) there are to force them out of the leadership by formal processes. It will also explore what factors help or hinder them in preventing that process being invoked.

The procedure for choosing leaders has two sides: it determines how people are elected *and*, directly or by implication, how they can be removed, threatened, or even sacked. Some prime ministers retire of their own free will. Others may be persuaded that their continued presence will be detrimental to their reputation, their party or their nation; reluctantly, but with a degree of consent, they stand down. To talk of prime ministers being sacked means removal, against their will, by their own supporters, and not defeat in parliament or in an election. It may be a vote directly on the leadership or a decision on any other item the leader regards as a motion of confidence. To examine whether prime ministers can be sacked, it is necessary to ask *to whom* they are answerable, to the party in parliament or to the party as a broader organisation, and *how* they may be called to account. In other words, are prime ministers vulnerable to party revolt?

In much of the debate on prime ministerial powers, people assume that prime ministers have become secure from internal challenge. John Mackintosh certainly believed so. After asking whether prime ministers could be sacked, he concluded that they could not be. Referring exclusively to Britain, he recalled that the only instance in the twentieth century when a leader was *forced* to resign because of the withdrawal of party support was that of Neville Chamberlain; and he argued that even then the final blow was cast by the Labour party's refusal to serve in a coalition under Chamberlain (Mackintosh 1974: Ch. 8).

The historical record since 1932 seems to support Mackintosh's point. The reasons for prime ministers leaving office can be categorised in four ways: electoral or parliamentary defeat, death or willing retirement, reluctant retirement, and removal by their party. On that basis, six British prime ministers have been defeated at the polls (Churchill in 1945, Attlee, Home, Wilson in 1970, Heath, Callaghan), four retired voluntarily (MacDonald, Baldwin, Churchill, Wilson in

1976), one was pushed (Chamberlain) while two, Eden and Macmillan, are placed between the 'willing' and 'reluctant' retirements by different commentators. None was actually sacked by their party. In Canada five prime ministers were defeated at the polls (Bennett, St Laurent, Diefenbaker, Trudeau in 1979, Clark); three retired at the time of their own choosing (Mackenzie King, Pearson, Trudeau). No prime minister was persuaded to retire or sacked. In Australia four prime ministers were defeated at the polls (Chifley, McMahon, Whitlam, Fraser), one by a parliamentary vote (Fadden), three died in office (Lyons, Curtin, Holt), one retired willingly (Menzies in 1966) and two were forced out of office by their parties (Menzies in 1941, Gorton). In New Zealand, two were persuaded to retire (Holland, Holyoake), two died in office (Savage, Kirk), and five lost elections (Fraser, Holyoake in 1957, Nash, Marshall, Rowling).

The analysis can be extended to include former prime ministers who continued as leaders of the opposition. Obviously it is likely to be easier to remove leaders of the opposition than prime ministers; they have fewer resources, less prestige and less patronage; they do not have the same national stature as prime ministers and their removal is likely to have fewer ramifications because it will not lead to the divisions within a government. Further, they have by definition lost office, and there seems to be increasingly less patience with defeated leaders in the 1970s and the 1980s than in previous decades. In practice in Britain three former prime ministers retired though how willingly is less certain (Attlee, Home, Callaghan) and one was sacked (Heath); in Canada two retired willingly (Bennett, St Laurent), two were sacked (Diefenbaker, Clark). In New Zealand two were forced out (Marshall, Rowling), one retired (Nash) and one died (Fraser). In Australia one died (Chifley), two resigned on the night of electoral defeats (Whitlam, Fraser), and one retired when it was clear that he had no support (McMahon). During the period two opposition leaders (Snedden, Hayden) who never became prime minister were removed by party room coup.

But vulnerability cannot be assessed only on the basis of the number of leaders who have been deposed. Tenure in office is too crude an indicator. First, it is possible to imagine a system where prime ministers are always vulnerable but where they have never been sacked because, aware that they are liable to challenge, they take precautions; in another system, where prime ministers are institutionally more secure, the occasional successful revolt might occur. Second, there is, in all countries, a trend towards making prime ministers more answerable to their parties. In the Conservative party more than elsewhere, it was assumed that a leader, once selected, had the right and responsibility to lead; leaders were not expected to be directly answerable to the party. The more recent attitude of many Conservative members is epitomised by the question raised by one of Heath's critics: was the leadership to be regarded as a freehold or a leasehold (Cosgrove 1979: 56)? Parties want leaders to be answerable. The demand for electoral success has become more insistent. In 1945 an ageing Churchill could stay on for six years as an ineffective leader of the opposition and return for another term as prime minister; in the 1980s there are few incumbent prime ministers who could reasonably expect to survive for long an electoral defeat. The record of the past may therefore provide only a limited guide to the new pressures that are developing.

Prime ministers do not always receive the uncritical support of their party colleagues. The reasons for which they lose favour are many: policy flexibility or inflexibility; action or inaction; a declining public image or unimpressive personal style. Each may create new problems or exacerbate old ones, and several consequences may result. The most likely is the fear that the government will lose the next election under the existing leadership, a growing feeling that a change in policy direction is needed for the ideological security of the party. Whether this is later turned into a desire for action may depend on a range of other circumstances, such as the proximity of an election, the availability of an ideologically sound alternative, or on the internal structure of the parties: that is, on the degree of ideological division or the existence of organised factions. Dissatisfaction or unpopularity does not of itself lead to a challenge, but it is a necessary condition. However, apart from an appreciation that the reasons for a challenge to the leadership may be disparate, what matters here is the degree to which prime ministers are then vulnerable.

Vulnerability and answerability are important components of the arrangements between leaders and followers. If leaders are answerable in some distinct way to their followers, they are obviously more restricted than those who are not so answerable. Non-vulnerable prime ministers may be able to face periods of unpopularity, both in their party or in the electorate, with greater equanimity. Government may therefore be more stable; hard decisions may be easier to take when consequences do not impinge directly on the leader's position, and governmental continuity may be easier to achieve. Vulnerable prime ministers may have to keep one eye on their backs; intrigue may become endemic whenever they are perceived to be doing a poor job. The potential for dismissal may be as important as the methods of election for structuring the relationship between leaders and followers.

AUSTRALIA

The leaders of all Australian parties are elected exclusively by the members of their parliamentary parties, sitting and voting together; that is, members of the Senate (with its 64 members) and the House of Representatives (with 126 members). The numbers involved in electing a prime minister are therefore small; when in 1974 Labor had a narrow majority in the lower house and was in a minority in the Senate, its caucus contained 93 people. When in 1977 the coalition had large majorities in both houses, the joint parliamentary parties included 121 members; 96 were members of the Liberal party which chose the prime minister.

Liberal leaders are generally chosen by exhaustive ballot. If no person has a simple majority after the first round, the one with the least number of votes is eliminated and further ballots are held until one candidate gets a majority. In the Labor party a preferential system is used, with the second, third and later preferences of the lowest candidates being distributed in turn until one person has a majority.

In both parties the leaders have to face regular election after each general election. This is often a formality, but it is not always so. Former prime ministers who have been defeated in an election may well be challenged; Whitlam was in 1976 and 1977, although neither attempt succeeded. But so too may prime ministers be challenged. In 1969 John Gorton won the election narrowly; his campaign performance was unimpressive and criticism of his casual and erratic style of government was publicly voiced by a senior minister, David Fairbairn. Fairbairn declared that he was not prepared to serve under Gorton again and that, if no-one else would stand as an alternative for leader, he intended to. Once the inevitability of a ballot was created, the deputy leader of the party, William McMahon, also announced his candidature. Gorton won on the first ballot, but the precedent was set. When in the last week of the 1980 campaign it appeared likely that Malcolm Fraser might lose or at best win narrowly, there were already rumours of moves to replace him. In the Labor party, where only one prime minister has ever won two elections consecutively, the possibility has never arisen.

Elections are not the only time that an incumbent prime minister can be forced to face a challenge. One can be mounted at any party meeting which is attended by all ministers and backbenchers in both houses. In the Labor party some notice for such a move is prescribed by the rules which state that a leader's position can be challenged only at a special meeting called for that purpose. In practice no such challenge has been made to a Labor prime minister since 1916. Then the party split over the issue of conscription; the state branches of the party, who controlled the preselection of party candidates, were bringing great pressure on many members to remove the prime minister, W.M. Hughes. A special meeting of caucus was convened, and a vote of no confidence was moved. However Hughes and his supporters walked out of the meeting before the motion could be put to the vote. He re-formed his cabinet with those ex-Labor members who had supported him and later coalesced with the conservative opposition (Weller 1975: 438–39). The lack of challenge since then is scarcely surprising: Labor governments are rare and the leaders who have taken the party to power have great internal standing. But then no Labor prime minister has survived for more than four years.

In 1983, for the first time, a Labor leader was deposed. Bill Hayden, as leader of the opposition, had survived a challenge from Bob Hawke by five votes in July 1982. Despite claims that the issue was to be closed until the election, discontent with Hayden's leadership continued and was exacerbated by a poor by-election result in December. Faced with the probability of an early election, a group of parliamentary leaders who had supported Hayden in July told him that they would switch sides. Rather than take the fight to caucus where he knew he would lose, Hayden stood down, almost simultaneously with the announcement of an election. Hawke was duly anointed to replace him. It was a further indication of growing intolerance of leaders faced with possible electoral defeat.

In a Liberal government challenges are even easier to mount. As there are no standing orders governing the procedures of party meetings, no formal notice of a challenge need be given. Leaders, even prime ministers, can be removed by a majority of one. On two occasions, indeed, prime ministers have been removed through party room opposition.

By 1941 Robert Menzies had become increasingly unpopular with the Liberals who objected to his frequent absences overseas. Since the parliamentary numbers were evenly balanced, they feared that an election fought under Menzies's leadership would be disastrous. Some were also personally hostile. On 28 August Menzies met his party colleagues and, faced with consistent criticism which he thought unlikely to abate, he resigned. He was replaced by Fadden, the leader of the Country party, in the hope that Fadden would bring greater cohesion to the government. The action of ministers and backbenchers publicly attacking their leader was criticised by the war historian, Paul Hasluck, himself a candidate for the party leadership in 1967: 'If the party had lost confidence in him as its leader the traditional expectation would have been that a party meeting would be called and a vote taken on the question of leadership of the party' (1952: 502). In fact such a vote was not taken but Hasluck's comment indicates that there was an accepted procedure for removing a prime minister which should have been used. The effect would probably have been the same.

In March 1971 the Liberal prime minister, John Gorton, was removed by a party room revolt. The week before his defence minister, Malcolm Fraser, had resigned, attacking Gorton's style of operation and his failure to consult. At the same time many Liberal back-benchers were concerned at the party's electoral image, because in parliament Gorton was being dominated by the leader of the opposition. Gorton convened a party meeting at which one of his supporters moved a vote of confidence in his leadership. The vote was tied. Gorton used his casting vote against himself, declared the motion lost and the leadership vacant. McMahon was immediately elected in his place. This challenge illustrates the modern Liberal style. First, there is a motion of confidence in the leader or one to declare the leadership vacant; only if the leader loses in that ballot is there need for alternative candidates to announce that they will stand. Similar tactics were used in opposition in 1975 when Fraser replaced the party leader. His supporters had made one attempt at a coup in November 1974, in which the leader was only given one day's notice of the challenge. In March 1975 there was a motion to declare the leadership vacant; when it succeeded Fraser announced his intention to stand (see Kelly 1976).

In April 1982 Fraser, who had by then been prime minister for over six years, was himself challenged. In April 1981 his minister for industrial relations, Andrew Peacock, had resigned from cabinet with a scathing attack on Fraser's style of leadership; in his resignation speech he used the same phrases as Fraser had done ten years earlier when attacking Gorton. Since Peacock was widely regarded as a possible successor to the leadership, his retreat to the backbenches provided a focus for the feelings of dissatisfaction that had developed towards Fraser's leadership and policy direction. Rumours of a challenge were common, particularly when Fraser fell ill just before the Commonwealth Heads of Government Meeting in Melbourne in October 1981. The media were continually counting numbers on each side (Seymour-Ure 1982). Then on 3 April the Liberal government of Victoria (the state from which both Fraser and Peacock come) fell after 27 years in office. Anticipation of this defeat, in which federal economic policies were an issue, coupled with a disastrous federal by-election result, brought the rivalry to a head. Not only was Fraser regarded as an electoral liability, but a new style and new policies were considered desirable. Fraser convened a Liberal party meeting 'to settle the question of the leadership'; he deliberately held it soon after the Victorian election, before his opponents were ready. Even on the day before the meeting it was unclear what tactics would be used. A vote of confidence, determined by an open show of hands, was one possibility; a 'spill' motion (by which all leadership positions were declared vacant) followed by a secret ballot was another. In the event Fraser declared that he understood that there was a desire for a vote on the leadership, that he was prepared to submit to it and that he would be a candidate. He won with exactly two-thirds of the vote—54 votes to Peacock's 27.

Fraser's success can be attributed to several factors: his record of having won three elections; the solidarity of most of the ministers behind him; and the belief that Peacock did not have the weight required of a leader. Yet these factors had not prevented the challenge. When Fraser was defeated in the 1983 election, he resigned the party leadership on the night of the polls. Not only did he publicly take the blame for the loss, but he probably also knew that, even had he wanted to retain the leadership, the difficulties of collecting votes for a defeated opposition leader were much greater than for a successful prime minister.

It is apparent that in Australia an intra-party challenge to the prime minister can be mounted at any time. Any majority, however small, is enough to replace a leader, who cannot postpone for long a party meeting if a substantial part of the party wants one. Whenever the internal opponents of a Liberal prime minister consider they have the numbers, feel sufficiently strongly that it is necessary and have an alternative candidate, the leader's position is in danger.

Successful challenges have not happened often, but the ease with which they can be begun has broad political implications that need to be drawn out. First, there is never any doubt that the new party leader will be prime minister. In theory, only the governor-general can commission a new prime minister, but in practice it would be inconceivable for the defeated leader to try to hold on to office or ask for a dissolution. Second, the ease with which challenges in the party room can be organised means that the other traditional methods of removing a prime minister—cabinet or parliamentary revolt—are less likely options. Certainly, apart from one parliamentary defeat in 1929, no government has been brought down by people who still claimed to be part of its party. Since there is a recognised method for changing leaders, it is expected it will be used.

NEW ZEALAND

In New Zealand, as in Australia, parliamentary leaders are elected by members of the parliamentary party. In the National party that choice has to be officially ratified by the Dominion Executive, although since the 1930s this has been a formality. Once elected, the National leader does not have to face re-election; he has effectively been elected for life or until other circumstances intervene. The Labour leader has to face re-election once in the term of each three-year parliament. For a time the occasion for that ballot was the beginning of the third year of each parliament, but it was later brought forward to the opening of the session in the second year or the first caucus meeting of that year. A new leader, if elected, therefore has two years to establish himself in the eyes of the voters as an alternative prime minister.

The distinction between the procedures of the two parties has made little difference in practice. Of National's five leaders, one never became prime minister and was removed, at the instigation of the Dominion Executive of the party, after a mere four years. The three succeeding leaders—Sidney Holland, Keith Holyoake and John Marshall—all served as prime minister. Holland was persuaded to retire in 1957, two months before an election, by a deputation of three ministerial colleagues. He was replaced by his deputy, Holyoake, who lost the ensuing election but won office three years later. Holyoake retired in 1972, ten months before an election. His leadership had been questioned for some time and, according to one observer, his retirement was a result of slow strangulation rather than political assassination. His decision was taken after he had finally raised the subject for discussion in caucus and was persuaded that he should go. What is uncertain is whether, in either case, the caucus would have forcibly removed Holland and Holyoake if they had not stepped down. There is no doubt that, whatever the public explanations may have been, both were reluctant. In the small political environment of New Zealand, loyalty to the party leader was regarded as essential. Deputy leaders have always taken over the top job.

Since 1972, however, loyalty has been less important as a constraint on the removal of leaders, primarily as a consequence of the confrontationist style of Muldoon. In 1974 he ousted Marshall from the leadership of the opposition. Marshall had provided little direction after National lost the 1972 election and was widely considered to be unable to stand up to Kirk in parliament. Moving in utmost secrecy (so that the New Zealand press did not get a hint of the intrigue until it was complete), Muldoon's backers gathered the support of the majority of caucus while Marshall was overseas. The Dominion Executive passed a unanimous vote of confidence in Marshall (an indication, as so often is the case, that votes of confidence are only passed when confidence is lacking). It also demanded that caucus give asssurances that there would be no change before the next election. In practice, the motion gave caucus the excuse to debate the issue. Then Marshall asked members of caucus in a confidential letter whether they wanted the leadership put on the agenda of the next caucus meeting. It was a strategem of asking for votes without doing so openly. When the majority replied that they did, thereby indicating their desire for a change, Marshall resigned. Though a formal vote was never required, he was pushed out because caucus clearly wanted someone who could effectively oppose Kirk. After Muldoon was elected leader unopposed in caucus, the Dominion Executive endorsed that decision (for a brilliant account, see Jackson 1978b; for an insider's account, see Chapman 1980: 82–7).

The precedent of 1974 perhaps created a new set of rules for the National caucus. In 1980 there was an attempt to replace Muldoon, then prime minister, with Brian Talboys, the deputy leader. It was organised by a group of the younger and more effective ministers— hence tagged the 'colonels' coup'—who collected signed letters of 26 members of caucus (a clear majority) which demanded a change in the National's leadership and a greater degree of consultation. Both Muldoon and Talboys were overseas. The rebels gave Muldoon a warning of their demands and roused his political fighting instincts. Using the external organisation to bring pressure on MPs through their local branches, fighting very publicly and calling in the dissident members individually to discuss their complaints, he detached one or two of the leaders. The Dominion Executive demanded that the leadership question be settled. By the time the next caucus meeting was held, Talboys was not prepared to stand. If the rebels had a majority, it was marginal and it seems that Talboys had no stomach for a continuing fight. The challenge fizzled out, Talboys retired at the next election and Muldoon installed as deputy a loyal colleague who had no pretensions to the top job. He has ensured too that there is no obvious alternative among those who are regarded as possible successors.

In the Labour party also, loyalty was a dominant feature of political life. From 1935 to 1962 the party had only three leaders—Michael Savage, Peter Fraser and Walter Nash. Each served as deputy before being elevated to the top position. None was challenged. Savage and Fraser died as leaders; Nash retired in 1962 at the age of 80. He was succeeded by Arnold Nordmeyer, a former minister of finance whose 'black budget' of 1958 was regarded as a principal cause of Labor's electoral defeat in 1960. Nordmeyer lost the 1963 election, then the support of caucus. When the time for the election of the leader arrived, Norman Kirk had the numbers and replaced him. The tradition of a natural succession had died.

In 1974 Kirk died in office and was replaced by Bill Rowling, who defeated the deputy leader in a caucus ballot. Rowling led the party when it lost office in 1975 and again in 1978; the party had no obvious replacement. The one new hope was David Lange, an Auckland lawyer who was elected to the deputy leadership after only eighteen months in parliament. In February 1980, at the meeting in which the regular election was considered, Rowling was re-elected unopposed. Late that year, soon after the National party had been divided by the colonels' coup, Lange's supporters tried to displace Rowling. Rowling narrowly survived a caucus ballot, reputedly by his own vote. The fact that there was an official time when a challenge could be made did not stop members making one whenever the numbers were there—or seemed to be. In 1983, after losing the 1981 general election, Rowling declined to stand again and Lange replaced him. The pressure on leaders for electoral success is indicated by Lange's own statement that he would not survive a defeat in the 1984 election.

In both parties the challenges of the last decade have stripped away the vestiges of loyalty that acted as a cement for party leadership. Even in the intimate politics of New Zealand, a ruthless attitude to leaders who appear likely to lose the next election has created precedents which have increased their vulnerability. What might in the 1950s have been regarded as unthinkable is now a regular subject of discussion.

BRITAIN

In Britain, from 1965 to 1980, the two parties used similar methods to elect their leaders; but since then, their procedures have become very different. Before 1965 Conservative leaders 'emerged', chosen by a process of consultation among the party elites. In practice that meant selecting the person who was most acceptable as prime minister, because between 1922 and 1965 no-one was first elected leader of the party while in opposition. Leaders usually resigned when they saw fit; the persistence with which Churchill hung on to the prime ministership, despite the almost unanimous view of his cabinet colleagues that he should retire, shows how much the decision lay in the prime minister's hands (see Seldon 1981: 40–54).

Since 1965 the Conservative leader has been elected by the Conservative members of the House of Commons. Both Heath and Thatcher were chosen by this method and both while the party was out of office. In the first ballot the leading candidate needs both a majority and a margin of 15 per cent more votes over the nearest rival—to ensure that the leader reflects some consensus in the party. If this is not achieved a second ballot is held with new nominations.

Thus compromise candidates can enter. A simple majority is sufficient in that second ballot.

Although Heath did not obtain the required percentage, he did get a simple majority. The other candidates then withdrew and there was no need for a second ballot. But, once elected, there was no available mechanism for removing him, or formally challenging his hold on the leadership. While he was prime minister there was no hint of a move to unseat him, but after he had lost two elections in 1974, demands for his removal swelled. The electoral defeats were only one of the reasons for the desire for change. His relations with his backbenchers had often been difficult and strained, and there were feelings that new policy directions might be required. This dissatisfaction culminated in a meeting of the 1922 Committee of Conservative backbenchers which almost unanimously demanded that Heath put his position to a vote. One member asked whether the leadership was freehold or leasehold: Heath thought it should be the former; the 1922 Committee and his critics demanded the second (Cosgrave 1979: 56; for details of Heath's unpopularity, see Norton 1978).

Forced to act by party demand, Heath commissioned a committee headed by Sir Alec Douglas-Home to establish a procedure by which the party could elect—or remove—a leader. The committee adopted similar procedures to those used in 1965, allowing for three ballots, the last of which would decide the issue by a process of preference distribution. In the first ballot Thatcher gained more votes than Heath, but not an absolute majority. Heath then retired from the contest. In the second ballot she gained a clear majority over the four new candidates who entered the race.

These two contests were fought while the party was in opposition, but they set important precedents. The rules devised by Douglas-Home also included a provision for the leader, whether or not prime minister, to face a ballot within six to nine months of the opening of a new parliament, or within 28 days of the beginning of each new session if there was a challenger to the incumbent (Cosgrove 1979: 58). No such challenger has yet emerged, but there is now a formal process by which a leader can be opposed. Early in 1983, when Thatcher was particularly unpopular, 'there was even talk of running a candidate against her at the beginning of the new parliament' (*Times* 2 August 1983). The Falklands war and then the electoral triumph ended that proposal, but it was apparently being discussed.

Conservative ministers do not meet with backbenchers in regular party meetings; at times they may be invited to address the 1922 Committee, but they are not members of that committee, nor are any formal votes taken there. It therefore appears that if a substantial part of the Conservative parliamentary party do want to change their leader at any except the prescribed time, there are no procedures to allow it. If there is no challenge, then the prime minister is 'constitutionally safe for another year' (*New Statesman* 16 October 1981).

The leader of the British Labour party was until 1981 elected by the members of the parliamentary party by a process of exhaustive ballot. After each ballot the candidate with the lowest number of votes was omitted and a further ballot held on a later date until one person received an absolute majority of votes; the elections of Attlee, Gaitskell, Wilson, Callaghan and Foot were all conducted by these means. While the party was in opposition the leader had to be chosen annually and the incumbent could be challenged. When the party had a parliamentary majority, the leader—in practice the prime minister—had to submit to an election at the beginning of each parliament. This was largely a formality since the leader would have just won a general election. In 1945 Morrison had argued that Attlee should not accept a commission to form a government until his position as leader had been confirmed by a meeting of the parliamentary party. Attlee ignored the suggestion, which was based on the hope that he, Morrison, might be elected instead of Attlee to head the Labour government (Donoghue and Jones 1973: 338–43). Nor in later cases did Wilson seek to confirm his position before forming a government.

Since the 1979 election the process of leadership election has been changed drastically. The most important decision required that the leader of the party be elected annually by a national conference. The electoral system, accepted by the Wembley conference of January 1981, gave unions 40 per cent of the votes, and the constituency parties and the parliamentary party 30 per cent each—in the latter case considerably less than most of the parliamentary party wanted (*Times* 21 March 1980). The system was used for the first time in the election of the deputy leader in September 1981 when Denis Healey narrowly defeated Tony Benn. In 1983, after Foot resigned, the conference elected Neil Kinnock.

The reasons for the change were complex. Much of the extra-parliamentary left wanted to ensure that the parliamentary members were more responsive to their wishes and would adhere more closely to their policies; both Wilson and Callaghan had shown at times an impatience with the demands of the party organisation. Further there was an argument, espoused particularly by Tony Benn (1981: 22–30), that the prime minister was far too powerful and should not control the conference. The move was therefore designed to make the prime minister more amenable to the party wishes by being made more widely answerable to the rank and file.

Yet in the debate over the methods that should be used to elect leaders, little attention was given to means that could be used to remove the prime minister at other times. Some members of the left did make suggestions; for instance, Benn's supporter, Michael Meacher, wanted Labour prime ministers to submit their records to conference for approval between 18 and 36 months from the date of the preceding election. But no such suggestions were taken up. The resolution finally adopted at Wembley did include a clause that, as Mostyn Evans, general secretary of the Transport and General Workers Union, argued, 'gave the necessary stability to a Labour prime minister because when the party was in office there could be an election [for the leadership] only if a motion to that effect was carried at annual conference' (*Times* 26 January 1981).

This seems a strange definition of stability: the result may be that Labour prime ministers are secure from revolt within the parliamentary party but could be forced by a vote of annual conference to face a ballot. However, if conference were to dismiss a prime minister who retained the support of the parliamentary party, the tensions created would be vast. It would mean imposing a prime minister on to a reluctant party—a process unlikely to happen in practice unless the party is ideologically divided in an irreconcilable way. If the move were made because electoral defeat was looming, it is unlikely that a prime minister would still retain the majority support of the parliamentary party.

Tony Benn has suggested that there are still mechanisms available at other times. If a prime minister abused his or her power, he or she 'would be overthrown by his or her Cabinet colleagues through a collective resignation or by Labour MPs through a withdrawal of support in the Commons. Either of these events would precipitate a change of leader, or a general election' (Benn 1981: 39). Such a suggestion raises several questions. First, how would the Labour conference react if *its* duly elected leader was then removed at the initiative of precisely those groups from whom the power to elect leaders has been so bitterly wrested? Indeed it is surprising that Benn, the advocate of outside election, should rely on such traditional methods to control a prime minister. Second, if a prime minister did resign, how would he or she be replaced—by the parliamentary party or by a conference that would take time to convene? The rules state that, in the case of a leader resigning, the deputy leader becomes leader with full powers (i.e. not acting leader) until the next conference can duly choose a successor. But the circumstances would surely lead to a badly divided party if a coup had removed the conference's leader. Besides, it has never been made clear under what procedures a coup could be mounted. While

Foot was blundering towards the disaster of the 1983 election, discussions about changes to the leadership were common, but little attention was given to the question of how a leader could be forcibly removed. The Economist (31 July 1982) concluded that 'the only way he can be removed is by provoking his resignation'.

Obviously the threats of cabinet or parliamentary revolt are potent weapons that may create restraints on a prime minister; every prime minister needs co-operation and consent. Yet it is questionable whether those mechanisms could be utilised; they have not been in the last 50 years. At times the Callaghan government was defeated in the House of Commons, but his opponents within the Labour party always supported the government on votes which it declared to be a vote of confidence. Nor is it likely that a collective resignation in a cabinet selected by a prime minister could be easily orchestrated. Most prime ministers are likely to retain some loyalty among those they choose. It may be argued that these methods are effective because in the past they have acted as a deterrent and have not had to be used. But the evidence could equally be interpreted to suggest that they are no longer valid in practice.

Indeed both of Benn's proposed methods of removing prime ministers are alien to twentieth-century precedents. Some prime ministers have been 'persuaded' to retire voluntarily, but this moral pressure, in Britain at least, was exerted in the days when leaders emerged, rather than were selected. It is less certain, although still not impossible, that similar tactics could be adopted now. A prime minister who wants to hang on to his or her position could with justification point to the fact that there are existing mechanisms and invite the critics to use them. It does not mean that prime ministers who make a spectacular blunder or major error might not be persuaded to resign; but that is different from saying they are being forcibly removed. As one observer has commented, 'Those who live by the vote must be killed by the vote' (New Statesman 16 October 1981). The existence of formal mechanisms will make the use of traditional pressures more difficult to use on a stubborn leader. When these mechanisms have been deliberately ceded to a broader section of the party, traditional methods have clearly become no more than political myths.

CANADA

In Canada the leaders of the three national parties have each been elected by a convention of delegates for the past 50 years and that process is now well-established. It ensures that all sections and regions are represented in the choice of the national leader—an important factor in a country where the parties often have few or no representatives elected to parliament from some of the provinces. The number of participants is large. The Liberal convention of 1968 had 2472 delegates; 1584 of them were elected by constituency organisations, the other were MPs (130), university student delegates (130) and ex-officio delegates. The latter group included Liberal candidates defeated at the previous election, provincial leaders and the representatives of various party organisations and subordinate bodies. The PC convention had 2411 delegates, of whom 1320 were constituency delegates, 95 were MPs, 116 were university student representatives, 428 were ex-officio and the remaining 452 were appointed as delegates-at-large (they consisted of leading members of the party not otherwise selected or eligible to attend the convention) (Courtney 1973: 120–3).

Leadership conventions are held when the leadership is vacant. Thus the Liberal party, which has governed Canada for most of the last 60 years, has held only five leadership conventions—in 1919, 1948, 1959, 1968 and 1984. At two of these the results were almost foregone conclusions: and there was no real doubt that St Laurent would win in 1948 and Pearson in 1958 and indeed in 1948 Mackenzie King carefully manipulated the convention process to ensure the outcome he wanted (Whitaker 1977: 171–8). In 1948, 1968 and 1984 the convention was, in choosing the leader, also choosing the prime minister.

Before 1966 there was no mechanism available for convening a convention unless the leadership was vacant. When asked in the early 1960s if a Liberal leader could be deposed, Lester Pearson stated: 'There is no institutional way ... we haven't had to dispose of leaders. We've had very few leaders. As you know, I'm the fourth... The leader deposes himself. I don't know what other arrangements there could be' (quoted in Engelmann and Schwartz 1976: 243).

The difficulties that can emerge when prime ministers lose the confidence of their colleagues were shown by the divisions that occurred in the PC cabinet of John Diefenbaker. In 1963 several ministers decided to move against him in cabinet in an attempt to replace him. Diefenbaker heard of their plans, hastily convened a meeting of the parliamentary party before the cabinet met, and received a vote of confidence there. The cabinet rebels thus were unable to depose him. Therefore the constitutional and party consequences of a such cabinet revolt remain speculation; no one can be certain whether cabinet *can* remove a prime minister. Diefenbaker then called a general election at which his minority government was defeated. The divisions in the party thus led to Diefenbaker's loss of the prime ministership, though not the party leadership. After the 1963 election, the PC party was split in a bitter internecine fight until 1966 when its annual meeting voted for the convening of a leadership convention, with the intention of deposing Diefenbaker. Throughout the period Diefenbaker retained the support of the majority of the parliamentary party; at the last minute at the convention he announced that he would again be a candidate but was resoundingly defeated. The events that led to his fall illustrated that support from caucus alone was not enough; the leader had to maintain the support of the extra-parliamentary wing of the party too (Perlin 1980: 24–8).

Both major parties accept that to leave the timing of an unsuccessful leader's resignation entirely to his or her personal judgement can create problems. At the national meeting of the Liberal party in 1966, the party debated how leaders could be controlled. One delegate, now a senior minister, argued that 'the party must have its check reins to keep the leader close to the party', and wanted automatic conventions within two years of each parliamentary election. Eventually the conference accepted that a resolution calling for a leadership convention would be placed on the agenda of the first biennial conference to be held after each general election. If the resolution was adopted after a secret ballot, a leadership convention would be called within a year (Courtney 1973: 100–1). Thus once during the life of each parliament the biennial conference could pass judgement on a Liberal prime minister by deciding whether he or she should face re-election. Trudeau was never threatened by that process. After his electoral defeat in 1979 he had agreed to stand down when the defeat of the Clark government interrupted his retirement plans and catapulted him back into office. In 1980 87 per cent of delegates opposed a leadership convention, most of the malcontents coming from the western provinces where Trudeau was particularly unpopular (*Globe and Mail* 7 July 1980). In 1982 there was an attempt to institute a secret ballot on the need for a leadership review every two years, instead of once in each parliament. The vote on the motion was turned into a vote of confidence for Trudeau and the convention overwhelmingly rejected the proposal (*Globe and Mail* 6 December 1982).

In 1969 the Progressive Conservatives formally moved in the same direction, but they distinguished between periods when the party was in government and those when it was in opposition. If the party was in opposition, and had failed to increase its standing in the house by 20 per cent at the previous election, the first post-election general meeting of the National Association would vote in a secret ballot on a motion calling for a leadership convention. Later a vote on the lead-

ership at each convention was effectively allowed. While the party was
in government, no resolution could be put to a general meeting unless
it had received formal notice that the prime minister had lost a vote of
confidence in caucus. In other words, to depose an unwilling PC
prime minister required first a vote of no confidence to be passed in
caucus, then a motion calling for a leadership convention to be passed
by the annual meeting, and then a contest (Courtney 1973: 102–4).
The whole process would most likely take a year and would almost
inevitably be totally destructive to a ruling party that tried to use it,
even though it was unlikely that a prime minister who had lost the
confidence of both parliamentary and extra-parliamentary parties
would still want to appeal to the wider party membership gathered at
of the convention. In practice none of these mechanisms has been used
to convene a leadership convention while a party was in government.

The new procedures did however lead to a change in the PC leadership in opposition. Two general meetings passed a vote of confidence in Joe Clark by opposing the call for a leadership convention, but
the percentage of the votes supporting him dropped to around 67 per
cent. Clark therefore stated that he would resign and recontest the
leadership. He handed over the parliamentary leadership to a close
colleague and campaigned vigorously. However he was defeated on
the last ballot by Brian Mulroney, who had never held elected office.
Of course, he was not *forced* to resign; the procedures merely allowed
the level of discontent to be indicated. Even so the process was prolonged and time-consuming, possible in opposition but almost unthinkable in government.

Clark's defeat brought about a review of PC procedures. The important question was to what degree should leaders be answerable? In
the month before the 1983 ballot, Mulroney claimed to support Clark,
but insisted on 'the importance of the principle of a review of the
leadership by secret ballot at regular intervals' (*Globe and Mail* 7 December 1982). But it was considered that the process led to instability.
First, the incumbent was running against ghosts; no alternatives had
to declare themselves. Also, the reasons for the vote might vary: some
who voted for a leadership convention may have been Clark's supporters who saw the need to clear the air. Second, the procedures did not
specify what size of majority was considered a satisfactory endorsement. It needed more than 50 per cent to require a leadership convention, but how far above that was a leader still safe? When those factors
are added to the PC's chronic dissatisfaction with its leadership, it is
easy to see how an *annual* vote of confidence can be regarded as
destabilising.

After Clark's decision to stand down, the PC convention changed the rules. If a leader became prime minister, there would be *no* review. If not, there would be a vote on the need for a leadership at the next national meeting (*Globe and Mail* 31 January 1983). That change made PC prime ministers almost totally secure.

By the standards of Britain and Australia these mechanisms are complex, but they are a move, albeit a small one, in the direction of answerability in Canada. They restrict to a degree the right of leaders to hold office as long as they want, but they probably would only be used against a leader of the opposition. The impact on a government of trying to remove a prime minister would be too great. Punnett's judgement remains true: 'If the leader is electorally successful the party can hardly afford to replace him, and if he is electorally unsuccessful it may be difficult to replace him if he is not prepared to retire quietly' (1977: 53).

The constitutional expert, Eugene Forsey, agrees: it would require 'a revolutionary situation to make a party get rid of a prime minister' (*Globe and Mail* 20 July 1982). Trudeau's position in 1982 and in 1983 emphasised the point. Speculation about when he would retire was frequent; sections of the party, particularly in the west, would have liked to dump him; polls suggested that the Liberal party would fare better under John Turner's leadership. In 1976 he did say that if cabinet reached a consensus that he should resign, he would (Radwanski 1978: 278), but that would have meant cabinet had someone else in mind. Such unanimity was unlikely to be achieved. It was generally acknowledged that the timing was entirely in Trudeau's hands. Everyone else had to wait; there are no usable mechanisms to speed a reluctant prime minister on his way.

FACTORS AFFECTING VULNERABILITY

From these brief surveys some lessons can be drawn about the factors that make prime ministers more or less vulnerable to internal party revolt in the type of parliamentary system examined here.

Constituency

The first, and most obvious, lesson is that prime ministers are answerable to those who elect them. The broader the constituency, the more difficult it is to call together and the less vulnerable the prime minister is likely to be. For instance, Mackenzie King, leader of the Canadian Liberal party from 1919 to 1948 and prime minister for much of that period,

> placed great stock in the fact that he was selected by a democratic conven-
> tion and not by the parliamentary caucus. On the rare occasions when the
> parliamentary caucas began to growl ... he more than once silenced the
> parliamentary wolves by emphasising that he was the representative and
> leader of the party as a whole, not merely the parliamentary party. What
> the parliamentary group did not create, it may not destroy, at least not
> without ratification by the party 'grass roots'. (Courtney 1973:128)

Diefenbaker similarly argued in 1967 that 'only a party convention
had the right to undo what a similar convention had done eleven years
before' (Courtney 1973: 129). Canadian prime ministers have always
had a dual responsibility—to the parliamentary caucus with which
they must work on a regular basis, and to the broad party that elected
them. To lack the full confidence of the former might indeed make life
difficult, but it need not be immediately fatal.

There are always logistical and political reasons that make it difficult for a broad constituency to assert its authority, however unques-
tioned that may be. It takes time to organise a leadership convention
and considerable pressures to have one convened. The results are likely to be unpredictable if the prime minister uses the considerable resources available to seek for votes. Further the costs in terms of public
division were regarded as too high for the Liberals in 1968 when
several cabinet ministers were competing for a leadership that was
voluntarily vacated. The image of a divided and internally competing
party was regarded as electorally damaging. A campaign against a
fighting incumbent could only be destructive. It has never been
attempted.

Contrast the Canadian situation with that of Australia or New Zealand. There the constituency is defined, limited and undisputed. There
is no cost in convening a meeting; even if parliament is not sitting,
four days are enough to recall party members from anywhere in the
world, as happened in Australia in April 1982. There is no doubt that
prime ministers owe their position to the parliamentary party, and to
it alone. Appeals over the head of parliamentarians to members of the
party as a whole would serve little purpose. If a prime minister is to be
removed it can be done speedily, at any time and without delay.
Obviously the removal of any leader will indicate that a party is internally divided, and splits will probably be evident for some time.
Nevertheless if the execution is expeditious, the wounds that occur
can heal far more quickly.

In the British Conservative party too the process may be easier
because the constituency is limited. Even though in 1974 there may
have been no formal mechanism to remove Heath, the fact that the
1922 Committee was *part* of a defined group and, with its executive

newly elected in October, could be seen to represent that part, gave its demands a certain legitimacy. Presumably, when the party is in government and with a formal mechanism now existing, the committee could act again, though doubtless with less weight, against an incumbent prime minister. With the Labour party, the extension of the electoral suffrage to the party conference will probably make it more difficult to challenge a prime minister at any but the official opportunity.

Influencing the constituency

An important question raised by the numbers involved is the degree of control over the constituency that the prime minister may exert. As Chapter 2 illustrated, in Australia both Liberal and Labor parties are federations of six state branches which are responsible for the selection of the party's parliamentary candidates and for the process of selection that each parliamentarian must face before every election. Prime ministers thus have little influence on the careers of parliamentarians. Indeed MPs are more likely to be threatened if they ignore the interests of their state branches, who therefore become important forces in leadership challenges. The choice of ministers is constrained too; a Labor cabinet is elected by the parliamentary party, with the prime minister distributing portfolios. The prime minister thus controls promotion within the ministry, but not access to it. That depends on factional alignment or broad support. A prime minister's support may be useful; it is not crucial. A Liberal prime minister chooses ministers, but has to take account of coalition, bicameral, state and factional forces; freedom of choice is limited, both in original choices and in reshuffles (see Chapter 4). In practice most ministers in the 1982 challenge to Fraser did remain loyal to him, but that was not true when Gorton was toppled in 1971. Prime ministerial patronage remains extensive but clearly has its limitations as members may be all too conscious of alternative pressures. Regional party pressures are often strong.

The federal structure of the party has important implications because the prime minister cannot control the various centres of power. A prime minister who can work closely with the state executives can appeal to them to bring pressures on those whose support is wavering; Fraser tried to gain a vote of confidence from the state executives in 1982, but failed. Where, as in the Labor party, factions are dominant, success will depend on the leader's own links. It becomes possible for individuals to maintain a strong power base in a province or state and to develop their own reputation. This is particularly true in the Cana-

dian PC party whose leaders have been provincial premiers. Politicians with a strong regional base can exist independently of the prime
minister's patronage.

In the British Conservative party the central party machinery is
under the direct control of the party leader. MPs are not regularly
threatened with the withdrawal of their nomination and the prime
minister is exclusively responsible for the selection and dismissal of
ministers. The focus is therefore more likely to be on parliamentary
than on extra-parliamentary pressures and prime ministerial patronage
remains influential. In New Zealand, National prime ministers have
no impact on selections, although they control promotion to the
ministry. Labour prime ministers there control neither.

When the constituency is wider than the party in parliament, prime
ministerial influence is far harder to exert. In Canada federal party
organisation is often ephemeral, particularly in those provinces where
the ruling federal party is weak. The prime minister's influence over
many delegates to the convention is likely to be more through reputation than patronage, particularly in those regions where he or she is
well-known. In constructing a ministry too, the prime minister has to
take account of more factors than Australian leaders, because linguistic, ethnic and religious links are also important. In the British Labour
party, where the new methods of election have been designed in part
to reduce the leader's influence, the capacity to influence the constituency will depend more on factional links than direct patronage.

Federalism splits up the party organisation in Australia and Canada.
It creates more party groupings which can exert pressure. It makes it
more difficult for the central organisation (itself usually weak) or for
the prime minister to influence parliamentarians if the party in parliament is the arena in which a leader is to be threatened. It may also
assist the prime minister because the forces that want to overthrow
him or her are likely to be divided. In assessing vulnerability the size
of the constituency has to be coupled with the accessibility of that
constituency to prime ministerial pressure.

Formal opportunity

Even if the constituency is clearly prescribed, that in itself need not
make the prime minister vulnerable. What is also required is the existence of formal occasions on which challenges can be launched, or at
least a set of rules that allow that opportunity to be created. In New
Zealand, Australia and Canada prime ministers and their cabinet meet
regularly with backbenchers in party meetings. Those meetings discuss legislation that ministers propose to introduce into parliament

and provide a regular and private forum for free-ranging criticism of ministers' proposals. Australian and New Zealand party meetings can, as we have seen, be used to challenge at any time; Canadian meetings cannot. Even though in Australia and New Zealand (except for the National party) there are formal times at which leaders have to face election, challenges are not limited to those occasions. In the British Conservative party, the constituency that elects the leader may be the same as in Australia but the rules do not provide for regular or formal ministerial-backbench meetings. Instead there is a formal occasion or set of occasions, at the beginning of each parliament or each session, when a prime minister can officially be challenged. There is no other occasion when the 'electoral college' meets as a body.

The existence of such prescribed occasions has two effects. First, it is highly unlikely that a prime minister who has won or retained office will have his or her leadership immediately challenged (although, as in Australia in 1969, it *can* happen). Second, it presumably increases the difficulty of mounting pressure at any other time. If there are no rules determining when a prime minister's position can be challenged, then incumbency is in a sense always under review. But once procedures are codified, they can be appealed to as a means of staving off dissatisfaction at other times; grumblers can be told to wait.

Prescribed and exclusive times for challenge have other impacts that help protect a prime minister. Changing the leader is a traumatic exercise and always a last resort, considered because party members can see no other way of avoiding an electoral defeat or of ensuring that the leader adheres to party policy. It would be suggested when other methods, such as cabinet pressure and persuasion, have failed. On only a few occasions, under any system, will a party be so divided, a prime minister's reputation so poor, and fears of defeat or misdirection so great that a challenge will be considered. Such challenges will generally have to be made when all these factors come to the boil, but it is unlikely that the right moment will often coincide with the moment when the formal review takes place. Further, if this is true of a parliamentary party which elects a leader, the chance of an outside body exercising its formal rights is likely to be even more limited; the political reverberations that would be created by an extra-parliamentary body removing, or seeking to remove, a prime minister would be too great.

An alternative prime minister

The fourth important criterion for assessing the vulnerability of prime ministers is the need for an alternative. No leader can be replaced by a vacuum. An alternative person has to be promoted, even if he or she is not actually a candidate.

Under some sets of rules an alternative candidate is a *sine qua non* of a challenge. The position of a British Conservative prime minister is put to a ballot *if* there is an alternative candidate. That means that some leading figure must be prepared to take on an incumbent prime minister in face-to-face battle. Few people have the prestige or perceived ability; even fewer of those may be willing to face charges of divisiveness and disloyalty. To challenge a prime minister may put one's career at risk; one's reputation might be harmed irreparably. It is one thing to stand without any expectation of winning when the party leadership is vacant, as a means of indicating a future interest; it is quite another to take on an active prime minister. The rules therefore protect a prime minister.

By contrast in Australia in the Liberal party there is a scope for a 'spill' motion, so that no alternatives have to declare their interest until the leadership is actually vacant. Such a process eases the pressures on the potential replacement who may be able to promise continued allegiance to the elected leader—for as long as he or she holds the position.

Nevertheless, whether or not a candidate has to be announced before the poll, rebels need to be agreed on somebody. There has to be an accepted candidate who is widely regarded as a legitimate successor. In New Zealand the 1980 colonels' coup was possible because Talboys was a possible prime minister; after his departure Muldoon was secure because those who were dissatisfied had no obvious person around whom to group. Indeed, generally prime ministers will try to ensure that there is no obvious alternative around whom support can coalesce. Wilson 'never had less three or four [crown princes] and at one time had ... six' (Wilson 1976: 51–2). Rivals are discouraged, watched and, if necessary, cut down to size.

Whatever the system, the alternatives have to be prepared to stand and campaign. If they refuse to be considered, the exercise is futile. Discussions of replacing Attlee with Bevin ended abruptly when Bevin was not interested (Brown 1971: 50). A challenge to Thatcher needs a distinguished figure around whom to rally; who will play that role? The colonels' coup failed in the end because Talboys did not have the stomach for a close and bitter fight. In Australia Fraser became more vulnerable when Peacock left the cabinet because he could provide a leader on the backbench around whom opposition could—and did—consolidate. It is far more difficult to arrange a coup from within the cabinet where ministers are expected to identify with government policy, in public at least.

The need for a clear alternative may be less obvious when extra-parliamentary bodies help to determine the leadership. In Canada to call for a leadership convention in theory opens the gates to anyone. Even so, when the prime minister is determined to resist deposition, challenging ministers risk their own positions in cabinet. The difficulty of finding an alternative is increased once formal procedures for removing the leader have been established. The process creates problems, particularly for opposition leaders. Their performance is consistently compared, not against one potential rival, but against several. A leader seeking support is thus constantly shadow-boxing with unannounced rivals. Those in the Progressive Conservatives who wanted a leadership convention need not have united in favour of any new alternative. Until the convention was called, that positive commitment was not required. It makes it difficult to retain wide support when not, as a prime minister is, protected by collective responsibility.

However it seems that Canadian prime ministers have been less concerned about the development of powerful ministers, perhaps because they do not see them as rivals. The great difficulty involved in removing leaders gives them security; and the need for ministers to oversee much of the patronage in their own provinces gives them an independent, but not necessarily threatening, power-base. The traditional role of the Quebec lieutenants like St Laurent, the strength of individual ministers like C.D. Howe and Walter Gordon who in some ways were more dominant than their prime ministers, illustrates this. Yet conflicts of personality seem endemic in Britain and Australia. The explanation must partially be that in Canada ministers may be regarded as potential leaders—when the job is vacant; in Australia and Britain they are considered as immediate rivals more readily.

THE IMPLICATIONS: ACCOUNTABILITY OR STABILITY?

Vulnerability is thus seen to depend on four factors: the constituency, the influence that can be exerted on that constituency, the opportunity for and the existence of an alternative. The narrower the constituency, the less easy it is to control, the more frequent the opportunity and the less the need for a specific alternative, then the more vulnerable the prime minister is. The institutional arrangements in the four parliamentary systems under discussion are summarised in Table 3.1, which suggests that *at the moment* Australian prime ministers are the most vulnerable, Canadians the least.

Of course institutional factors are not the only ones that may deter-

Table 3.1 Factors for vulnerability

Party		Constituency	PM's influence	Opportunity	Need for alternative
Australia	Labor	narrow	low	unlimited	no
	Liberal	narrow	medium	unlimited	no
Britain	Labour	broad	low	annual	yes
	Conservative	narrow	high	annual	yes
Canada	Liberal	broad	low	rare	no
	Conservative	broad	low	rare	no
New Zealand	National	narrow	high	unlimited	no
	Labour	narrow	low	unlimited	no

mine the vulnerability of leaders. Some leaders may be regarded as tougher than others, and opponents will be more wary of taking them on. Poor health may provide extra opportunities; so might circumstances beyond the governement's control. Nor are the existing institutional constraints immutable: new rules cause new politics. If Benn's proposals to remove some of a British Labour prime minister's resources, for instance the choice of ministers, are adopted the prime minister's position will be weakened. Any faction which has control of the party may, for ideological or electoral reasons, seek to change the rules. If coalition governments become necessary, that too may alter the situation. Further, the attitude to leadership may vary. In Britain, Conservative leaders are regarded with a degree of deference that would be unknown in any Labour party. In Australia, Liberal leaders are given greater freedom to succeed, but treated with less patience when they fail, than their Labor counterparts. Yet these factors, important though they may be, will operate within a party framework and must abide by some 'rules of the game'. Institutional constraints will structure the role of the prime ministers.

The choice is between stability and answerability. Vulnerable prime ministers are, and feel, immediately answerable to their parliamentary party. While non-vulnerable prime ministers obviously do not ignore the cabinet and parliamentary colleagues with whom they must work, they are less in danger of immediate challenge.

There are some important implications. Vulnerable prime ministers must pay constant attention to the backbench, and to public image. If their party fears they may lose the next election, it may take preventive action. If government policies are considered ill-advised, supporters might start considering alternatives. The reputation of prime ministers is being constantly assessed, often in comparison with those of potential alternatives. They can ill-afford to sack popular senior ministers, who might act as the centre of an internal party opposition. Rumour can be a deadly device as party opponents try to destabilise the situation and cast doubt on their leaders' ability (see e.g. Seymour-Ure 1982). If a vulnerable prime minister is doing badly, it creates the conditions for constant plotting and intrigue; while the uncertainty lasts, all the prime minister's attention will be directed toward survival—governing must wait. On the other hand, vulnerability does create answerability. The prime minister must listen to the party, must heed the views of influential colleagues and must keep an open door. However dominant personally, he or she can not afford to ignore the power-base.

A non-vulnerable prime minister can, to an extent, remain immune from these immediate threats. That immunity is comparative only; no leader can afford to have too rebellious a backbench or too fractious a cabinet. However if the prime minister is not answerable, there may be more open criticism, more grumbling, and a greater feeling of frustration among backbenchers who feel that they have been ignored too much, or else merely taken for granted. Prime ministerial arrogance or intolerance may be less dangerous to a non-vulnerable leader. On the other hand such a government may have greater stability. Intrigue may be less as the party has, except for prescribed moments, delegated responsibility to the prime minister. Leaders are less worried about their backs or about factions within the party. In other circumstances, this stability may be regarded as an unfortunate inability of the party to influence an ineffective prime minister.

Both answerability and stability have their advantages and disadvantages. However, there is no doubt that, in the last two decades, the trend has been towards greater answerability. That trend has important implications for discussion of prime ministerial power. Prime ministers will not often be removed by internal revolt; they have too many resources for that. But the mechanisms for change illustrate that, as prime ministers become answerable to their parties, so in times of difficulty their power is likely to be curtailed.

4

Prime Ministers and Patronage

In discussion of prime ministerial power, the right of prime ministers to appoint, dismiss or shuffle ministers always looms large. So does the capacity to wield extensive patronge in civil service appointments, in honours lists and in the filling of numerous positions, honorary and paid, to statutory authorities or other government bodies. The power of patronage, it is argued, helps prime ministers to cement their position and to bring ministers or others into line on issues of policy.

Crossman (1963: 51) has argued that prime ministers can exercise their authority because they sit at the apex of both the bureaucratic and party systems and therefore can use their powers of appointment to control both. The power to reward, to promise and to dismiss makes people malleable and sympathetic to the prime minister's interests. Crossman (1972: 63) believed that a minister's future lies entirely in the hands of the prime minister: there is 'nothing much I can do about it—except succeed, and so build up my own strength'. Through patronage prime ministers are able to determine the government's personnel and therefore to shape its priorities. Patronage can also protect prime ministers in times of difficulty; too many people are, or hope to be, selected by them.

Statistics indicate the large number of positions that prime ministers can influence. Benn (1981: 26–7) points out that, between 1945 and 1976, seven prime ministers appointed 309 cabinet ministers, 1185 non-cabinet ministers, 586 hereditary or life peers, 118 baronetcies, 264 knighthoods, 85 chairmen of nationalised industries and 35 chairmen of royal commissions: a total of 2564 major appointments and honours. If the other patronage positions, such as permanent secretaries, ambassadors, chiefs of staff and heads of security agencies, are added, Benn calculates a total number between 5000 and 7000. Rose (1980: 6) and Sedgemore (1980: 57–62) provide more detailed figures for each prime minister. Sedgemore, counting the number of different appointments not merely the individuals affected, shows that Attlee appointed 50 cabinet and 188 non-cabinet ministers during his time as prime minister; Wilson made 100 cabinet appointments and 403 non-cabinet ones if his two terms are combined. In Australia the total numbers are naturally smaller, but the patronage available at any time is still considerable. When John Gorton became prime minister in 1968 after Holt's death, he promoted two ministers to cabinet but left all but six in their previous positions. After the 1969 election he changed the portfolio of all eight Liberals in cabinet and of seven of the ten non-cabinet ministers. In his seven years as prime minister, Malcolm Fraser's appointments or reshuffles affected 20 cabinet and 43 non-cabinet Liberal ministers; these included changes in portfolio and/or promotions to cabinet rank. The numbers of non-ministerial appointments that need cabinet approval are fairly large too: in 1978/79 185 appointments were endorsed by cabinet, 206 in 1979/80, 187 in 1980/81 and 210 in 1981/82 (PMC 1979, 1980, 1981, 1982). Over four years the total was 792. As the cabinet handbook makes clear, before any of these appointments can be brought to cabinet for approval, they must be cleared with the prime minister. Although prime ministers may not initiate all appointments, they have a practical veto if they want to use it.

In Canada, patronage seems to loom larger than in Britain and Australia. Canadian politics are more concerned with brokerage than with ideology, and it is accepted practice that ministers will dispense jobs and contracts to party allies. During the long rule of Mackenzie King, those firms which gained government contracts in exchange were expected to make contributions to party funds (see e.g. Whitaker 1977: 104). Quite *who* was to be responsible at the federal level for the distribution of patronage was less obvious; under Mackenzie King, leading ministers from different provinces were generally the people responsible for patronage in those areas and the prime minister was content to leave it to them. In the 1970s the process became more centralised.

In ministerial terms Canadian prime ministers make a wide range of appointments. When Lester Pearson became prime minister, he appointed 25 ministers; during his five years as prime minister, 15 new ministers were appointed, there were further 37 changes of portfolio in that time. During Trudeau's initial term, 28 ministers were in his original cabinet and 29 new ministers were appointed, so 57 people held cabinet rank and there were 98 changes of portfolio. On top of that, Pearson appointed 30 parliamentary secretaries and, up to 1974, Trudeau had appointed 44 (Matheson 1976: 72–3).

In New Zealand 16 ministers were appointed in 1961 by Holyoake and 15 others held office in his eleven-year reign. Muldoon chose 22 originally and 15 more between 1975 and 1982. Since each minister may hold two or three portfolios, reshuffles have been fairly common; Holyoake made 35 changes and Muldoon 32 between 1975 and 1982. The amount of government patronage outside the direct public service is also considerable. An answer to a parliamentary question in 1971 listed ten pages of almost 2000 jobs, large or insignificant, that had been filled by the government (NZ *Parliamentary Debates* vol. 375, Sept.–Oct. 1971, 3879–92).

If in terms of numbers the extent of patronage seems impressive, it still has to be shown how this gives prime ministers power. Several questions need to be asked. Are there practical constraints on its use? To what extent do prime ministers have independence to make free choices, or must they take into account the views of others? The point is not to deny that prime ministers have greater powers of patronage than their colleagues, or that they use them to their own advantage. It is to explore the ways in which institutional and political factors may influence the use of patronage.

THE CHOICE OF MINISTERS

Prime ministers choose their ministers in all parties except for the ALP and New Zealand Labour party, where cabinets are elected by the parliamentary party. The impact of the electoral system will be discussed later, but first it is necessary to see what limits constrain the choice of the prime ministers. Prime ministers can never pick a ministry of all the talents, even from within their own party. A cabinet is a party cabinet, not merely a group of executives; it must reflect the tensions and structures of the party. Merit and anticipated performance are therefore not the only criteria; other factors need to be considered and may force the prime minister's hand.

Regional representation

Political parties are coalitions of one type or another. In federal systems, whether the parties are integrated or confederal, the provinces or states are distinct political units that need to be seen to be formally represented. The Australian and Canadian cabinets therefore function as arenas for regional representation as well as executive action.

In Australia state representation must always be taken into account. Under a Liberal–NCP coalition government, a Liberal prime minister will always choose at least one minister from each state and not too many from any of them. If one of the smaller states has an abundance of talent and has already provided four ministers, as Western Australia did between 1977 and 1980, then the path of promotion for other members from that state will be blocked until that number is reduced. Some balance has to be maintained between Victorian and New South Wales ministers; since all but one leader of the Liberal party has been Victorian, there is generally a fear that Victorian members will gain a disproportionate share of the spoils.

Those unofficial but freely acknowledged limits on choice have two effects. First, when a Liberal prime minister initially forms a ministry, the last few positions may be filled by representatives of particular states who are chosen because of their origin rather than their talent. Second, when resignations occur, there is often pressure to replace the minister with another representative of the same state in order to maintain the perceived balance of state interests.

However in Australia there is no demand for all states to be represented in *cabinet*. In a Liberal-NCP coalition the ministry is divided into a cabinet and a group of outer ministers. From 1975 to 1983 neither Tasmania nor South Australia provided a cabinet minister. It is true that for outer ministers access to cabinet is easy (Weller 1980); further, the senior ministers from each of these states may be co-opted to cabinet when decisions of particular importance to their state are to be made. But regional representation has not been extended to the membership of cabinet itself.

In Canada, where the provinces are more conscious of their separate identity, the pressures for regional representation are greater. When this is combined with the fact that neither of the larger parties can be assured of representation from every province, the flexibility available to the prime minister in the choice of ministers is further circumscribed. In recent years the Liberal party has had little or no representation from the western provinces. Anyone elected from there almost automatically becomes a minister. Where no-one is available, the representation is created by the creation of senators or even occasionally by persuading political opponents to cross the floor and join the ministry. (When that tactic attracted the Albertan, Jack Horner, to the Liberal cabinet in 1978, it failed to achieve its purpose of revitalising the Liberal cause in Alberta because he lost his seat at the next election.) Since the PC party has few representatives elected from Quebec, those who do win there are likely to be chosen for cabinet fairly quickly, even if, as in the Diefenbaker ministry, their influence is soon seen to be limited. At the same time the number of ministers who can be chosen from the Maritime provinces is likely to be limited and, for the Liberals, a balance has to be maintained between representatives from Quebec and Ontario.

These demands for representation also have an impact on the degree to which the prime minister can manipulate the structure of cabinet. With the brief exception of the Clark government, there has been no attempt to split the ministry into a cabinet and an outer group. The most telling argument against such a proposal has been that, by reducing some ministers to second-class status, the representational function of cabinet would be undermined. The experience of the Clark government merely emphasised that problem. When Clark announced the membership of his inner cabinet, there was an immediate complaint that British Columbia was not represented. The omission was quickly rectified by adding one person to the inner cabinet, but the point was obvious: the regions require representation in what is perceived as the highest decision-making body, the full cabinet. It may be true, as one former minister commented, that the growth of television has made the task of representation less vital and therefore the influence of local power-brokers less distinct, but the practice is still pursued in the distribution of jobs even if not in the allocation of real influence.

By contrast in Britain and New Zealand there are few regional pressures. The secretaries of state for Scotland and Wales are always in cabinet and are usually drawn from the members elected by those areas. This may lead to a limited choice, particularly for a Conservative leader, but thereafter regional pressures seem to be few. Indeed the lack of direct links between many British MPs and the areas they represent would make it difficult to see MPs there fulfilling a representational role. In Australia or Canada MPs are conscious of the need to identify with local, or at least state or provincial, needs. In Britain that sense of identification is often much more limited. In New Zealand the South Island needs to provide some ministers and the prime minister has to ensure that Auckland does not provide too many. Otherwise the country is sufficiently small to avoid more regional demands.

Bicameralism and coalitions

Parliamentary forms require that prime ministers select ministers to represent the government in their upper houses. In Canada the leader in the Senate may be influential—the minister there in 1980 was also chairman of one of the important cabinet committees and hence a member of the Priorities and Planning Committee (P&P)—but other Senate ministers are often appointed for purposes of regional representation. The Senate itself has little power.

In Britain the number of ministers in the House of Lords will vary although it will always be greater in a Conservative government where some hereditary peers like Carrington are effectively career politicians. Three peers were in cabinet in Thatcher's first 1979 ministry and in her post-election reshuffle in 1983. Several junior ministers may have been appointed to the House of Lords as a means of allowing them to take office: C.P. Snow, Lady Young and Lord Crowther-Hunt are examples. However, the number of ministers there will be a matter of convenience; there is no quota to be filled.

New Zealand, having a unicameral house and no need for coalition government, avoids both problems.

By contrast to the House of Lords or the Canadian Senate, the Australian Senate is a powerful house. It is capable of bringing government to a halt, as it did in 1974 and 1975, and even destroying a ministry. Its members are elected and therefore do not owe their position directly to the prime minister. It is seen as a forum for an active and influential political career, in which any office except those of prime minister, deputy prime minister and probably treasurer is open to its members. As a chamber it is jealous of its independence and authority, and its members want decent representation in the ministry and in cabinet.

In the 1960s only the leader of the government in the Senate was in cabinet; he was nominated for his party position by the prime minister. The other ministers, between three and six in number and generally including one from the Country party, were in the outer ministry. Any attempt to reduce the Senate's ministerial numbers was strongly opposed. By 1981–82 their influence had indeed increased. It then provided six ministers, five of whom were in cabinet. In part this was because of the acknowledged talent of the senators; two had been promoted rapidly to the cabinet just because their performance was seen to be good. In part it was because the events of the mid-1970s, when the Senate had stopped supply twice, showed that it could not be ignored.

Additionally an Australian Liberal prime minister has to negotiate with the NCP leader about the terms of the coalition. Although there is no doubt that the two parties *will* enter an agreement because in federal politics they have co-operated very closely, the number of NCP ministers and the positions they hold will always be open to discussion. When relations between the leaders are tense, as they were in 1969, a written agreement may be drawn up. Often it will merely be verbal. In practice the NCP has generally provided three cabinet ministers and three outer ministers (one of whom, up to 1980 but not since, was in the Senate). For the last twenty years NCP ministers have held those portfolios of particular concern to country areas— Trade, Primary Industry and Transport. The actual choice of personnel is the prerogative of the NCP leader, although it seems likely that the prime minister could have a veto if he or she felt strongly enough.

Religion or ethnic groups

In Canada several other factors are also taken into account. There is a need for linguistic representation, so Francophones do not feel isolated. Within the ministers from Quebec, there is usually an Anglophone to represent the substantial English-speaking minority there. At least one woman will be chosen. Increasingly the ethnic communities will also be considered.

In Australia, Britain and New Zealand, with much greater homogeneity of language and ethnic background, those pressures do not exist. In the past the Liberal party has tended to be mainly Protestant in composition although the former deputy leader of the party, Phillip Lynch, was a Catholic, but that reflects too the nature of the Australian establishment from which it draws its support. Religion is not seen as a bar to advancement. One woman has usually been chosen in recent years (although few are available, particularly in the House of Representatives to which, before 1980, only four had been elected). Susan Ryan, elected by the Labor caucus in 1983, is Labor's first female minister. But in discussions of likely choices, religion and group representation do not seem to be relevant factors. In Britain it has usually been true that at least one woman has been in cabinet in recent years, but the other factors mentioned here do not seem to have been important.

Factionalism

Diefenbaker reputedly commented that he presided over a cabinet made up of his enemies. There must be moments of frustration when most prime ministers would echo that statement. It emphasises the nature of cabinet formation and political parties. All parties are coalitions of diverse groups with different interests. Even if these interests lack formal organisation and can be best described as 'tendencies' rather than 'factions', their existence needs to be acknowledged in the structure of cabinet if internal harmony is to be maintained.

As a result many leading members of the party cannot be left out. Some must be included because of their status. In Canada those who polled well, for instance in the leadership convention that elected Trudeau, were automatic choices. In Britain a Labour prime minister has to include those beaten in the recent leadership contest if their support was substantial. Leading members of the shadow executive must also be included because they were elected in opposition. In Australia the party's leading spokespersons and state branch power-brokers will be given early preference. Indeed wherever a prime minister first forms a government it is possible to predict the majority of those who will be selected because most have some independent standing or, in federal systems, their own power-base.

This does not mean that *every* leading figure will be in the ministry. Thatcher could drop Robert Carr from the frontbench when she was elected party leader; she never offered Heath a position. Fraser decided to exclude Don Chipp. In themselves these may be indications of prime ministerial authority. So they are, within limits. As Alderman (1976: 132) has pointed out, the power of the prime minister lies not so much in the right of appointment as in the power of choice. Someone has to be selected. Prime ministers may be able to leave out one or two rivals, but it seems unlikely that their choice goes beyond that. Thatcher could ignore Heath, but could not exclude from the ministry, or even from cabinet, many of the 'wets' who supported Heath. Their status was too great. As a result, her first cabinet included a majority of people who were not her supporters. Fraser could not exclude Peacock as well as Chipp, even after relations with him deteriorated. Further, after Peacock's resignation in April 1981, Fraser got him back into cabinet at the first credible opportunity. Wilson and Callaghan both chose Benn as a cabinet minister, even if they were out of sympathy with his ideas and despite what were, in their eyes, frequent breaches of collective responsibility. Presumably it was safer to have him in cabinet than out. They also had to ensure that there was a correct balance of youth and experience, a suitable number of trade unionists and some contact with the national executive of the party.

Size

The size of the ministry in all four countries has grown over the past decades. There is considerable debate about what constitutes an effective size for a decision-making body if business is to be completed expeditiously and a sense of direction is to be imposed. Northcote Parkinson (1957: 41) argues that the maximum number is between 19 and 22.

Yet the pressures on prime ministers to increase the number of ministers is considerable. In Australia this has increased gradually. In 1901 there were 9 ministers, and at one point in 1904 only 8. By the 1930s there were 15 and by 1950 20. Then, in 1956, Robert Menzies decided that cabinet was becoming too large and he split the ministers into two groups, a cabinet of 12 and 10 ministers who were outside the cabinet. In the next few years the number of outer ministers increased gradually until there were 16 in 1972. The Whitlam Labor government kept 27 ministers, all of whom were in cabinet. When the Liberal government was re-elected Fraser initially appointed a cabinet of 12 and an outer ministry of another 12; by 1981 this had crept up to a cabinet of 15 and an outer ministry of 11. The Hawke government kept the same inner–outer cabinet structure and the same number of ministers. It seems the Australian ministry has settled down at around 27 people.

In Canada the number of ministers has also grown gradually. There were 16 ministers in 1926, 23 in 1963, and 28 by 1968. By the early 1980s the cabinet had well over 30 members. In Britain the cabinet was reduced to 15 under Heath, but it is generally around 24. However the number of paid positions in the ministry is now around 100 (Rose 1974: 367). Various pressures maintain its large size as Wilson explains:

> I had often been attracted, as is every Prime Minister, by the idea of a smaller cabinet, not just marginally smaller by one or two, but something not much larger than half the average size of a post-war Cabinet. On this occasion I made a real effort to see whether I could appoint a Cabinet of no more than eleven or so—with other departmental heads outside the Cabinet—along the lines of the two, very differing, War Cabinets in two world wars. But when I drew up such a list, the impossibility became clear. A Cabinet as small as eleven is possible only if it consists almost exclusively of two or three key departmental heads, such as the Foreign Secretary and Chancellor, together with non-departmental ministers and 'overlords' (in the first Churchill Cabinet even the Chancellor was not a member). But all experience was against the appointment of 'overlords', with the divided responsibility between an ivory tower chief on the one hand, and on the other, ministers with statutory duties responsible to Parliament. There is another problem. Prime ministers who have tried to keep numbers down by leaving out of the Cabinet the minister ultimately responsible for, say, education, agriculture or transport, have alienated very important interests, indeed essential components of our Society ... Trying to work to a list of eleven and twelve, which I prepared as an experiment, proved conclusively that my hopes must remain unrealized. (1971: 662)

The size of cabinet is thus related to functional and patronage problems. A large cabinet adds to job prospects: more people can be satisfied. There is inevitably a set of competing demands in discussing the size of cabinet: notions of efficiency on the one hand and political and representational pressures on the other. The latter have generally forced the prime minister to keep the numbers high. When cabinet is perceived as too large, ideas of inner cabinet committees are floated. These are considered in Chapter 5.

Field of choice

The usefulness of patronage depends on the uncertainty of being selected. That may depend on the prospects for promotion that people have. In Britain and Australia the field of choice for prime ministers is generally that of parliamentarians. It is possible to appoint people to the House of Lords. Occasionally people may be found safe seats in the Commons in order to get them into cabinet—Frank Cousins and John Davies are recent examples, although neither was successful as a minister. Few people enter parliament with the expectation that they will immediately become ministers, let alone members of cabinet. It is accepted that some parliamentary apprenticeship is needed. Senior ministers have generally had a lengthy parliamentary career.

If the field from which ministers can be chosen is limited to members of parliament, it is also true that not all MPs will be suitable (see Rose 1974: 369–70). Some are too old or too young, too inexperienced or proven failures, too lazy or too disinterested. If one-third to one-fifth are ineligible, the final choices are even more restricted.

In Australia similar assumptions are made. Although the constitution allows people to be chosen as ministers without a seat in parliament as long as they get one within three months, no-one has taken advantage of that clause to attract notables to the ministry. Two people (Lyons and Menzies), both with ministerial experience at state level and both to be later prime minister, became cabinet ministers directly after their election to federal parliament. Several reach office within two years of their first election to parliament. Indeed in the Liberal party, a member who has not reached the ministry within eight years has probably missed his or her opportunity (Weller and Grattan 1981: 36). A long parliamentary experience, following the British tradition, may not be a requirement for ministerial office. However a parliamentary seat is. Given the lack of influence of prime ministers over the process of the preselection of candidates, they do have to select from the available parliamentary pool. The implications of this have been spelt out clearly by Sir John Hoskyns (1983: 144):

> The overwhelming impression of government, to an outsider, is of a rather small world; perhaps too small for what it has to do. A small policy-making monopoly, with salary tariff barriers to repel outsiders; a cabinet formed from a tiny pool of talent; the cabinet of 1995 already for the most part sitting in the commons; the key posts filled again and again by the same cast of players.

If the British house of 650 is small, the Australian political community of 189 is much smaller, and the New Zealand pool is minute.

A *large* majority in New Zealand means a party of 55; a bare one includes 46. Out of these, 18 ministers, two or three undersecretaries, the whips, the speaker and committee chairmen have to be chosen. It is also generally accepted that new members do not immediately become ministers; a three-year term on the backbenches is expected. As a result, some prime ministers have no effective choice at all. In 1975 the National caucus contained only 30 people with parliamentary experience, from whom Muldoon had to select 26 to join him in official position. As Jackson said (1978a: 66), it was 'virtually a non-choice'.

In Canada the same assumption has never been as true. A parliamentary career is often seen as part of the career of a successful man, by no means the finale. Politics is not a career in itself. Leading Liberal ministers like John Turner and Donald McDonald have left parliament to pursue a business career. Yet, because of the Canadian process of electing leaders, both were still regarded as potential candidates for the Liberal leadership when Trudeau stepped down. A continued period in parliament is therefore not a prerequisite for leadership.

Further, all Liberal prime ministers have sought to encourage extra-parliamentary notables of perceived ministerial calibre to enter parliament. Mackenzie King appointed eight provincial premiers to his cabinet and sought other leading personalities so often that he 'effectively minimised the value of a parliamentary career as an important consideration for future appointments to the cabinet' (Courtney 1973: 94). He recruited St Laurent direct to cabinet as his Quebec lieutenant and then ensured his succession to the leadership. Since 1948 the civil service has produced several leading Liberal ministers. Pearson, Pickersgill, Sharp and Drury were all former deputy ministers who went straight into cabinet. Indeed, Pickersgill's transition must be one of the most remarkable in any Westminister system. He attended a cabinet meeting on 12 June 1953 as clerk of the Privy Council Office; when cabinet adjourned for lunch he was sworn in as minister and returned to the meeting at the foot of the table as secretary of state (Pickersgill 1975: 185). He had been 'selected' for a safe seat in Newfoundland (with which he had no previous connections) by the provincial premier, Joey Smallwood. Seldom can promotion to political office have been so fast, or the jump from civil service to politics so small.

C.D. Howe and Walter Gordon were businessmen who came into cabinet when they chose and largely on their own terms. Under Pearson's leadership the 'three wise men' (Marchand, Pelletier and Trudeau) were carefully recruited and rapidly promoted. Lalonde moved from the PMO to the cabinet; Coutts would probably have done the same if he had not lost the by-election. Pierre Juneau, the head of a statutory commission, was appointed a minister before he had a seat. It may be true that, as the process of candidate selection becomes more decentralised, so the prime minister may have less influence over the composition of the pool from which ministers are chosen, but that decline is only relative. The lack of importance of a parliamentary career can be seen by the speed with which ministers reach executive rank. In Pearson's 1963 cabinet, just over 50 per cent of the ministers had *less* than six years in parliament; 38 per cent had less than one year. In part that can be explained by the near annihilation of the Liberals in 1958 and the lack of many safe seats. But in 1968, in Trudeau's first cabinet, 80 per cent had less than six years experience in parliament (Punnett 1977: 60). The field of choice for a prime minister is larger if well-qualified individuals can be persuaded to run and win.

Within parliament, the field of choice can be seen from the percentage of the parliamentary party that is appointed to the ministry (see Table 4.1). British prime ministers have more jobs at their disposal most of the time than their Australian and Canadian counterparts. Only when the government parties elsewhere have narrow majorities (Trudeau in 1972; Gorton in 1969) or are in a minority in the Australian Senate (Fraser in 1980) do the figures in Canada and Australia compare. New Zealand prime ministers are able to offer portfolios to well over a third of their parliamentary colleagues; further they need not worry about upper house representation. That must assist their position.

Prime ministers have the luxury of creating a new cabinet only when they win office. If they inherit a cabinet, most ministers are likely to stay on. Thereafter, the reconstruction of the ministry is a more *ad hoc* process as retirements or resignations, voluntary or otherwise, create vacancies that can be filled individually. It is there that the influence of prime ministers over backbenchers can be exerted. When there is a whole cabinet of jobs to be filled, there are obvious candidates. When there is one job, there may be several possible appointees, all of whom have some expectations. Muldoon's 1975 cabinet was gradually changed over the ensuing eight years, without any massive change. But Muldoon was an expert at dangling the carrot before his backbenchers. He could promise possible rewards as a means of consolidating his power; when under challenge in 1981 he met backbenchers individually and managed to detach some from the rebel cause. Fraser's final cabinet retained only half its original members. The new entrants came in at the bottom of the list, grateful for the chance. Prime ministers do not need many vacancies to dangle before the multitude of pretenders to maintain a sense of dependence. Once in office, between elections and after a successful re-election, this is a powerful and persuasive weapon. A prime minister in for one term obviously can do less than survivors like Fraser, Trudeau and Muldoon.

Table 4.1   Ministerial appointees as a percentage of government MPs

Britain			*Canada*		
Wilson	1964–70	37	Pearson	1963	18
Heath	1970–74	26	Trudeau	1968	18
Wilson	1974–76	30	Trudeau	1972	26
Callaghan	1976–79	36	Trudeau	1974	19
Australia			*New Zealand*		
Gorton	1969	25	Nash	1957	40
Fraser	1975–77	21	Holyoake	1960	36
Fraser	1980	36	Holyoake	1966	40
			Kirk	1972	37
			Muldoon	1975	37

Sources: Rose (1980: 6), Punnett (1977: 62), Hughes (1977, 1981), Alley (1978: 107).

BARGAINING

So far the discussion has assumed that those whom the prime minister has chosen want to serve, that it is, to use Alderman's (1976) term, a situation of command. But it does not necessarily follow. As Alderman has persuasively illustrated, prime ministers in Britain have frequently had to come to arrangements with people they want to have in cabinet. The bargains may be about status and cabinet rank or about portfolio; or the chosen person may have to be persuaded to serve at all. Not everyone is in a position to bargain; most will be given no choice. Indeed as the number of what King (1979) has called career politicians has increased, for whom political office is the target and purpose of a political career, so the capacity to bargain may decline. Nevertheless it seems that enough people have turned down high offers to make it important to see what the bargains are.

In Canada the concept of politics as a part-career and the attempts to encourage the introduction of notables may give those people particular influence in setting their own terms. Pearson and Gordon both initially declined invitations to enter politics; the timing was theirs. Gardiner put conditions on the portfolio allocated to him. Marchand would not stand unless seats were also found for Pelletier and Trudeau.

In Australia, where politics is generally a full-time career (living in Canberra makes other means of support almost impossible for everyone except lawyers and farmers), office is perhaps more important. It is difficult for a backbencher who has not reached office to retire to the business world, where he may be regarded as a political failure. Even then office is not always accepted without condition; when Fraser sought to demote Eric Robinson from cabinet to the outer ministry, the offer was peremptorily dismissed. Other people have been prepared to retire from politics comparatively early—in their 40s and 50s—when the challenge of the job or their interest in it declined. Yet the career structure suggests that it is less easy for backbenchers to bargain in Australia than in Canada or even Britain.

Australian and Canadian prime ministers have to construct a cabinet within a variety of constraints that will limit many of their choices. At the senior level of the party, the leading figures in part pick themselves. The greatest choice is available when a ministry is being constructed for the first time. For the last few jobs the opinion of the prime minister will be crucial. Yet even there the question that will be asked is not simply 'Who is the best person to appoint to the ministry?' but, for instance, 'Which of the available South Australians in the House of Representatives is best suited for appointment?' Similar questions are asked in Canada.

In Britian and New Zealand the prime minister has few of these regional or bicameral pressures. Even then some consultations may take place. In New Zealand prime ministers have traditionally held straw polls, asking backbenchers whom they would like to see chosen, although whether it made any difference to the choice is less certain. In 1960 Holyoake and Marshall wrote the names of possible ministers and portfolios on the back of visiting cards and shuffled them around until the best combination was achieved: the final choice remained the prime minister's. As the existence of career politicians becomes more widespread, so the capacity of some ministers to bargain may decline. In the exercise of constructing a cabinet the British prime minister has a much freer hand, even with the factional constraints that exist.

AN ELECTED MINISTRY?

In their dislike of prime ministerial patronage, both Benn and Sedgemore advocate a series of reforms that they believe would properly reduce the prime minister's power in Britain. One of these is the election of ministers by the parliamentary party and the need for prime ministers to submit for the approval of the parliamentary party their allocation of portfolios. But they do not consider in what way the results achieved by these means would differ from the existing situation.

The selection of ministers by the prime minister is certainly the most common method of choosing a ministry, but it is not a necessary part of a parliamentary system nor an essential part of the prime minister's authority. In Australia the Labor party elects its ministers after it has won an election, a process it has adopted consistently since 1909. In New Zealand a similar process has been used since 1935. There is no doubt, however, that prime ministers in Britain and Canada will seek to maintain their prerogative. Attlee, for instance, thoroughly disapproved of the Australian system, calling it totally wrong and arguing that if the party could not trust its leader, it should remove him (1954: 156). Nevertheless the Australian example does illustrate an alternative method of choosing ministers in operation and provides evidence against which Benn and Sedgemore's hopes can be judged.

In the Australian Labor party, one of the basic principles of action is that democratic procedures should be followed, so that all decisions are taken by vote and all officials are regarded as delegates responsible to those who elected them (Crisp 1955; Weller 1975). This belief is extended to ministers; they were elected by caucus and are held responsible to it. In the first meeting of the parliamentary party after an election, the ministry is elected by a series of ballots; in 1972 and 1974, seven took place. First, the four parliamentary leaders were each elected in a separate ballot. In 1972 they were returned unopposed; in 1974 the positions of deputy leader in the House of Representatives and leader in the Senate were contested. Then there were two ballots, one to elect four ministers from the Senate, the other to choose ten members from the House of Representatives. With representation from the two houses thus assured, the final ballot, open to senators and MHRs, was held for the last nine places in the ministry. The allocation of portfolios was then left to the prime minister.

Many decisions were taken on the structure of the government before the party won the 1972 election. It had been agreed that the party should retain a ministry of 27 that the Liberal–CP government then had; 27 positions meant 27 jobs, a strong incentive for a party that had been out of office for 23 years. Caucus had also decided in opposition, by a majority of one, that the party would not create an inner and outer cabinet, but that all 27 ministers would be of equal status and in the full cabinet. In these areas the options for the prime minister were cut off.

In 1982 there was little competition. It was agreed between the three main factions that the shadow executive of 22 would be elected and then the other five jobs were distributed on state and factional lines. The chosen group won easily, although three left-wingers trailed the others by ten votes; whether this was by design, to ensure that they were the most junior ministers, remains disputed.

In New Zealand the 1972 cabinet was elected by caucus, with many of the senior members who had been out of office for the previous twelve years getting their opportunity at last. But the real choice was small; 20 cabinet members and 3 undersecretaries were selected from the 36 experienced members who were nominated (Jackson 1978a: 66). Kirk *could* not have chosen a very different group. Nor, some participants argued, would he have.

How much difference in personnel did the system of election bring about? Probably not much. The choice of the Australian caucus in 1972 was predictable and conservative. In 1972 the previous leaders were elected unopposed. In the first ballot for MHRs, those who had been members of the shadow executive since 1969 were then elected without exception to the cabinet. It would have been impossible for the prime minister to leave out any of these people; they had long records of service in opposition and were seen to deserve a ministerial chance. In the final ballot one or two of those whom the prime minister wanted elected failed to get the numbers, but that was all. If the prime minister had had a free choice, there would have only been a difference of two or three people. In 1982 Hawke could not have afforded to leave out all the members of the left; one or two individuals may have been different, but Hawke needed broad support and to have immediately had revenge on his party opponents would have dented the image of consensus he was trying to build.

In 1974 the conservatism of the choice was re-emphasised in both countries. In Australia a new ministerial election was required after the election. Only one new minister was elected, and he replaced the one minister defeated at the polls. Every other minister was re-elected. In New Zealand, after Kirk died and Rowling replaced him, the whole cabinet faced re-election. Rowling appealed to caucus to be loyal to those who had been in office for less than two years. He was *too* effective for every minister was returned, though he would have like four or five changes and, given the choice, would have made them.

There are occasions when the prime minister has cabinet ministers whom he finds personally incompatible. The election of Eddie Ward and Arthur Calwell in 1943 occurred despite the opposition of the prime minister, John Curtin. But whether, if given the *personal* responsibility for choice, Curtin could have left both of them out seems more debateable. The advantage of the system of election is that, while it removes the power from the prime minister, it also removes the blame. Those left out can only hold their colleagues responsible.

ALLOCATING PORTFOLIOS, RESHUFFLING AND SACKING

The power of appointment is only one of the areas of prime ministerial patronage. There are three other important powers: the allocation of portfolios, the reshuffling of ministers and the right to sack.

In Britain all the powers are used extensively. Some ministers may be able to demand particular porfolios if the prime minister wants them in cabinet badly enough, or they may be able to put conditions on their acceptance (Alderman 1976). More often, prime ministers can allocate jobs without hindrance. Attlee switched the positions he was to give his two senior lieutenants, Morrison and Bevin, at the last moment. Morrison and George Brown wanted to become foreign minister, but neither was appointed at the time he most wanted the job. Wilson switched the portfolios that Richard Crossman and Michael Stewart had held in opposition, in part, it was believed, to keep Crossman too busy to make trouble. Attlee not only put people where he wanted them, but did not always consult them about the choice of their junior colleagues.

The allocation of portfolios can be used to balance possible rivals—Brown and Callaghan in economic portfolios in 1964—or to isolate policy areas. Thatcher's 1979 cabinet may not have included a majority of her supporters, but the economic portfolios did. Howe, Biffen, Joseph and Nott, and later Lawson, Tebbitt and Parkinson, were all members of the 'dries'. Having selected her people, Thatcher could then keep economic policy-making in the economic committee of cabinet chosen on functional lines (Burch 1983: 411).

Reshuffles too are common in Britain, and are usually obligatory. Benn did not want to shift from Industry to Energy, but had little choice. Leading members of cabinet, led by Foot and Castle, protested against Wilson's attempt to demote their left-wing colleague Judith Hart. After several traumatic meetings Wilson got his way. But even that had been based on an earlier agreement with Roy Jenkins, who had threatened to resign if a different colleague was moved out of cabinet (Castle 1980: 413–16). There are therefore limits, but not many. Thatcher has changed the head of *all* the fourteen main departments at least once since 1979; by October 1983 Trade had had *five* ministers in four years. Ministers are often learning new jobs, the prime minister alone remains constant. It has its advantages for prime ministerial authority, if not for good government.

In Britain, ministers are regularly sacked. Attlee recalled it as one of the hardest jobs of a prime minister, but he, like his successors, needed no reason to ask for ministerial resignations; it was assumed to be within the prime minister's prerogatives. The most spectacular example was Macmillan's 'night of the long knives' when he discarded a third of his cabinet. Ministers left Wilson's cabinets in a constant trickle. Callaghan got rid of Short and Castle when he took over as prime minister despite protests from Foot at Castle's removal (Castle 1980: 725). Thatcher has gradually removed many of her critics—Stevas, Gilmour and then Pym, seen as her only possible rival—and several other cabinet members too. Sackings are regarded as an unfortunate but necessary part of the job.

There are limits to the use of this power. Some ministers are regarded as better in cabinet than out of it, regardless of their reputation. When a reshuffle has taken place, ministers are probably safe for a time, at least to provide an opportunity to vindicate the prime minister's judgement. Some may be sufficiently powerful to be in effect invulnerable: perhaps Callaghan and later Jenkins in Wilson's cabinet and certainly Foot under Callaghan. Or they may be so closely associated with the prime minister's views that to sack them would be too personal a move. Not everyone is vulnerable, but in general it is true that the British prime minister has considerable authority over most of cabinet.

The ease with which British prime ministers can or do sack ministers who are well-established and of cabinet rank is not typical of parliamentary systems. In Canada, Australia and New Zealand it does not occur at all frequently. In Canada Mallory's (1971: 80) comment that 'a minister once appointed is extremely hard to get rid of' was true up to the time of writing. In considering the reason for which ministers left office before 1974, Matheson (1976: 118) lists only two who failed to be renominated, although there were several who resigned for personal reasons. Writing of Mackenzie King, Gerald Wright (1976: 291) commented: 'the need for a balanced ministry made the threat of dismissal almost a nullity, as it has been since'. In restructuring his ministry after the 1974 election, Trudeau broke with earlier precedent by dropping several ministers, perhaps establishing for Canada a precedent often followed in Great Britain (Van Loon and Whittington 1976: 323). Some others went in 1976, and returned to office in 1980. Canadian prime ministers *can* sack but the regular removal of ministers between elections does not seem to have followed, although three parliamentary secretaries were dropped in September 1981. Instead, vacancies in cabinet are caused by the use of external patronage or by accepting the resignation of ministers who chose to return to private life or business. At no time does it appear that there have been on the backbenches several senior ex-ministers with a grudge against the prime minister. Indeed, leaving parliament is not a bar to leadership ambitions. Temporary exile from politics is a positive advantage as that individual is not associated with a government's failures.

The second reason for the comparative lack of sacking is the very function of representation that a cabinet fulfils. If ministers are not appointed only for their administrative capacity, then there are other reasons needed for their removal, although not necessarily for their reshuffling.

In Australia it is unusual for prime ministers to return serving cabinet ministers to the backbenches. In the last twenty years only one minister of cabinet rank has been dropped, purely because he was not up to the job. When new prime ministers have taken over from within a party—Gorton in 1967 and McMahon in 1971—they dropped in each case two or three junior members of the ministry, in part to reward their own political friends. In 1980 Fraser too dropped the most junior member of the ministry and tried to demote another from cabinet to outer-minister rank for party political reasons. But most people stayed. When ministers did leave the cabinet, they invariably left the parliament, either on personal grounds or to lucrative government appointments including the governor-generalship, the high commissionership in London and sundry ambassadorial appointments. They were not left smouldering on the backbenches.

In several cases ministers have been effectively sacked for other reasons: one was accused by a royal commissioner of 'committing an impropriety'; another brought a colour television set into the country without paying duty and so his resignation and that of the minister responsible for customs (who had been told about the incident, although how fully is uncertain) were both demanded. In these cases public outrage seemed to make their removal easier than toughing it out, and the prime minister's hand was forced. But the prime minister's final decision always depends on political calculations; when leading NCP ministers were accused of administratives bungles, Fraser chose instead to try to fight back. They were close colleagues and he did not want to lose them.

On occasion ministers may have sufficient cards to refuse to go. When Fraser wanted to remove an ineffective minister of defence out of cabinet, if not out of the ministry, he was reputedly told the minister would resign from parliament, causing a by-election which the government would probably lose. The minister stayed in cabinet, although a job with no real responsibilities was created for him.

The problems in sacking ministers are caused in part by the pressures of representation, but more by the vulnerability of the Australian prime minister. No leader wants one or more prestigious party members on the backbench who can act as a focus for discontent. David Fairbairn's refusal to serve under Gorton gave Liberal rebels a figurehead; Peacock's resignation in 1981 led directly to a challenge to Fraser. The preference is for leading members of the party to be in the cabinet, or right out of parliament if any real choices are available.

In New Zealand the small size of the political community creates other restraints. Prime ministers have always kept undated but signed resignations from their ministers in their safe, but they act only as a reminder of who notionally has the power. In practice New Zealand prime ministers rarely sack ministers. When Marshall became prime minister in 1972 he persuaded some ministers, who intended to retire at the election due that year, to stand down early. But that was with their consent to some extent. More often prime ministers cover for their weaker colleagues because of the collective involvement.

There has been one marked exception in the last twenty years. In 1982 Muldoon sacked a minister, Dennis Quigley, who had been one of the leaders of the attempted coup in 1980. Muldoon waited his opportunity and when Quigley was *publicly* critical of government policy, Muldoon demanded his resignation. 'Pour encourager les autres', observers say. This is evidence that it can be done—it does not have to be done often. All the same, it was an exceptional case that would probably have forced the prime minister to act in any of the systems under review. And Muldoon did have to wait for a mistake. British prime ministers would not feel so restricted.

Labo(u)r prime ministers in Australia and New Zealand have special problems; since they did not choose ministers, there is some doubt how far they can remove them. In 1975 Whitlam sacked two ministers for misleading parliament; he then effectively had to take his decision to caucus for endorsement. In the Hawke government a new rule was introduced to allow the four parliamentary leaders to ask for a minister's resignation. It is likely to be used only if the minister has been responsible for some notable error, not for administrative mediocrity. Even in that case it is not in the prime minister's hands alone.

In 1974 the New Zealand government gave Kirk the authority to change up to two members of cabinet; it was a recognition that some changes might be required. The power was never used; in any case it probably could only have been used in exceptional circumstances.

In Labo(u)r cabinets in Australia and New Zealand, ministers are conscious that they owe their allegiance as much to the caucus that will re-elect them as to the prime minister. They are therefore less concerned about their position.

If sacking is a less powerful weapon in Canada, New Zealand and Australia, what of the power to allocate or reshuffle? It seems more potent. Once access to the ministry has been achieved, promotion within it becomes important. Certainly some bargains may be made in Canada by notables whom the prime minister wants in cabinet, but thereafter it seems that everyone, even senior ministers, may be affected by reshuffles. In the PC cabinet of 1979, only six ministers got the portfolio they had shadowed. In 1983 almost all Trudeau's senior ministers had their jobs changed. In Australia deputy leaders of the Liberal party are elected by the parliamentary party and therefore hold their position independently of the prime minister's patronage. Traditionally they have the right to select their portfolio, but it is not always granted. McMahon was moved out of Treasury to Foreign Affairs against his will after he had challenged Gorton for the leadership in 1969; Lynch was not returned to the Treasury in 1977 after his temporary resignation when his financial affairs were under investigation, although it is less clear whether he still wanted the job.

When reshuffles occur some bargains are made. When the Treasury was split in 1976, Lynch was told he could keep both jobs if he wanted to; he did. When a senator was promoted into cabinet from low in the ministerial ranking, the minister who might have expected that promotion was reputedly promised that he could attend cabinet whenever he wanted. Yet many ministers are given jobs they don't want or know nothing about (see Weller and Grattan 1981). Some may be consulted; most are told where they are going. In the allocations of portfolios, both Liberal and Labor prime ministers have virtually unlimited authority and use it.

Portfolios are allocated to some people because the job is hard and the prime minister hopes they may stumble. In New Zealand, George Gair is scarcely Muldoon's favourite colleague and he has been given successively hard jobs. Other possible rivals have been kept in the one portfolio for a long time, so that they cannot develop the broad expertise regarded as necessary for a potential leader. Kirk balanced the jobs, so that one minister also had a colleague with close functional responsibilities; no-one therefore had too much independence. In Australia ministers from the Senate have been given jobs to ensure that the portfolio is removed from close examination by a sharp opponent in the other house. In Canada Trudeau occasionally appointed an inexperienced minister to foreign affairs, so that his own links with that policy area could be close. Hawke has deliberately isolated left-wing ministers in portfolios that have only limited involvement elsewhere in the government. Portfolios are therefore allocated for personal, party political, parliamentary or policy reasons. Few have been able to demand particular choices—except in Australia under the coalition. In terms of *regular* influence, the allocation of portfolios is a more powerful weapon than the selection and sacking of ministers.

The cumulative effect of these powers is also important. Prime ministers who use them gradually shape their cabinets to suit their needs. Thatcher's first cabinet may have included many of her factional opponents. At the time of the September 1981 reshuffle, a *Times* (15 September 1981) editorial commented that: 'She has in the past been commendably but excessively puritanical in not introducing the traditional Prime Minister's caucus of "King's men"'. But since then the promotion of ministers who supported her views has continued. After the 1983 election, her cabinet still included some unsympathetic to her economic strategy, but the majority of ministers in key positions were clearly her ideological allies. Opponents may not have been excluded, but they were outnumbered.

In Trudeau's case, leading members left politics (perhaps with the intention of returning); in New Zealand they are left isolated in cabinet. As the powers to remove are less distinct, so the development of a prime minister's group is less easy to achieve, particularly over a short period. Any prime minister who lasts as long as Trudeau or Muldoon will inevitably discover with whom they can work best and rely on them. But it takes time.

PATRONAGE AND PRIME MINISTERIAL INFLUENCE OVER MINISTERS

It is often assumed that power over appointment, dismissal and promotion makes people more malleable to the prime ministers' influence. Yet this seems only party true.

For access to the ministry, subservience to the leader may be one route to preferment, but it is by no means the only route. According to Aneurin Bevan, there are two strategies: 'to crawl up the staircase of preferment on your belly' or 'to kick them in the teeth' (Crossman 1972: 46). Even if the first is seen as more predictable, the second is possible. Bevan and Benn were both chosen by Labour leaders; Michael Foot, never one to compromise his position, became indispensable. In Australia both inane but noisy backbenchers and analytically acute critics have been promoted to keep them quiet. Opposition to a prime minister is not an assurance that a person's chances will be reduced. Senator Chaney led the opposition to the prime minister's demands that Senator Reg Withers, found guilty of an 'impropriety', should resign—and was selected to replace him.

Second, the selection of some ministers means that others are passed over. Some of the latter may believe that, as a result, their only chance of promotion will be with a different leader. Whatever their views about whether the alternative is preferable, they will support change if the opportunity arises. The use of patronage does not only make friends.

Once selected, the calculations are different. Crossman argues that prime ministers hold every minister's future in their hands and there is nothing that the ministers can do about it. It is easy, of course, to exaggerate the detailed interest that a prime minister may take in each minister. Kaufman argues:

> While you need to take a close interest in what the prime minister says and does, do not imagine that he will in return be watching everything you do. Some ministers do seem to believe this. They get the notion that every speech they deliver, every slip they make or every small success they notch up, is somehow being noted by the prime minister ready for a grand end-of-term report. While he is not unaware of your activities, do not be foolish enough to believe that he is keeping a close check on your every move. For one thing, he has given you a job to do and simply expects you to get on with it. Secondly, he simply does not have the time. (1980: 78)

That is indubitably true in a large system like Britain. A senior British minister commented that, contrary to popular belief, he did not live in daily fear of losing his job. Some people feel secure because they are newly appointed in a reshuffle, because they have a power-base in the party or because they represent areas. Others may be safe because they are reluctant politicians who would leave politics without undue regret if moved (as some of the Canadian imports) or because they could embarrass the government by resigning from parliament. Particularly in Canada and Australia where sackings are rare unless the minister commits some major error, ministers are not in constant fear of dismissal. One New Zealand minister, out of favour with the prime minister, commented that he was in office because he had to be; he was senior and not at all afraid for his job.

Promotions in reshuffles are far more likely to be useful inducements, but they are related to performance as perceived by the prime minister and, to an extent, by colleagues. Political standing in cabinet cannot be ignored. To achieve it, subservience to the prime minister in policy issues is not always the best way. For much of the time ministers know that they will be living with their position, and do not expect any immediate change.

The power of appointment and dismissal, within whatever constraints, is a blunt instrument, so dramatic in its effects that it always has wide implications. Every prime minister is severely constrained in how that power can be used; however, those constraints are much greater in federal systems like Australia and Canada or in small systems like New Zealand. In none of those cases can prime ministers select or dispose of ministers with the ease of the British. In the Labo(u)r parties, the power to choose and fire has also been removed from the prime minister's hand.

APPOINTING HEADS OF DEPARTMENTS

The heads of departments in three of the countries are 'political' appointments in the sense that all are in effect chosen by the prime minister, with or without widespread consultation.

In Australia from 1977 to 1984 there was a formal procedure prescribed by the Public Service (First Division Officers) Act. A committee of three headed by the chairman of the Public Service Board and including two other permanent heads drew up a short list of 'established' candidates, people who could reasonably be expected to be promoted and usually at senior levels in the service. That list was presented to the prime minister. If someone on that list was chosen, they held the position for life. The prime minister was not bound to select from that original list; he could ask for names to be added to it or go beyond it and select a 'non-established' candidate who would then retain the position for a contracted period or for the life of the party's government, whichever was shorter. In the process the two people of central importance were the prime minister and the chairman of the Public Service Board. The prime minister could consult with the head of PMC or others.

The Hawke Labor government intends to remove the distinction between established and non-established candidates, as part of a proposal to create greater flexibility in the senior levels of the public service. Its White Paper, *Reforming the Australian Public Service* (1983), proposes that the chairman of the Public Service Board provide a list of candidates to the prime minister after an executive search has been completed. Decisions on the 'appointment, unattachment or transfer of Departmental Heads will be made by the Governor-General in Council, in accordance with the recommendation of the Prime Minister, after consideration by Cabinet' (p. 10). The prime minister remains the person to make the final decision.

Ministers may be consulted about the choice of their permanent heads. When Chaney moved from Aboriginal Affairs to Social Security, the permanent head soon followed. But that does not necessarily occur. The previous head of Social Security was appointed without the minister, Senator Margaret Guilfoyle, being consulted. Sometimes the prime minister will never have met the person who is recommended, but will agree to a recommendation from the Public Service Board. He is likely, in all circumstances, to discuss proposals with the head of his own department.

However there has been a tendency for many appointments to go to those whom the prime minister does know. One minister complained: 'PMC is very much the department through which one goes if one wants to be a permanent head and that, I think, is devastating. I think it is the most serious administrative problem facing the government structure' (quoted in Weller and Grattan 1981: 195). The criticism may be a matter of opinion, the observation is accurate. In January 1983 the heads of four senior departments, Finance, Social Security, Employment and Industrial Relations and National Development, were former deputy secretaries of PMC. The prime minister's hand—in that case, Fraser's—was clear in all cases. When the Hawke government was elected, three new permanent heads were created, all of whom had within the recent past served at senior levels in PMC.

In Canada and Britain the process may have less statutory authority. The Canadian prime minister is advised on appointments by a deputy minister. Under Trudeau, the former clerk of the PCO, Gordon Robertson, maintained this responsibility when he became head of the FPRO. After his retirement it reverted to Micheal Pitfield of the PCO. As in Australia, service in the PCO seems to be an advantage. Pitfield was an officer there before being appointed to his first deputy ministership elsewhere. Of the deputy ministers in the powerful central co-ordinating departments in 1982, three, Ian Stewart of Finance, Gordon Teschke of Economic and Regional Development, and Gordon Smith of Social Development, were all formerly senior PCO officials. They were all well-known to the prime minister and this clearly was not to their disadvantage.

Consultation with ministers may take place. It depends in part on the prime minister's approach. One civil servant, who later became a minister, claimed that Mackenzie King asked some ministers, but not others; St Laurent did his best to see that ministers were not displeased; Pearson, a long-time civil servant, tended to tell ministers whom they would get; Trudeau gave ministers the first opportunity to nominate someone, but if he did not like the choice he ignored it. Earlier attempts by Trudeau to appoint Stewart to Finance had been blocked by the minister (*Macleans* 24 May 1982: 22).

The role of the prime minister in actually making the choice is important. Deputy ministers are aware their job is in his gift. Indeed a divided loyalty—to minister and to prime minister—is deliberately fostered so that deputy ministers are continually conscious they are working for the whole government, and not just for the one minister.

In Britain appointments to the level of permanent secretary or deputy secretary are normally made on the recommendation of the Senior Appointment Selection Committee, chaired by the head of the civil service and composed of permanent secretaries. As Lord Armstrong has commented, this advice is usually accepted because those on the committee are likely to know far more about the people. Some prime ministers generally accept the recommendations, but not all. Thatcher is known to send names back for reconsideration and to use her own channels to check on the views of likely candidates (Stephenson 1980: 42). It is also true that those who have worked closely with the prime minister are likely to have the inside running for promotion. Principal private secretaries to the prime minister invariably become permanent secretaries when they leave the prime minister's office. In her first three years in office, Thatcher was able to fill eleven of the 23 most important permanent secretary positions which became vacant by retirement, and has taken a close interest in the process. She has ensured that those chosen fit her mould (Burch 1983: 410; *Economist* 22 October 1983).

Yet if prime ministers can heavily influence the appointment of permanent secretaries, what of the powers of removal? In Britain it is hard to move a permanent head. Castle failed to shift Sir Thomas Padmore; Benn's disagreements with his secretary ended only when Benn was shuffled elsewhere. Permanent secretaries are generally seen as permanent and changes to their position as being tantamount to undermining the concept of the neutral civil service. That factor obviously has some impact on permanent secretaries.

In Canada it is accepted that deputy ministers (a most suitable term for the heads of departments) serve during the government's pleasure. Changes of government will lead to the expectation of a *few* changes; demanding Pitfield's resignation was one of the first acts of Clark's government. In Australia, even if it is difficult officially to remove permanent heads, it can be done. Sometimes they are willing to be moved around. If they are unwilling, it is possible to abolish the department, declare all positions vacant, and then reconstitute it, perhaps with slightly different functions and with a new head. That has on occasion been done, leaving a permanent head without a department.

In Australia no permanent head is truly permanent. Since the machinery of government is in the prime minister's hand, so are the choices. In 1983 Hawke wrote to his new ministers telling them that they would not be allowed to change the permanent heads, as some had hoped to do. That decision was final. However, when the Review of Commonwealth Administration in 1983 recommended the regular rotation of permanent heads every five or seven years, it pointed out that in practice the turnover was quicker than that. Its proposal has now been accepted by the government's White Paper; if rotation is accepted, then the shifting of permanent heads who prove to be incompatible with their ministers will be much easier. The tradition of the 1950s and 1960s of long-serving heads has been changed.

Only in New Zealand is the system substantially different. There, permanent heads are 'section 29' appointments. The chairman of the State Services Commission selects a committee of three from a panel elected by the permanent heads. The ministers might have the name of the choice mentioned to them, in case they feel they could not work with that person; in those circumstances they might be able to impose an implicit veto. But they do not choose the new permanent head; nor, once selected, can the mandarin be removed.

Obviously, when a head of the Prime Minister's department is selected, the prime minister is consulted. With such a sensitive relationship, it would be impossible to operate otherwise. But there is no consistent and formal way in which the prime minister can exert influence; informal influence will spring from his consistent interaction with leading officials, who know what he thinks of possible choices. Importantly, therefore, the selection of permanent heads in New Zealand is not part of the prime minister's prerogatives.

But how much influence does the power of *appointment* give the prime minister? Van Loon and Whittington (1976: 391) suggest that it gives 'some measure of control over individual departments even if a minister becomes recalcitrant or remiss'. But they add the crucial condition that 'since the deputy minister usually works in very close contact with his ministers and at arms length from the prime minister, this power is more formal than real'. Further, new permanent heads will develop a sense of identity with their departments so that, even if they did emerge through PMC or the PCO, their new position takes precedence and they will compete for influence for their own departments and their own minister. Obviously it helps if the permanent heads are well-known and trusted by the prime minister. When Callaghan was prime minister, six permenent secretaries had previously been his private secretaries; so he could occasionally get a private view that he trusted. It helps too that they have a network of contacts at the centre to facilitate the accomplishment of their department's wishes. They will also know the prime minister's likes and dislikes. Their appointment might make the centre easier to work. It does not make all permanent heads that come through this route subservient.

At times, when prime ministers are particularly activist and making demands on departments, *usually* through the Cabinet Office/PCO/ PMC, permanent heads may wonder for whom they are actually working; some feel these direct demands make their position difficult. They realise that the continued existence of their *department* (in Australia and Britain—in Canada departments are created by statute) depends on the prime minister's decisions on machinery of government. At times they may feel that they have some obligations to the government as a whole—hence the practice of 'looplining' or informing the centre of the less practical nature of their minister's proposals (Weller and Grattan 1981: 67–8)—or the use in Britain of the Central Policy Review Staff (CPRS) as a means of undercutting ministers. At times, by the judicious positioning of public servants who have worked directly to the prime minister, the illusion of a spider's web may be created.

Yet most of the time prime ministers do not directly contact permanent heads. If they want information or action, they may either speak to their ministerial colleagues or ask the head of the prime minister's department or cabinet office to relay their request. Some prime ministers, like Muldoon, are punctilious in maintaining the formal working procedures. Of course the fact that such requests are relayed make the permanent heads aware that the prime minister is looking in their direction. More often, prime ministers have the opportunity to meet the influential permanent heads in cabinet committee where they can be questioned in detail and, in Canada and New Zealand, may participate in debate almost on equal terms. Certainly there is an awareness of the ever-ready presence of the prime ministers and of their influence exerted through the central agencies. To be out of favour with the latter may lead to a lack of advancement from the former. Yet as a general statement it does not seem true that prime ministerial control of the broad picture has much day-to-day influence. Benn (1981: 48) argues that, as long as permanent secretaries feel that their ministers have retained the confidence of the prime minister, they will support them. That is certainly true in all similar systems. If that confidence is missing, Benn believes permanent secretaries will undermine ministers' positions and use the network to secure their own positions and interests. Nevertheless, if ministers are able to impose a sense of direction on the department, they can ensure that, on most issues, the civil servants will direct their loyalty towards them.

OTHER AREAS OF PATRONAGE

Governments also control a variety of other patronage jobs, from the heads of nationalised industries, crown corporations or statutory authorities to the honorary membership of boards.

In Canada the discussion of the way that this patronage is distributed is extensive. Canadian parties, far more than their Australian and British counterparts, are tied together by patronage rather than by ideological bonds. In govenment they suffer from what one writer calls 'an obsession with patronage' (Wearing 1981: 156). For much of the time patronage was decentralised. Mackenzie King left its distribution to his provincial ministers. In particular, the Quebec lieutenant was largely responsible for determining who got which position in that province.

For a time Trudeau attempted to centralise the process. After his election in 1968, he established in the PMO a series of 'regional desks', so that his staff could oversee appointments. This step was regarded with particular suspicion by ministers and by the extra-parliamentary branch of the party. The latter appreciated that, if it was to have any clout, it needed to participate in patronage decisions and indeed set up advisory committees to help in its allocation (Wearing 1981: 148–57). The advisory committees did not work. Ministers were too jealous of their prerogatives. Nor did the 'regional desks'; they were disbanded after the near-defeat of 1972 led to charges that the prime minister had become too distant from the party machine. To an extent patronage was returned to the earlier system of ministerial control. In 1981, for instance, Trudeau defended the practice of giving regional responsibility to cabinet ministers and, for the first time, 'released a list outlining the regional political jurisdiction of members of cabinet' (*Globe and Mail* 26 February 1981). In some cases ministers unashamedly admitted its value: 'Is it wrong', said one minister, 'to favour a past political supporter over someone else if the two have equal ability?' (Wearing 1981: 153). The system of prime ministerial centralisation did not work, even though the degree of prime ministrial involvement may still be greater than it was under Trudeau's predecessors.

The extent and importance of patronage in Canada are great. Between 1968 and 1977 around 200 former Liberal candidates or their spouses had received appointments (Wearing 1981: 153). Later 52 former Liberal ministers were put on the government payroll, often for long periods with lucrative contracts (*Macleans* 7 March 1983). The Senate was used to create suitable by-election vacancies, to reward unsuccessful provincial Liberal leaders, to remove ministers from the firing line. Even Michael Pitfield, former clerk of the Privy Council, got a seat there. Government contracts are rewarded to former Liberal ministers. In Canada, it seems, patronage is the oil in the political system.

When the PC government won in 1979, one section of the PMO, headed by a defeated candidate, was responsible for drawing up a list of people suitable for appointment by a PC cabinet. One frequently expressed regret was that the cabinet did not move fast enough, or ruthlessly enough, in putting their people into patronage positions.

Next time, they argued, it would be different.

In Austraila the cabinet handbook requires that all potential appointments are cleared with the senior minister from the state in which the appointee resides. They can be raised in cabinet only after the prime minister has approved. PMC maintains a list of government appointees. In the past under the Fraser government the department of Administrative Services also maintained a list of people who were 'appointable' and safe on political grounds. Names could be added only by a minister. Initially this list was maintained at the instigation of Senator Withers, the leader of the government in the Senate, the minister of administrative services and a senior member of cabinet. He saw his role as being the 'minister for politics' and maintaining the list was one of his functions. But after his departure, the portfolio was downgraded and the minister was both junior and less politically acute; the list therefore fell into abeyance. The process has reverted to an ad hoc operation in which political reliability is one important factor. Looking at appointments in government instrumentalities like the Australian Broadcasting Corporation (ABC) and Qantas, there is no doubt that political factors are important in the choice of personnel.

In Britain the prime minister has exclusive control over peerages, over the honours list and over appointments to a range of commissions, boards and other quangoes. The extent of the positions available was shown by Benn and Sedgemore's lists quoted earlier. There is a section of the No. 10 office that maintains lists of potential candidates, including ecclesiastical posts. There is no restriction on their choices.

The House of Lords is a particularly useful chamber to which potential ministers can be appointed or tired backbenchers or ministers retired without disgrace. In a society where honours are often treasured, the range available to prime ministers is extensive.

In New Zealand the Cabinet Office maintains a list of all cabinet appointments; they can be extensive. Often ministers will consult the caucus before appointments are announced, but whether they pay any attention to its decisions is less certain. If the prime minister wants someone appointed, that decision will be made.

How much influence does this give prime ministers? Many appointees are already people of distinction who do not regard government service as an ultimate ambition. Certainly they appreciate public preferment, but in some cases it may be due reward for party or public services. As a time for reappointment draws near, there are no doubt many statutory officers who become conscious of the need to remain on good terms with the incumbent government, but to see this as an extension of the prime minister's influence, rather than the government's as a whole, may be special pleading (as I believe it is with Benn and Sedgemore).

Besides, to appoint people to boards or statutory offices is not to control them. Many of those who would seem to be malleable turn out to be determined to protect the prerogatives of their new positions. It is quite possible, as Richard Marsh (1978: 112) discovered in appointing Cecil King to the Coal Board to counterbalance Robens, 'to be too clever by half'. In that instance King and Robens hit it off so well that they became even more dominant than Robens had been on his own. In Australia, appointments to the board of the ABC have often seen the need to show their independence of the government which chose them. Failing to reappoint powerful statutory officers with a high public profile because they disagree can be politically expensive, although it can be done.

Obviously it would be wrong to deny that many so-called independent statutory officials and boards do spend much of their time anticipating government reaction and trying to avoid conflict. Where prime ministers are known to have strong views, they will have an important input to decisions. And some place-seekers will ingratiate themselves with prime ministers. But it does not follow that the powers of patronage allow them to influence day-to-day decisions.

Where the power of patronage may indeed be influential is in the promises it holds:

> The problem of patronage is really a problem that begins long before the honour has been awarded. It stems from the relationship that is set up between the party leader—as donor—and those who may wish—as applicants—to receive the award. This relationship lies at the heart of the matter and extends the influence of patronage far beyond the numbers of people who, in the event, actually receive an honour. (Benn 1981: 24)

Whether referring to ministerial or other positions, the deference that patronage may create before appointment may be of value to all prime ministers.

CONCLUSIONS

Prime ministerial patronage is widespread, important and influential. Its impact may be subtle and difficult to identify. Yet it must always act within limitations. Politically prime ministers must balance their cabinet; bureaucratically they must maintain some morale in the civil service and maintain a smoothly operating machine. Much of the time they will rely on their colleagues for advice, even though some choices are obviously their own. It is too easy to add up the number of jobs within the prime minister's gift and draw conclusions from that gross figure. In Canada and Australia the pressures of federalism have impacts on its use. In Canada patronage is far more important as a means of maintaining party prestige than elsewhere. In New Zealand it is often shared out among the party. Other sources of power have to be used to supplement the wielding of patronage; by itself it would seldom be adequate to ensure loyalty or subservience if that were its intention. In some areas, indeed, the strength of patronage is an illusion.

5

Prime Ministers in Cabinet

Prime ministers set the agenda for cabinet meetings, decide which ministers will be cabinet members and determine what cabinet committees will be formed and what their authority will be. They chair the meetings of cabinet and their summary of discussions becomes the basis of the formal decisions. These powers are common to all prime ministers, except in some instances the leaders of the ALP and New Zealand Labour party. They shape the content and tone of debate in cabinet and provide the means by which prime ministers can determine the directions in which the government intends to go.

Prime ministerial powers in cabinet fit two categories: 'setting the arrangements' and 'running the proceedings'. The former is concerned with structural factors such as the agenda and the distribution of powers through the creation of cabinet committees; the latter relates to informal judgements made about how best the processes can be run and how a decision should be reached.

The use of rules is only one means by which prime ministers may get their own way within cabinet. Their influence may also be personal. They may be tougher, intellectually superior, more aggressive or more determined than their cabinet colleagues. It takes many of these qualities to get chosen in the first place, but the calibre of those colleagues should not be underestimated. In most cabinets there are several people with ambitions to become prime minister who may have many of the characteristics needed for success; it is not personality that determines their outlook but their position at that time. Intelligence and personality may assist in the dominance of prime ministers but they are not necessarily the cause of it.

Some prime ministers can control cabinet because they have been around for so long, either as prime minister or as a senior minister. Macmillan, for instance, was ten years older than most of his colleagues and had a longer memory of past events (Sampson 1967: 129). By the early 1960s Menzies had not only been prime minister for over ten years, he still was seen as the founder of the Liberal party who had brought it out of the political wilderness. Trudeau in 1983 had been prime minister almost continuously for fifteen years, far longer than all but one of his senior colleagues. In 1983 Muldoon had held office for eight years, long outlasting those among his contemporaries who proved to be effective ministers. Also he had been the only National minister to hold the Finance portfolio since 1969; his breadth of knowledge and experience therefore gave him a considerable advantage. Since many issues are in a sense re-runs of earlier problems, these prime ministers may know what has been tried before, what arguments were used and how they were demolished.

Factors that spring from ability and longevity assist any minister in attempts to influence cabinet colleagues, but more is required to prove the argument that prime ministers can dominate cabinet. To personal characteristics are added mechanical and procedural weapons. What is important to judge is how far, within the four systems, these weapons provide prime ministers with freedom to maneouvre, and to what extent their use is limited.

CABINET

Whichever system of government is being discussed, there is a danger of overestimating the capacity of cabinet and thereby of blaming it for failing to achieve objectives that lie beyond its proper powers. In both conventional and less conventional accounts of policy-making, cabinet is allocated a heroic role. Whether these purported functions are traced back to Bagehot, to contemporary political reformers or to theorists of organisation and management, cabinet is seen as the central source of authoritative decisions and pronouncements. It co-ordinates, directs and arbitrates. It resolves disputes, disposes of formal business and legitimises decisions made elsewhere.

However, cabinet arrangements are much more fragile than is often proposed, and its influence is difficult to exert in precise ways. That is not surprising. It is, after all, a committee, and committees are noted for the frustrations that they engender. Cabinet is unusual not in its abilities but in the forces operating on it and in the expectations that its mystique arouses. It is involved in continuous struggles to manage the unmanageable, routinise the extraordinary, systematise the disorderly, and co-ordinate the incoherent. Its agenda includes matters of great importance, matters of detail too gritty to be dealt with elsewhere, and matters that appear retrospectively insignificant but were perceived to be politically sensitive at the time. How it deals with business depends on the particular mix of incentive systems involved;

ministers come to the cabinet room with established personal anti-pathies as well as points of policy agreement.

Further, cabinet may not always get its way. While from its own perspective everything ought to come to it, elsewhere in the political machine its role is much less central. Government activity continues within each ministerial area of responsibility, with or without the minister's knowledge. That must necessarily be so. Cabinet's resources are limited; they can easily be spread too thinly or marshalled too erratically. In order to maximise its influence cabinet arrangements need constant care and consistent organisation. This care is not secured automatically; its presence depends primarily on the prime minister's wishes.

Gordon Walker (1972: 159) has warned of the dangers of asking the wrong questions about cabinet and then concluding that it is not working properly because it is failing to do something it was not designed to do. Crossman had clear ideas on how cabinet should *not* be run—the way that Wilson ran it. He deplored the failure of cabinet to formulate political and governmental strategy, the isolation of senior ministers from each other and from the prime minister, the ways in which important business eluded systematic cabinet attention, and the shifting alliances of ministers and civil servants who came together to deal with particular items and then dispersed. Further, he recorded with disappointment Wilson's private and evasive style of leadership. In Crossman's view, Wilson handled issues as they came, trying, now confidently, now pessimistically, only to ensure political survival. Crises were to be endured rather than circumvented by forward thinking. Achievements happened rather than came from conscious and co-ordinated striving (the above paragraphs are drawn largely from Hawker *et al.* 1979: 51–2).

Crossman argued that what was essential was a small 'inner' cabinet that could determine strategic directions and settle the important disputes—as long as he was a member of it (Jordan 1978). He believed that by this means some broad political direction might be achieved. But Gordon Walker held that 'cabinet is a constitutional mechanism to ensure that before important decisions are reached, many sides of the question are weighed or considered'. He rejected the view that cabinet did not 'make policy' or 'works less satisfactorily if it must think for itself or act without a brief' because 'cabinet is not meant or designed to do either of these things' (1972: 160).

Crossman believed that the failure to provide a coherent strategy or set of priorities was Wilson's fault. Gordon Walker believed that that type of co-ordination is impossible. Both views have implications for the way that prime ministers *ought* to relate to cabinet. Crossman thought the prime minister should give positive leads, arguing both that British government had become prime ministerial and that Wilson, as prime minister, was not prime ministerial enough. According to Gordon Walker, the prime minister's main function is to extract sensible, consistent and considered decisions out of cabinet, and to make the machinery of consultation work. Wilson (1976) largely accepted the latter role.

George Jones (1975: 57) argued that

> The Prime Minister's role is to advise, encourage and warn his colleagues: not to do their jobs for them. He may involve himself in one or two areas of policy, which seem most important at the time or with which he is publicly associated, but he lacks the administrative resources and the knowledge to make a significant impact on a wide range of governmental responsibilities...
>
> The Prime Minister is conductor, but from time to time he feels like reverting to his old position as leader of one of the principal sections; yet he also knows perfectly well that a chamber orchestra has to be led, and directed, in a style which recognizes that this is a group of highly-skilled, hand-picked players some of whom may feel confident that they too could direct.

Within cabinet prime ministers must play many roles, at times simultaneously, at times consecutively. They must keep the cabinet reasonably unified, ensure that acceptable and administratively feasible decisions are reached, take care that due consultations have taken place, maintain some consistency in different areas of policy, and provide a tone, a sense of direction or collective purpose.

Every recent survey of the operations of cabinet argues that it needs effective prime ministers to run smoothly. Their position gives them more resources than other ministers and in recent years, some argue, they have made greater use of those resources. Relations between prime ministers and cabinets can still vary widely, but prime ministerial preferences are crucial. It is easier for a prime minister, by wilfulness or omission, to disrupt the smooth working of cabinet than it is to ensure that it operates smoothly. How a prime minister chooses to work, and within what constraints, becomes important.

Because the proceedings and sometimes even the structures of cabinet are secret, it is often difficult to obtain accurate information about what has happened there. Yet an understanding of the environment undoubtedly helps to discuss the prime minister's powers. Here normative views of what part prime ministers should play often direct the argument. We are concerned more to ask what use prime ministers make of cabinet and how the procedures may assist either the leader or their colleagues.

THE AGENDA

In all four countries the agenda of cabinet is officially drawn up under the auspices of the prime ministers. They decide what will be discussed, what will be left off and at what position on the agenda each submission will appear. The use of this power has been regarded as one of a prime minister's most potent weapons, but how detailed or exclusive this power is may differ from system to system.

In Britain the first two items on the agenda, parliamentary business and foreign affairs, are fixed. On the first item the chief whip reports on the parliamentary situation, and on any related matters that might affect the progress of the government's programme; ón the second foreign affairs ministers may brief their colleagues on the international situation. Ministers can notionally raise any questions relating to these areas that have not been mentioned by the speakers. Under the Heath government two other areas of policy, relations with the EEC and Ulster (after direct rule had been imposed), also became standing items on the agenda (*Listener* 22 April 1976).

In practice, in Britain as elsewhere, much of the planning of business is done by the officials of the Cabinet Office. An increasingly sophisticated system of forward cabinet planning has been developed, in which the deputy secretaries are provided with details of likely departmental proposals. These items can then be fitted into a more regular pattern for consideration by cabinet or one of its committees. Much of the time recommendations about the agenda are proferred to the prime minister by the secretary of cabinet and accepted. The system has to an extent become bureaucratised.

In Canada the cabinet agenda has been largely standardised and the process of deciding where submissions will be considered has been '"automated" with a minimum of squabbling as to which forum should consider a given proposal or where it should appear on the cabinet agenda' (Radwanski 1978: 146). As the system of 'envelopes' has developed, under which the Priorities and Planning Committee (P&P) determine an overall figure for each committee which then settles the details, that process of decentralisation has continued (see Borins 1982). Most decisions are therefore made by the PCÒ. Occasionally an item may be delayed, when it may be logical to take some items together and at a time when the political climate is more suitable. The exceptions are those items that go direct to P&P. In Canada it is acknowledged that there are two ways in which issues can be settled—a fast route through P&P, and a slow lane through the normal channels. What goes directly on the agenda of P&P depends very much on the interests of the prime minister.

Table 5.1 Number of cabinet documents and meetings, Canada 1969–79

	1969	1970	1971	1973	1974	1975	1976	1977	1978	1979
Memorandum	784	781	829	683	611	634	494	493	483	635
Discussion papers	N/A	N/A	N/A	N/A	N/A	N/A	N/A	292	226	249
Draft bills	N/A	N/A	N/A	N/A	N/A	N/A	N/A	57	89	68
Committee reports	487	716	593	628	668	647	607	657	656	595
Cabinet meetings	73	77	75	58	57	57	64	62	56	75
Committee meetings	369	350	285	218	257	283	257	272	207	206

Note: No figures were kept for 1972, so the composite July 1971/72 figures have been omitted.
Source: PCO.

In Australia too the agenda is determined by the prime minister on the advice of the secretary of PMC. Ministers are required to provide planning details to the cabinet secretariat to allow sensible timetabling of items. There is a set of items required to be brought to cabinet, but ministers may in addition bring items for which they want advice or cabinet support.

In New Zealand the agenda is in practice drawn up by the secretary to the cabinet. Cabinet usually considers executive council items, engagements and cabinet committee reports first. Thereafter what is listed depends on what the ministers choose to bring. As long as the submission fulfils the formal requirements laid down in the cabinet handbook and, where appropriate, is accompanied by a Treasury note, it will be listed. Within the agenda the items are grouped according the portfolio so that the order has no significance. Generally the prime minister receives the agenda of the next cabinet meeting at the same time as the ministers.

An important factor is the number of items on the agenda. In Britain, in addition to the regular items, the agenda will include from four to nine items. In Canada, where much of the work is done in committee, most memoranda will be listed in an appendix to the agenda and will be raised for discussion only if a minister has requested it in writing to the prime minister before the meeting. Numbers of memoranda or discussion papers are listed in Table 5.1. The *average* number of memoranda or discussion papers was between ten and twelve per meeting.

In Australia the agenda is much fuller. Tables 5.2 and 5.3 give the equivalent figures. These show that cabinet considered far more items than in Britain and Canada, although New Zealand usually had around 40 items on a normal agenda.

Table 5.2 Ministerial, cabinet and committee meetings, Australia 1972–80

Time	Weeks	Full ministry	Cabinet	Standing committee	Ad hoc	Total
Whitlam government						
Dec. 72–Apr. 74	70	N/A	69	130	23	222
May 74–Sept. 75	73	N/A	59	58	82	199
	143		128	188	105	421
Fraser government						
Dec. 75–May 76	24	4	28	33	8	73
May 76–Nov. 76	24	4	29	35	13	81
Nov. 76–Apr. 77	24	3	39	49	10	101
Apr. 77–Oct. 77	24	6	73	51	46	176
Oct. 77–Mar. 78	24	3	37	60	25	125
Mar. 78–Sept. 78	24	6	90	67	72	235
Sept. 78–Dec. 78	16	2	37	47	35	121
Jan. 79–June 79	26	7	54	194*		255
July 79–Dec. 79	26	8	43	130*		181
Jan. 80–June 80	26	5	43	150*		198

Table 5.3 Submissions to cabinet, Australia 1971–80

Time	Weeks	Submissions	Papers	Total	Av. per week
McMahon government					
Oct. 71–Oct. 72	52	550	—		10.5
Whitlam government					
Dec. 72–2 Oct. 74*	86	1304	—		15.2
June 74–May 75*	52	662	—		12.7
May 75–Sept. 75	13	284	—		21.7
Fraser government					
Dec. 75–Dec. 76	54	972	28	1000	18.5
1977	52	877	194	1071	20.6
1978	52	1045	618	1663	32.0
Jan.–June 79	26	312	364	676	26.0
July–Dec. 79	26	397	314	711	27.2
Jan.–June 80	26	401	389	790	30.4

There are three resources open to prime ministers in cabinet: they can keep items off the agenda; they can flood it with items; or they can list them in an order most convenient to themselves. Keeping items off is not a problem, according to most Australian ministers, at least not in their own area. That is to say, all items that they wanted discussed were listed, if not immediately, then within two or three meetings. But, of course, they could not influence the listing of items in which they did not have an interest. In Canada most submissions are listed automatically for consideration by committees, except in those areas of policy in which Trudeau took a particular interest such as constitutional change and federal-provincial relations; these items might go directly to P&P or even be settled bilaterally. On a few occasions the prime minister might choose to delay discussion on an item until a more propitious time. In New Zealand no ministers recalled difficulty in the listing of items for their own portfolios. It was agreed that the process had almost become automatic.

In Britain the evidence for prime ministerial control seems to be stronger. Devaluation was never discussed by the Wilson government. Castle (1980: 367) claimed that Wilson 'had effectively de-natured Cabinet ... Cabinet's agendas have never been thinner'. Elsewhere Castle (1980: 427) showed considerable concern about whether items would appear. Thatcher did not discuss the Falklands crisis with the full cabinet; at times the war committee simply reported to it. Callaghan was, according to a senior official, 'arbitrary and despotic' in declining to list items, but even so the official believed a strong minister could still get a proposal discussed. All prime ministers could use their powers to get discussion removed to more suitable arenas.

Complaints about exclusion from the agenda often relate to the inability of ministers to discuss areas of policy with which they are not directly concerned; it is not so much an inability to get action on their own items. On the question of devaluation in Britain, it seems probable that the chancellor and the minister for economic affairs were content to make decisions without discussions with full cabinet, as long as the prime minister listened to them. Under Whitlam, foreign affairs was discussed only once—and then after protest. For a time Whitlam himself was minister for foreign affairs and later preferred to settle foreign issues in co-operation with the minister, who was a close colleague. In other words, if the responsible minister is prepared to settle issues in consultation with the prime minister, then the exclusion of cabinet is possible. If ministers want an item discussed that lies within their responsibility, it seems that they can usually achieve it.

Cabinet can also be manipulated by putting too much on the agenda. If cabinet is designed to allow full discussion of all angles, then packing the agenda may be an equally effective way of controlling it as trying to isolate cabinet from some issues. This tactic was used most frequently by Malcolm Fraser. He worked extremely hard, but the pressure on his ministers was great too. Inevitably few of them could be fully prepared for cabinet meetings; one commented that he read about one-tenth of the cabinet papers carefully and 'if anyone says he does more, he is lying'. Many agreed that they skipped over difficult or technical items (see Weller and Grattan 1981: 110–12).

An over-full agenda has three consequences. First, many items get scant attention when they deserve more; many of the political consequences are not adequately considered. Second, temporary deferment to ask for more information is often an easy expedient. It does not mean that a 'decision deferred was a decision made', to use Wilson's phrase (Barnett 1982), but rather that as more items return to cabinet the agenda becomes cluttered. Cabinet discusses one item several times, rather than several items once and properly. According to a senior public servant, it is the 'desecration of the cabinet system' (Weller and Grattan 1981: 95).

The third implication is the most important for this discussion. Too large an agenda cedes influence to those who are best briefed, are intellectually the most acute or have the most stamina. In the Fraser cabinet the prime minister, the treasurer, the minister for finance and, in his capacity as leader of the Country party, the minister for trade, were briefed on most items. The prime minister was given a briefing note that had both procedural and often policy implications. When that was added to Fraser's diligence and toughness, it meant that he knew more about most items than anyone except the sponsoring minister. The size of the agenda also means that on some items discussion is limited to a small group. Items of great political moment may be discussed, but other issues are not. This clogging of the agenda—and the capacity it provides for a well-briefed prime minister to dominate discussion—is a result of timidity of ministers and the prime minister's desire to remain well-informed.

There is a need to be wary of reading too much into the number of submissions. Some may be no more than reports for information of colleagues; others may be passed without debate. At the last cabinet meeting before Christmas in New Zealand, the agenda often looked like a clearance sale, with up to 90 items to be disposed of. In a normal agenda of 40 items, it is unusual for more than five or six to be debated at length. In Australia the recommendations of cabinet committees might be relisted for final authorisation. Yet, even with these caveats, there is no doubt that the large agenda in Australia and New Zealand gives a distinct advantage to dominant prime ministers like Fraser and Muldoon.

However the length of the agenda may indicate a greater collective emphasis. In New Zealand there are specific limitations on expenditure that can be taken without submission to cabinet and many ministerial decisions that do not involve more than one department must also be brought to cabinet for approval (Talboys 1970: 3). In Australia since 1978 the minister of finance has been authorised to approve minor expenditures bilaterally with ministers without cabinet consideration, but the ceiling is fairly low. Items that have an impact on federal-state relations are required to be brought to cabinet. Perhaps partly because of the narrower range of choice from which ministers are drawn, and hence weaker ministers, more decisions are taken collectively and formally in cabinet. Discussion may be brief (75–80 per cent of submissions in New Zealand are approved as recommended), but the prime minister is still better able to keep informed of what ministers are doing in small polities like Australia and New Zealand by packing the agenda.

The third tactic is the determination of an item's place on the agenda. Castle was conscious of this, complaining once: 'Top salaries were supposed to be today's priority in Cabinet but as usual it was allowed to be pushed to bottom place when other matters are argued interminably' (1980: 247). Often an item could be rushed through around the end of the meeting (see e.g. Barnett 1982: 103). Australian Labor ministers too recall that major decisions, such as the purchase of land in Woolloomooloo, have been passed rapidly at the end of a meeting.

> The ultimate lesson, if a chief secretary wants a paper through quickly, is to ensure that there are many other politically contentious items on the Cabinet agenda. It does not always work, but from time to time I have managed to obtain approval for a paper in thirty seconds before 1 p.m. as Cabinet was almost breaking up. It cannot, of course, be done if the paper is new or controversial and, more importantly, *it cannot be done without the cooperation of the Prime Minister.* (Barnett 1982: 111—emphasis added)

Less is known about the order in which items are taken in the other countries. Most accounts indicate that prime ministers in Canada and New Zealand have largely ceded the routine of drawing up the agenda to their supporting staff and that items are usually taken in the order listed. Where the agenda seems excessively long, both Fraser and Muldoon have warned ministers that they would stay until it was completed—an effective deterrent on debate. But shuffling the agenda in the British manner is not frequently recorded.

Prime Ministers may also determine what else cabinet may discuss. In New Zealand some prime ministers, such as Holyoake and Kirk, permitted items off the agenda to be brought to cabinet; others, particularly Marshall and Rowling, refused to allow debate on any items that were not properly documented. 'Items-off' could in some cases be raised without giving the prime minister prior warning. In Canada, 'emerging issues' brought up with the consent of the prime minister could be discussed at the end of cabinet meeting. In Australia, there was provision for 'under-the-line' items—issues for which there had been no time to prepare a formal submission or which ministers wanted to bring to the attention of their colleagues. Under-the-line items needed to be cleared in advance with the prime minister (Cabinet Handbook 1983: 19). Under the Fraser government, they were taken first and sometimes took a large part of the meeting; under Hawke they are shifted to the end of the agenda. In Britain the standing items provided the opportunity for raising these types of issues. In all cases it was up to the prime minister to decide whether to permit discussion.

The influence that the agenda gives the prime minister needs to be kept in perspective. The development of the agenda and the requirement for full and informative submissions are comparatively recent. Consider the advantages that accrued to prime ministers before the cabinet system was bureaucratised. Mackenzie King did not have cabinet meetings on fixed days; he had no agenda and went from item to item without notice; then he told the secretary to cabinet the result. Pearson allowed ministers to present proposals with little supporting evidence. Trudeau's system of requiring committee consideration, of ensuring proper routines and the circulation of submissions, may have helped to keep the centre aware of what was being done; it certainly assisted other ministers to become aware of the broad directions of government policy and allowed them to prepare more for cabinet discussion. Further the increased demands made by cabinet offices to meet the requirements of submissions (for e.g. see Weller and Grattan 1981: 220–21; Cabinet Handbook 1982) assist *all* cabinet in decision-making. The importance of the agenda needs therefore not to be overstated in the routinised cabinet offices that now run all the cabinet systems.

CABINET COMMITTEES

In each country some of the work of cabinet is delegated to cabinet committees for decision. The membership of these committees and their terms of reference are decided by prime ministers. Decisions on whether or not appeals to full cabinet will be allowed are also in prime ministerial hands. It has been argued that cabinet committees are a means by which prime ministers can circumvent cabinet by stacking the membership, or by manipulating the results. The result, in policy terms, is seen to be great. For instance, a permanent secretary in Britain commented that in the Thatcher cabinet 'The monetarist minority ... prevailed in economic and industrial policy because they had strategic control of the key departments and cabinet committees... The doubters and dissenters were either being given no opportunity to

mount a challenge in full cabinet or were unable to do so effectively'
(Pliatsky 1982: 178).

The existence of cabinet committees is now well–documented,
although for a long time it was kept secret in Britain. The arguments
for that secrecy, as expressed in a memorandum from Callaghan to his
ministers, were that publication could be 'misleading or counterproductive'. It would be asked why some committees did not exist, or
whether decisions made in committees indicated a lack of status. He
suggested that details of the ad hoc committees, numbered as GEN
and MISC under successive governments, could not be published as
their subject-matter was sensitive and they were often ephemeral. Besides, publication 'would make it harder to make changes' (*New State-
man* 10 November 1978). In 1981 Thatcher too argued that to provide
any details of committees, except those standing committees whose
membership was initially announced in 1979, 'would not be consistent
with the doctrine of collective responsibility, as it has developed in
this country' (*Times* 10 February 1981). Gradually more knowledge of
the British system has emerged, while information on the Canadian,
Australian and New Zealand systems has been readily available for
some time (see Mackie and Hogwood 1983). Nor have any of the
problems anticipated by Callaghan been perceived in those countries.

The important question to ask about cabinet committees is whether
the power to select members and terms of reference, and the influence
that prime ministers have to determine the treatment of decisions, has
a great impact on their decisions. It is worth recalling that committees
fulfil a vital function in dealing with items that are not important or
controversial enough to be dealt with in full cabinet. Attention in full
cabinet does not necessarily depend on any notion of the intrinsic importance of a topic, however gauged. It depends on the political sensitivity of the item. Heath was one prime minister who believed that,
even so, too much was referred to cabinet (*Listener* 22 April 1976).

In Canada the system of committees was developed by Trudeau to
a degree of sophistication not matched elsewhere. The shape of the
committee system went through several stages. In 1980 there were
thirteen including three co-ordinating committees, P&P, Legislation
and House, and Treasury Board. Trudeau himself chaired P&P, the
Public Service Committee and the Security and Intelligence Committee. At an earlier period there was also a Federal-Provincial Relations
Committee whose membership was identical to that of P&P: the two
were later combined.

Most of the committees are functional; they deal with subject areas,
such as Foreign Affairs and Defence, Economic Development and Social Development, or with areas, such as Western Affairs. The choice

of chairman was in the hands of the prime minister, but all were ministers with functional responsibility in the subject areas. Occasionally they may have electoral responsibility; for instance, Lloyd Axworthy, the only minister from the Western provinces, was chairman of the Western Canada Committee.

P&P is the central committee; it has been called the executive committee of cabinet and at times the *de facto* inner cabinet. In the budgetary context it determines the size of envelopes—in August 1980 it settled these priorities at a special meeting at Chateau Lake Louise (Borins 1982: 67). It deals with problems of acute political sensitivity, the ones on which other committees cannot make a final decision, and with the areas in which the prime minister is particularly interested. Its membership—12 strong in 1980, 13 in 1982—was partly determined functionally and partly regionally. Thus the chairmen of the main functional co-ordinating committees, Economic Development and Social Development, each of which is supported by its own department, are both members of P&P. So is Yves Pinard, the house leader and chairman of six committees. Others, like Axworthy, are partly there in a representative capacity. Membership of P&P is prized, since non-members rarely attend. When changes to its composition are announced, such as the reshuffle on 6 October 1982, they provide a fair indication of who has risen or fallen in influence and status. When Clark tried to establish an inner cabinet without a representative of British Columbia, he soon had to revise his list when a storm of protest followed. Most of the time representation follows functional lines with P&P being the main exception. At times P&P decisions have been final; at others they have to be endorsed by cabinet. The difference is academic. It is inconceivable that a full cabinet would overturn a decision made by this group of senior ministers. However, even if P&P can deal with two or three vital issues, it cannot do everything.

Decisions of cabinet committees are not re-opened in cabinet. As long as the appropriate procedures have been adopted and the Treasury Board has approved any expenditure, the decisions are included in an annexure to the cabinet agenda and approved without debate. Items decided in committee can only be raised with the approval of the prime minister, and that must be sought in writing beforehand. It does not often happen (French 1979). The process of decision-making, intended to ensure collegiality and mutual support, can be time-consuming. An experienced minister, Mitchell Sharp (1977: 67), said he spent 12 to 15 hours a week in cabinet or its committees; that did not include time for preparation:

Trudeau would not have initiated this kind of system had he wanted to concentrate decision-making in his own hands. What he has achieved, however, is the reinforcement of cabinet solidarity and the principle of collective responsibility, and that is sometimes mistaken for the centralization of power in the hands of the prime ministers. (Sharp 1977: 67–8).

The formalised and well-established nature of the procedures makes the exceptions more obvious.

In Australia the existence of standing committees was first publicly announced by the Whitlam government in 1973. There were six standing committees, each with a nominated membership that was largely functionally derived; other members of cabinet were allowed to attend if they chose. Whitlam acted as chairman of three of the committees and determined what went to all of them. In the first eighteen months the committees met regularly but thereafter, largely as a result of Whitlam's choice, they met less often. Between December 1972 and April 1974, there were 130 meetings of standing committee (40 of which were legislation committees) and 23 of ad hoc committees; between May 1974 and September 1975 the figures were 58 standing committee meetings (including 39 legislation committees) and 92 ad hoc committee meetings. The membership of ad hoc meetings was less functionally structured. In 1975, for instance, the membership of the Expenditure Review Committee, which examined both new and ongoing spending proposals, consisted of the most powerful members of the government, even those who themselves had expensive proposals. But ad hoc committees, usually headed by the prime minister, were perceived to be easy to control.

Under Fraser membership of the standing committees was again made public and terms of reference were changed. An Economic Committee was initially appointed, but that was soon abolished when it became clear that all important items were referred to the full cabinet for decisions. The membership was determined on a functional basis; in the first set of committees, this arrangement meant that the main opponents to Fraser, Peacock and Killen, could be left off all the committees except the one dealing with defence and foreign affairs. In 1981 one of the reasons that Peacock gave for his resignation was Fraser's failure to include him, in his capacity of minister for industrial relations, on the Wages Committee.

After 1977 Fraser established on a formal basis the Co-ordination Committee. Before that time some items on which the cabinet could not reach a decision were referred to an unofficial leaders' committee for decision. That committee contained the leaders and deputy leaders of the two parties and the leader of the government in the Senate. The formal creation of the Co-ordination Committee established this on an official basis. Peacock complained that it had too much authority, with cabinet ministers occasionally being asked to leave the room while the committee made a final decision; none of his colleagues speaking in the same debate recollected those events.

In addition to the standing committees several ad hoc committees were created. After the elections of 1975, 1977 and 1980 expenditure review committees under various titles reassessed spending priorities. In 1980 it was formally called the Review of Commonwealth Functions, and issued a public report to parliament. Other ad hoc committees were created to examine particular items such as the communications satellite, and to draw out the ramifications for later decision by cabinet. Notionally standing committees had the right to make final decisions; ad hoc committees reported back unless specifically given authority otherwise.

The Hawke government has in large part followed the recommendations of a party task-force report in establishing its standing committee structure (*Quality of Government* 1983). It has also spelt out in some detail the process that a proposal needs to follow. There are seven functional committees and three co-ordinating committees. In some cases—such as the inclusion of ex-leader and former treasurer Bill Hayden on the Economic Committee—the choices were personal; most were functional. Proposals are first sent to the relevant committee for consideration; the recommendation of the committee is then listed on the agenda for the following cabinet meeting. The prime minister then reads through the items one by one to see if there is further debate. Generally committee recommendations are accepted, but they have not received cabinet approval until formally endorsed in this way (Weller 1983c).

In New Zealand the most important cabinet committee under National party governments, the Cabinet Economic Committee (CEC), has existed since 1949. Under Kirk a new body, Policy and Priorities, was created, partly so that its membership did not have to include some people whose portfolio required them to be on CEC. Policy and Priorities soon became the body that made the most important decisions (Roberts and Aitken 1980) and became an 'inner think-tank'. Under Muldoon CEC was returned to its former eminence. Muldoon himself was a member, although not its chairman; membership was a good indication of who was in favour and it was thought a considerable advantage for ministers to be members. A Committee on Expenditure dealt with the small spending items, while CEC looked at longer term strategy. Sometimes items were sent from cabinet to CEC for final settlement. As minister of finance and prime minister Muldoon could dominate CEC. He did not however directly involve himself in the activities of other committees, although he was kept in close touch with what was being discussed and decided.

Cabinet committees often officially have the power to make final decisions (with the exception of the Works Committee); they are meant to discuss policy, drawing public servants into their discussions, and then make a decision. Committee reports are on the agenda of each cabinet meeting, but primarily for noting. Their recommendations are seldom overturned and when a powerful committee like CEC brings a proposal to cabinet, it is unlikely to be challenged.

Usually committee decisions were not discussed again in cabinet, but they could be if the prime minister wanted. Kirk, for instance, was overruled in Policy and Priorities by six votes to one when he opposed any rise in state services. So he took the decision to a cabinet meeting when three of his six committee opponents were absent. There he lost by seven votes to eight. He then went to caucus where he finally got support for his stand. The incident illustrates the unique ability of the prime minister to re-open items, but also the need to get support. It shows the possible flexibility with which cabinet committees can be used.

In Britain lack of information makes precision more difficult. In 1979 Thatcher announced the names and chairmen of standing committees, but details of the ad hoc committees are not provided. There is no doubt that committees deal with much of the work—according to one estimate, they include 90 per cent of the volume, but only 10 per cent of the importance. The *Economist* (6 February 1982) did provide some details; in six years Attlee created 396 ad hoc committees; Wilson set up 118 in 1974–76; Callaghan 158 in his three years in power. In her first two and a half years, Thatcher created around 60. The memoirs of ministers illustrate the frequency with which they met in those committees and the subjects that they had to settle.

In all four countries the choice of chairman is important. In Australia, where there are probably fewer committees, all prime ministers have chaired the important committees themselves. Where they have delegated the responsibility it has almost always been to one of the leadership group. Hawke is nominally chairman of all but one of the standing committees, although he will probably only attend the Foreign Affairs Committee regularly. In Canada Trudeau deliberately delegated much of the responsibility as chairman to others, retaining for himself the areas of interest which are directed to P&P. Of the eight cabinet committees established by the Clark government, only the inner cabinet was chaired by Clark.

Chairmanship seems therefore to be more widely distributed, and more a matter of dispute, in Britain. Prime ministers may chair the important ad hoc committees (such as Thatcher's war cabinet). If an area is becoming controversial, they may take over the chair to help direct a conclusion they like, as Wilson did with the Industrial Development Committee in 1974 (Jenkins 1980: 208). Callaghan took the chair of some ad hoc committees, such as the one on the aircraft industry, in which he had a personal interest. Prime ministerial confidants are always more likely to be made chairmen than those less in sympathy, yet even so most chairmen take seriously the need to achieve some result. Barnett records of one committee: 'Tony Benn chaired our meetings—apparently it was the first time he had ever chaired a Cabinet committee—and tried very hard to get agreement to avoid having to go back to Cabinet. This was despite his own opposition to the whole exercise' (1982: 107).

All prime ministers have used their power to nominate the membership of committees to some extent. Castle complained of the European bias of the European Questions Committee (1980: 295). But it seems that most of the choices are marginal. Many ministers have to be there because of their functional responsibilities; obviously an economic committee must include the chancellor/treasurer/finance minister. At times they are able to insist on membership; when Prior was moved to the Northern Ireland Office, he successfully demanded retention of his position on the Economic Committee (*Economist* 10 October 1981). It was indeed a question for comment when Fraser left the minister for industrial relations off the Wages Committee. Particular ad hoc committees might include regional representation—in Australia every state was deliberately represented on the committee that investigated the prospects for a communications satellite. A committee like the Falklands Committee included the paymaster-general because he was chairman of the Conservative party, not for portfolio reasons. But most committees must be largely functionally derived.

That is the result of prime ministerial distribution of portfolios. Prime ministers can also choose the arena in which problems will be discussed, whether full cabinet or committee. This allows dominance of areas of policy by particular committees.

The single most important fact about Mrs Thatcher's first period of government is that the main thrust of economic policy was effectively hived-off from the scrutiny of the whole Cabinet. Apart from discussions on expenditure reviews, the Cabinet as a body did not consider the general economic strategy until July 1980: 14 months after entering office. And it usually only discussed the matter on an annual basis thereafter. Policy was contained within the Cabinet's 'E' Committee on Future Economic Policy, and more frequently in even smaller, less formal, groups of Treasury and economic department ministers centred on the Treasury and Number 10. (Burch 1983: 411)

The Times (14 March 1981) pointed out that the direction of economic policy depended on 'a shifting balance, not according to issue but to whether the decisions are taken by the economic ministers by themselves or in full cabinet'. As the quotation from Pliatsky at the beginning of the chapter indicates, economic policy can be dominated by the 'dries' because they have been put in the crucial portfolios; their control was strengthened in 1981 and 1983. Since they therefore have a majority on the economic committee, the prime minister can have crucial decisions delegated to them. Indeed Burch (1983: 415) has suggested that the 'wets', mostly congregated in foreign affairs jobs, did not try to interfere in economic policy because that might have led to a reduction in their control of foreign policy. Under Thatcher 'the tendency to compartmentalise government policy-making almost as a formal principle of organisation' was new (Burch 1983: 415). The prime minister's influence was in determining who got which job. Thus committees could still be functionally derived without reducing her control.

In Canada the membership of P&P and in New Zealand the membership of CEC are both indications of the favoured or the powerful. The occasional juggling of membership is a clear indication of the political climate. Muldoon has tended to keep his potential rivals off CEC; Trudeau ensured his close colleagues were on P&P, even if some regional representation was still required.

In the review of decisions, prime ministers generally have the right to re-open questions in full cabinet in all four countries; they also have the right to refuse to open questions. In practice it is accepted that questions can only be re-opened with the prime minister's approval, requiring an application in writing in Canada and the consent of the cabinet chairman in Britain, although it seems in Britain that on a few occasions Callaghan allowed Foot to re-open items on pay policy as a special prerogative (Mackie and Hogwood 1983: 37). The one constitutional exception in Britain is the rule that the Treasury cannot be overruled in committee; therefore if the Treasury does not accept the outcome, it has to be referred to full cabinet (Pliatsky 1982: 140). In general, it is accepted that, just as cabinet itself is a committee, so parts of cabinet can act with its full authority. Hence some Australian and British committees can act with full authority, while Canadian and New Zealand decisions are usually accepted in bulk at a cabinet meeting.

Throughout the process prime ministers are always kept informed by their cabinet secretariat on any likely sources of conflict. The cabinet secretariats service committees and, with the Canadian exceptions of the ministries of state for social and economic development, hold the main responsibility for briefing chairmen. The prime minister in Britain can intervene if he or she chooses. One prime minister always saw the minutes of a particular committee's decisions before they were circulated; on one occasion he stopped the circulation, on another he took the topic to full cabinet. The options were his. In Canada, Trudeau kept a careful check on the committee's proceedings on an issue in which he had a particular interest (Borins 1982: 72), although his role was less active elsewhere. Clark, on the other hand, wanted to be kept informed on everything. That is a matter of choice. In Australia, with the prime minister or one of a very small group as the main chairmen, control and oversight are even more centralised.

Prime ministers do not have to be present to be remembered in committee deliberations. Ministers in all countries acknowledged that their influence was everywhere when decisions were being made. If ministers knew the directions their leaders might follow, that had a considerable impact on the committee.

THE PROCEEDINGS OF CABINET

Within cabinet prime ministers have considerable scope to determine how issues will be dealt with, which parts need attention, what else may be discussed, and how decisions may be reached. There are the traditional skills of all influential chairmen, and here it is more difficult to draw distinctions between the influence of prime ministers in different systems.

Personalities affect style. Consider the perceived differences between Canadian leaders. Mackenzie King and Pearson were, according to one colleague, instinctive politicians; St Laurent and Trudeau were rational; those approaches affected the way they ran their cabinets. Another argued that Pearson appeared open, gregarious, bumbling and slightly helpless, but that he knew what he wanted and steered cabinet towards it. Trudeau was the opposite in all respects; he gave the impression of knowing what he wanted, but really did not try to direct cabinet except on a few issues. He was, said a mandarin, potentially powerful but generally permissive, patient and collegial in running cabinet. Gordon Robertson, clerk of the PCO, sat in cabinet with four prime ministers—Mackenzie King, St Laurent, Pearson and Trudeau. Of the four, Trudeau was 'the most likely to be guided by consensus and the least likely to impose his own views... He allows all kinds of discussion, invites it, encourages it, shows enormous patience' (Radwanski 1978: 152). Clark was more crisp and directive.

Prime ministers can also dominate the proceedings of cabinet by their intellectual weight and their preparation. Macmillan's 'chairmanship of cabinet [was] superb by any standards. If he dominated it (he usually did), it was done by sheer superiority of mind and judgement. He encouraged genuine discussion, provided it kept to the point. If he found himself in a minority, he accepted the fact with grace and humour' (quoted in Sampson 1967: 129). Kaufman points out that prime ministers often won because they did their homework (1980: 76). Attlee was efficient, well-informed and occasionally devastating; he could not stand unnecessary talk (Harris 1982: 403–5). Trudeau's capacity to home-in on the critical elements of an issue and to examine the consequences was marked, to the extent that the discussions of some cabinet committees resembled an academic seminar (Radwanski 1978: 145–6). In Australia 'Menzies was often, indeed mostly, the best informed man around the table because he read his cabinet papers' (Hasluck 1980: 9). Whitlam was hard-working, sharp and had an encyclopedic memory. Fraser controlled cabinet by 'superior knowledge... The prime minister is always terribly well briefed. But he's also voracious, he masters an enormous amount of detail' (quoted in Weller and Grattan 1981: 185). Muldoon was personally dominant, partly because of his detailed knowledge and partly because of his rough style. And, a disgruntled National backbencher added, because he was never challenged by 'the weak-kneed, lily-livered bastards who are there'. Personal characteristics are constantly at the fore in cabinet proceedings.

As cabinet chairperson all prime ministers can determine how an issue is treated. For instance, Harold Wilson argued that prime ministers can steer and guide discussion:

> The prime minister may wish to indicate how the discussion should be handled and decisions taken. He may, for example, say the question raises, say, three issues ... he may feel it right to remind the Cabinet that they have not met to review a broad policy decision, but are concerned with this or that point of implementation. (1976: 68, 69)

Several British ministers endorse this view. On one occasion 'H. [Wilson] issued a warning. We must all limit our speeches to ten minutes and would we please note we were *not* to reopen the general discussion ... merely to indicate what were our priorities for cuts' (Castle 1980: 483). Similar powers accrue to the prime minister in Canada, New Zealand and Australia.

Prime ministers may also decide when to rush items through cabinet at the end of the meeting (Barnett 1982: 103) or when to present cabinet with a *fait accompli*. When the British cabinet could not decide on an economic package, Callaghan announced that the chancellor and he would 'go away, make up a package and present it to the

House and party. If it was thrown out by the Party, that would be that' (Barnett 1982: 106). The cabinet had to ratify the Lib–Lab pact (Barnett 1982: 116). In Australia in May 1983 Hawke announced a royal commission into the security services without consulting cabinet, which had no option but to agree.

The approach to discussion often depends on the inclination of the prime minister. Some act as arbiters, others are initiators. While they must all be 'ever alert to issues which raise fundamental doctrinal passions' (Wilson 1976: 69), some see their responsibility as ensuring that there is, as far as possible, a consensus in cabinet and want to draw out views; others will make their own views clear and pull cabinet with them. In Australia Holt's cabinet meetings appeared unending as he insisted that ministers talked their way through to a conclusion which they could all accept. Gorton often, and Fraser occasionally, made it clear what they wanted early in the discussion and forced cabinet to follow. Thatcher has a tendency to make her position clear much earlier and more clearly than did Wilson, who was concerned to let views emerge. 'This meant that her colleagues either had to go along with her or chip away at her stated viewpoint. As a consequence, she often lost out to her cabinet, certainly more often than her predecessors' (Burch 1983: 412). Others argue that the prime minister ought to stand back: too early intervention can reduce collective responsibility. It is better to be prepared with the appropriate tough question (Barnett 1982: 41) to ensure that the implications of submissions are drawn out.

In New Zealand Holyoake sometimes adopted the disconcerting habit of asking one minister to explain to cabinet the implications of another minister's submission. It had the effect of ensuring that all the ministers read the submissions before the meeting. Holyoake led from behind, gently pushing the cabinet. Muldoon leads from the front. Because he is also minister of finance, he is unable to stand above the argument—and this is one of the reasons that the combination of portfolios which he holds has been criticised.

In part style depends on the degree of importance the prime minister gives to an item. According to his biographer, Trudeau had three categories into which items were notionally slotted:

> issues which he stakes out as his personal domain, in which he claims a prerogative to decide what should be done and how; issues in which he feels strongly about the goals to be obtained, but is open to discussion as to the means; and issues in which he takes no great personal interest, as long as what is being done strikes him as reasonable and consistent. (Radwanski 1978: 161)

Although the categories were not rigid, all the problems of national unity, including federal-provincial relations, the constitution and language policy, fitted the first category. So did US relations and nuclear proliferation. On questions that came within the other categories, he was much less concerned with detail.

In Britain economic and foreign affairs have always been crucial areas; thus as chancellor Healey 'had to work very hard to convince the prime minister' (Barnett 1982: 63) before any policy could be adopted. In New Zealand the combination of foreign affairs with the prime ministership ensured that the former area stayed within the prime minister's influence. Since 1975 when Muldoon took over the ministry of finance, in some important policy areas such as housing and agricultural support he effectively makes the decision personally.

On some occasions prime ministers choose not to bring items to an immediate conclusion, perhaps because the political costs of one minister losing are greater than any problems caused by delay. Mackenzie King deliberately drew out some battles in order to bring both sides to terms (Wright 1977: 287). Trudeau allowed the battle between Lalonde and Turner over a guaranteed income scheme to drag on until neither man appeared the loser and he had effectively defused the confrontation (Radwanski 1978: 157–8). In Australia Fraser would sometimes insist on cabinet taking two or more bites at the more complicated proposals, to ensure that most ministers understood the implications of what they were deciding (Weller and Grattan 1981: 127). In Britain Callaghan allowed a lengthy debate on the IMF proposals, even though he was determined that they would be accepted. Discussion served the useful political function of allowing dissident ministers to protest and let off steam (Dell 1980: 31; Pliatsky 1982: 156). It is the prerogative of prime ministers in all systems to hold up decisions where they see it as necessary or desirable.

Deciding how decisions are taken is part of the prime minister's prerogative. In Australian Labor governments prime ministers generally prefer to obtain a consensus, but when it cannot be achieved they have been prepared to take a vote, even though some of their colleagues are sceptical of the value of such a process. Occasionally their counting is considered unreliable (Weller and Grattan 1981: 130), but the traditions of the Labor party are sufficiently engrained to ensure that such a process is acceptable.

In British Labour governments, processes varied. Attlee never took a vote. Wilson often did in an informal way: 'Although we do not actually vote, ministers closely involved count votes. Prime ministers also count, indeed their counting is all that matters. In this instance the prime minister summed up that we were evenly balanced, and gave his casting vote for us' (Barnett 1982: 77). When the prime minister chose, he could interpret the vote as he pleased. Barbara Castle records (1980: 549):

> We made it ten clearly in favour of Tony [Benn]'s figure of 2½ billion; nine for the chancellor's figure, including H himself, and two wobblers. We thought the chancellor had lost but H summed up that there was a 'very slight' majority in favour of 3¾ billion, Eric [Varley] kept whispering to me that he thought Denis [Healey] would have resigned if he had been beaten.

Elsewhere Castle writes (1980: 532): 'H[arold] at work rigging cabinet is wonderful to behold, whether it is welcome depends on which side of the arguments one's interests lie'. Barnett recalls winning and ,losing cases primarily on the proximity to lunchtime: 'Cabinet democracy works in strange and mysterious ways' (1982: 103).

In the non-Labor parties votes are not taken (French 1979: 891). Heath and Thatcher merely sum up. Heath explained why votes could never be taken on important policy issues:

> When the Prime Minister finds that there is a difference in the Cabinet, he will recognise differences coming a long way off, and he will have done a great deal of preparation to avoid the differences crystallising. When, at a Cabinet meeting, he perhaps surprisingly finds a difference which is greater than he thought, he has to find a means of dealing with it. It may well be that, mentally, he is weighing up numbers around the table; and I have seen a Cabinet Secretary sometimes rather unobtrusively jot down names on two sides, and a Prime Minister can then form his own judgement about numbers. But the other reason is that it is not numbers which always matter. It is the weight of the individual, and his position. (*Listener* 22 April 1976)

In Canada Trudeau sought a consensus: 'Yes, consensus seeking, provided I am sure I can share the consensus' (Radwanski 1978: 171). Yet in Australia Fraser used to go around the table in the same way as Wilson in Britain. Jokes about eight to six decisions, with Fraser on the side of the six and summing up that way, were common. One participant described the process:

> We've had enough discussion round the table, and the prime minister says, 'I think we've all said our piece. Has anyone got anything fresh to say?' And the answer is no. At that point the outer minister has no say, but he's had the right—if he's been co-opted he certainly has the right; if not as a matter of common sense he usually has the right if he feels strongly about something, to say what he thinks. And it's a coincidence that he's in the room—he's in the room waiting for something to be dealt with. O.K. Whether he's co-opted or not, at that point, if the discussion has been pretty animated and disagreement has been very evident then the prime

minister will say, 'Rightoh, we'll just take the views of minsters, he starts with Robinson on his left-hand side or with Viner on his righthand side, in the order in which they're sitting—they're the two junior ministers in the cabinet—they go around the table in a clockwise or anti-clockwise direction getting views; and if people have felt strongly enough—and usually it's yes or no, where do you stand? I stand with the minister or against the minister who's brought the matter forward. And that's a vote in anyone's language. And if it's close, well, there's often a further animated discussion if it hasn't perhaps gone the way the leadership wanted it to go. Sometimes the leadership will accept the decision reluctantly, sometimes they'll, well, you can have a situation where the PM, the deputy PM, the Treasurer, are outvoted. Now it's pretty serious—if it's outvoted by one, they might really insist on a further reconsideration—don't overlook this or that. That's when you might find one or two ministers find it convenient to change their mind in the light of some new evidence. But it's a vote, and it's the position, and it's been talked through. (quoted in Weller and Grattan 1981: 131)

A former secretary to the British cabinet would disagree that there had been a vote: 'Collecting voices is one thing; I think voting is another' (*Listener* 22 April 1976). It depends on weight, not numbers. Occasionally, when prime ministers feel strongly, they can make decisions against the consensus.

How do ministers react to these processes? To some extent they accept it as part of the prime ministers' prerogative that they can manipulate the process to get their own way. As one Australian minister said: 'If he felt a very strong reason for not accepting a consensus, I think that if he persisted I would take the view that I would very seriously reconsider my own view and weigh it. He is leader and that demands high respect.' But not everyone was always happy. After one vote in the Wilson cabinet, 'Denis [Healey] snapped "I must say to you, Prime Minister, that these matters cannot be decided by a majority in cabinet". This is the first challenge to H's method of counting heads without calling for a vote, that I have ever heard' (Castle 1980: 464).

The last point begins to illustrate the limitations on a prime minister's capacity to sum up their way all the time. Senior colleagues must be respected and often courted. Callaghan 'always had to be sure of carrying his deputy, Michael Foot' on cost-cutting exercises (Barnett 1982: 89). He was considered essential to the survival of the government. At other times, even if the chancellor was in a minority, Callaghan might argue that he gave especial weight to his views and was therefore coming down on his side. The debate on the IMF in 1976 was one such example. In cabinet, even where numbers are counted, votes do not always weigh-in the same. Barnett, as chief secretary, was once outvoted eight to one in committee, but in cabinet 'with the Chancellor and the Prime Minister on my side, I was doing much better' (1982: 77). In Britain some ministers are regarded as particularly important to the government; Jenkins, it has been argued, was for a time as indispensable to Wilson as Foot later was to Callaghan.

An Australian prime minister acknowledged that sometimes he could force cabinet in a direction, but that could not happen too often: 'You certainly have to feel very strongly before you wanted [to prevail against a cabinet majority] because if you can't persuade your colleagues that you are right there is probably something wrong in your arguments' (quoted in Weller and Grattan 1981: 189). Colleagues accepted that if he felt strongly he could get his own way. One New Zealand prime minister accepted that he could 'steer' cabinet, but denied that he could 'direct' it.

Of course prime ministers will try to ensure that they know what the outcome will be. An Australian prime minister explained:

> If I'm worried about a submission I might speak to the minister involved beforehand and if I am worried about a submission (which doesn't happen too often) this probably means I'm not sure or certain about the outcome, about where a decision might lead us. So if you are speaking about it beforehand it's probably because you want to be able to see the way ahead, whatever decision cabinet might take and what its impact might be. (quoted in Weller and Grattan 1981: 184)

But the very fact that he needed to consult beforehand indicates that prime ministers cannot take support for granted. Cabinet is not a simple rubber-stamp for prime ministers' ambitions.

At times, in all countries, prime ministers lose. Thatcher was in a substantial minority in demand for cuts in public expenditure in 1981 (Burch 1983: 403) and had to live with the result. Fraser did not always succeed. Whitlam was overrruled on economic policy in 1974, and for a time effectively left the running to his deputy. Even Muldoon, often regarded as the most dominant of prime ministers, has (his colleagues insist) accepted cabinet decisions of which he does not approve, although not often.

In Australia non-Labor governments have the additional complication of being a coalition. Senior National party ministers have often made in part their own rules, and are largely beyond the control of the prime minister. Since under Fraser they were also the most experienced ministers, their impact was considerable; as one put it, 'You can get away with a lot if you are senior enough—and in the Country party'. Another very senior minister commented: 'It's legitimate for you to say, I feel very strongly about this and would you mind if I took it away and brought it back' (Weller and Grattan 1981: 128).

In Canada all English-speaking prime ministers have delegated considerable independence of action in Quebec affairs to their Quebec lieutenants. Even within cabinet a range of opinions is needed because of the representative nature of the institution. Yet uneven weight is accepted. One participant argued it was 'consensus in an in-group. With thirty men and women around a table, it's unavoidable that some people in the decision-making process carry more weight with the prime minister in a decision' (Radwanski 1978: 169). So the consensus is weighed and all prime ministers are cautious that they do not too regularly ignore the heavy-weight. Collective responsibility works best after discussion, even though prime ministers are mainly responsible for deciding what it means and how it is to be applied. They can use it to their advantage to dictate how ministers should behave, what is permissible and what conventions should be followed—and they do (Benn 1981: 28).

The evidence about prime ministers operating in cabinet—whether memoirs or biographies in Britain and Canada or structured interviews in Australia, Canada and New Zealand—illustrates how much time prime ministers spend in discussion and how, even if they know what they want, they do not always get it. Of course there are occasions when they impose their wishes on a doubtful cabinet—particularly on items which they consider important. But all, including Thatcher, have suffered defeats there. For the items that come as open questions—and some are too important not to—cabinet seems an arena which prime ministers in all four countries cannot entirely control.

INNER CABINETS?

Most prime ministers are accused at some time of bypassing cabinet and concentrating power in the hands of small group, whether made up of ministers, advisers or officials. These groups are often called kitchen cabinets, inner cabinets, cabals or cliques.

The precise nature of the criticism is often unclear. All leaders will have a group of people with whom they feel more comfortable, with whom they can readily discuss political events in a unthreatening atmosphere. Inevitably they will see more of these people than others. This may take them influential, but does it add up to a powerful inner group?

It may—but it is unlikely to be a fixed group. Trudeau was always close to the leading members of the PMO, but all its leading figures—

Lalonde, Roberts, Austin, Coutts—later sought an independent political career. Presumably they had a clear notion of the reality of personal power. Heath had his own group of supporters with whom he often met—it included Barber, Whitelaw, Carr and Carrington. Muldoon has his cronies, ministerial friends who are not the most competent but are the most congenial. Whitlam interacted with an ever-changing group, as ministers came in and out of favour. Chifley had an 'official family' of ministers and officials with whom he discussed policy. Fraser for a time had an unofficial 'leaders' group' of the four party leaders (and occasionally the government leader in the Senate). Wilson had a well-known staff at No.10 including Haines, Kaufman and Marcia Williams, although Haines's later accounts scarcely suggest cohesion within that group and some of its members constantly changed. Wilson also met regularly on Friday with the chancellor, the foreign secretary and the leader of the house to review the forthcoming week. The discussions often became general.

The important question is whether these groups constitute an inner power elite that can circumvent cabinet and replace it as the main source of authority. Kaufman has argued that the existence of these groups should not be seen as indicating a redistribution of power. He denied that there was a kitchen cabinet or that some members or ministers had peculiarly easy access to the prime minister. In his advice to a putative minister he said

> But, you will whine, he [the prime minister] would certainly pay attention to my important activities if I were one of his cronies. Ever since Harold Wilson dubbed Harold Macmillan's administration 'Government by crony', cronyism has been a dirty word in British public life. You will be surprised to find that the Prime Minister is unlikely to have any cronies, if you define such people as those who have access to him whenever they wish. Of course he has colleagues who were close to him in the past, ex-Parliamentary Private Secretaries, for example. But they will find that—and, to incredulous colleagues, will protest that—they now see little of him. They certainly cannot expect any special favours from him...
>
> You may feel that even though the Prime Minister is not blatantly favouring his old friends over you, your democratic rights as a Member of Parliament and Minister are being usurped by an undemocratically selected Kitchen Cabinet. Do not be too easily taken in. There is no evidence whatever that James Callaghan was the centre of such a body... Harold Wilson, on the other hand, is firmly believed to have had a Kitchen Cabinet. Certainly he would have had one if wishing could have created one. Richard Crossman ardently desired such a body to exist, with himself as a key member of it. (Kaufman 1980: 78, 80)

What then of official inner cabinets? Britain and Australia have ministers officially divided into members of cabinet and outer ministers. Access to cabinet for the latter varies (Weller 1980), but the distinction is clear. In Britain cabinet includes around 23 members, in Australia around 13. In New Zealand there is no distinction. In Canada Clark created a smaller 'inner cabinet', but Trudeau reverted to the all-in Canadian tradition when he returned to power.

Ministers are therefore *officially* regarded as of different weight when the cabinet's structure is created. In all instances there are further practical distinctions, usually in the form of cabinet committees. In New Zealand the CEC, in Australia Fraser's Priorities Committee and in Canada P&P are accepted as the most important. For a time Wilson had a Management Committee. Membership is sought and is in the prime minister's gift. These committees often make important decisions on budgetary or other political matters, and if cabinet's endorsement is needed it is a mere formality. In Britain the 'E' Committee, or the Falklands War Committee, has similar powers.

Are these then inner cabinets? Gordon Walker (1972: 87–101) argues that they are more 'partial cabinets', that is official groupings of senior ministers, with a nominated membership, official terms of reference and authority ceded to them by cabinet to make final decisions. Their main importance is that they have formal authority and that they are legitimate parts of the cabinet system, not a corruption of it. Of course on occasion they may in practice act as a means of legitimising what prime ministers have already decided to do, but they may also be a real forum of debate.

What the debate indicates is that the power to determine committee membership (in turn based on the distribution of portfolios), to determine where discussions are undertaken, and to control procedures gives all prime ministers a means of influencing outcomes. Prime ministers will always listen to different groups of advisers, but they do not need to create a mysterious inner cabinet for they already have the means of creating powerful partial cabinets—and they use it. In some systems the procedures are far more routine than others, usually because the prime minister has chosen to make it so.

CABINET PRIORITIES

The debate over inner cabinets draws attention to the problems of setting coherent priorities. Inner cabinets are said to be required because cabinets are too large for broad discussions and are thus unable to set clear priorities or devise coherent strategies (see e.g. Butt *Times* 9 April 1981). That claim is made as readily in Australia, with a cabinet of 13, as in Canada with a cabinet of well over 30 ministers.

Prime ministers are generally meant to be concerned with party strategy and with the general directions the government is taking. According to Crossman (1972: 76), 'the biggest task of the Prime Minister in any radical Government is to stop this fragmentation of the Cabinet into a mere collection of departmental heads'. Ministers in Canada and Australia argue that too much technical discussion or too much detail can depoliticise cabinet. There is a need to balance the narrow and the general.

There are two approaches. One is for the prime minister to take the main burden of that overview. The other is to persuade cabinet to act collegially. Many of the political and bureaucratic experiments in the last twenty years have sought to solve the problem by assisting cabinet collectively, as Chapter 6 explores in greater detail. Trudeau's early cabinet structures were designed to ensure that ministers knew what their colleagues were doing and understood the implications of their submissions before they were approved. The procedures were intended to increase collegiality. They were time-consuming and reduced ministerial independence in their own areas of responsibility (to the undisguised disgust of both ministers and mandarins from the more relaxed St Laurent and Pearson eras), but it was considered easier for cabinet to speak with 'one voice' after proper discussion. In 1975 and 1976 the Canadian cabinet went further. It set out to determine government priorities. The opinions of all ministers were sought and the threads were drawn together in an extensive exercise, but the final result was too general and too late (French 1980: 75–85). Political crises had determined the agenda. In the 1980s, starting under the Clark government, a system of expenditure envelopes was determined by P&P, within which sectors had to live. Canadian cabinet procedures have always appeared the most rationalistic.

In Australia and Britain attempts were made to establish institutions that could advise on government strategy, while drawing on bureaucratic and partisan skills. In Britain the Central Policy Review Staff (CRPS) lasted for thirteen years, but it became useful more as a task-force into policy problems than as a strategic planner (Pollitt 1974; Plowden 1981). In Australia the Priorities Review Staff (PRS) lasted a mere three years and never succeeded in its broader objectives (Weller and Cutt 1976; Boston 1980). In New Zealand no such group existed; the key cabinet committees (CEC under National; Policy and Priorities under Labour) were, according to one participant, far too busy to be strategic. The collective advice provided appears to have been less useful to ministers than their departmental advice. Ministers are usually conscious that they must fight for their corner. Besides, for bodies like the CPRS and the PRS, present political problems soon become more important than examining longer-term interests.

The other collective strategy is to take ministers away from the submission-regulated cabinet meetings to a forum where they can think about general strategy. The Canadian cabinet has regular 'think-ins'; the meeting of Meach Lake in June 1981, for instance, decided its priorities were inflation, industrial strategy and constitutional reform (*Globe and Mail* 15 June 1981). In Britain, Heath instituted the idea of 'Chequers weekends'. One of his ministers regarded them as essential. The Wilson government discussed devolution and the CPRS report on social services at such weekends. Edmund Dell is doubtful about their value:

> Every cabinet minister could deliver himself of such thoughts as he had accumulated either within his own head or from those of his officials. There were pleasant enough occasions. They made a nice break from work. Occasionally they served to suppress incipient revolts such as on devolution by showing up how much fight there actually was in the dissidents. They may have brought some satisfaction to those ministers for whom it was more important to have registered a view than to have persuaded colleagues. But as time passed it became clear, I think, that busy ministers increasingly resented the time devoted to them. (1980: 35)

Fraser occasionally held meetings of the full ministry. The Hawke government has decided to follow the Canadian example; it intends to hold meetings without submissions once or twice a year.

Looking back over the past decade, the record of collective priority-setting is not encouraging. It may be that priority-setting is in any case a chimera—always be either too general or too difficult. Although the Canadian procedures for the allocation of expenditure provide an impression of rationality and cohesion (an impression not always retained by a glance at its economy), it seems little better than the other countries at promoting collective directions. Decision-making is invariably sequential, and usually *ad hoc.* Even in Thatcher's cabinet the economic strategy of the 'dries' has often come adrift in the face of opposition from spending ministers. The lady may not be for turning, but her economic strategy scarcely seems to be a collective cabinet priority (Burch 1983: 403).

If the attempts to secure the adoption of collective priorities have failed, even greater stress is put on prime ministers. They alone can look at items from a general and a political perspective; they alone have to fit the pieces together. The tasks grow increasingly complex. Many, perhaps most, have difficulty in achieving it, because of the pressures of their job. Yet it is the function that observers expect them to fulfil. While they can, to a greater or lesser extent, manipulate the procedures of cabinet, the problem of priorities draws attention to the support that *they* get to assist in their job. This is considered in the following chapter.

6

Advising Prime Ministers

To ask what advice prime ministers need is almost the same as asking what their job is. Prime ministers need help to do whatever they choose to do, and the range of options open to them is much greater than that available to their ministerial colleagues. Yet at the same time discussions of the available support structures often develop into normative accounts of what prime ministers should do. Rose (1980: 26) has suggested that form follows function; yet often writers assume that, as they believe the functions of prime ministers should not change, there is no need for the form to vary either. These normative assumptions often camouflage the fact that prime ministers may be playing roles, legitimate in their own eyes, which vary from those preconceived notions. As a result form and function may no longer fit so neatly.

Discussions of the 'correct' advisory structure revolve around two themes: the need for partisan advice and the need for policy advice. The first raises the question of whether the support given by career civil servants, trained notionally to serve prime ministers of all complexions, is adequate for prime ministers' needs. Neutral non-partisan officials may be eminently suited for running the cabinet machinery and for ensuring the co-ordination and consistency of policy, but is their advice sensitive enough for the politically charged problems that prime ministers frequently face? Alternatively, do prime ministers need the assistance of political partisans who understand and share their own political outlooks and beliefs? Traditionalists abhor the growth of ministerial staff and other 'independent' sources of advice. It is necessary to ask how useful they are, what roles they can play and what the implications of these roles may be.

The second theme concerns the type of advice that prime ministers ought to receive. Should it be concerned primarily with the processes of central government or with detailed policy issues so that prime ministers may become involved in policy initiation? It is here that much of the normative debate occurs. Some observers and participants believe that prime ministers should *not* get into the detailed pursuit of specific policy areas; one person who worked in No. 10 argued that every time the prime minister got too involved in detailed policy, it was a disaster. Like Wilson, these people see the prime ministerial role as conductor of the orchestra and not as player of an instrument. Others have argued that prime ministers have increasingly, and as a matter of necessity, become more involved in the detailed development of specific policies. As a consequence they need supporting structures that can give them thorough and well-developed advice in those areas of policy and from their own perspective.

This chapter will explore three main issues: What type of support do prime ministers receive? What are the advantages or disadvantages inherent in that form? And are 'prime minister's departments' compatible with cabinet government and collective solidarity?

Several ways of describing the different roles prime ministers play have been suggested. Peter Bailey (1974) argues that a prime minister's two main roles are to act as team leader and to be the inspiration and initiator of policy for government. Such an approach distinguishes between policy role and cabinet role. A second approach considers the content of advice that a prime minister might receive—whether on procedural matters, on policy content or on partisan political matters. This is not to suggest that the three are clearly distinct, but organisational arrangements are based on the assumption that some bodies are *primarily* involved in one of these arenas, even if they must at times wander into the others. A third approach considers the interests of the prime ministers themselves. Thus the PCO in Canada distinguishes between prerogatives and priorities or interests. The former category relates to those functions that the prime minister has to fulfil, the duties that are part of the position; the latter are those areas to which the prime minister gives high priority and wants to devote energy. Any discussion of supporting structures can therefore concentrate on the prime minister's roles, on the types of advice needed or on the prime minister's interests.

AUSTRALIA

In Australia the prime minister's main bureaucratic support is the department of the Prime Minister and Cabinet (PMC) (see PMC 1979; Mediansky and Nockels 1975, 1981; Yeend 1979; Hawker *et al* 1979: Ch. 4; Weller and Grattan 1981: Ch. 9). On 30 June 1981 the department had a total of 432 staff. It was then organised into eight divisions. Two of these, the Cabinet Office (with 35 staff) and the Parliamentary and Government Division (with 36), serviced the prime minister as team leader. The Cabinet Office provided the secretariat for cabinet and cabinet committees and ensured their smooth programming—a major task since in 1980/81 there were 82 meetings of cabinet, 176 meetings of cabinet committees and a total of 3661 decisions of cabinet or its committees to record and circulate (PMC 1981: 11–13). The Parliamentary and Government Division's responsibilities included a variety of legal questions, relations with parliamentary and party committees, all machinery of government and ministerial arrangements, and senior appointments, although primary carriage of the last three items lay with the Public Service Board which also reported to the prime minister. The large Operations Division included the Office of Ceremonial and Hospitality, provided support staff for the other divisions and dealt with the prime minister's voluminous correspondence. These areas therefore supported the prime minister as team leader; they maintained the smooth running of government machinery as far as possible.

Five divisions were functionally organised to cover all areas of government activity: the Economic Division, which also dealt with resources policy; the Communications Division, which included industrial relations, cultural activities and federal-state relations; the International Division; the Trade and Industries Division; and the Welfare Division. These divisions contained between 17 and 33 people each. They provided the prime minister with a brief on any item coming to cabinet or on any other question of interest to him. Again that task was substantial. In 1980/81 alone 1664 submissions or memorandums were submitted to cabinet. Since June 1981 parts of the department have been reorganised to meet the emerging priorities of the prime minister, but the basic structures are still as outlined above. Members of PMC have played a leading role in co-ordinating policy and acting as chairmen of major task forces. In 1975 a member of PMC acted as chairman of the official committee that provided data for the expenditure of the then Labor government. In 1981 another member was the chairman of the officials' committee that supported the massive review of commonwealth functions. The permanent head of the department chaired four of the official committees that provide backing to the standing committees of cabinet. In a sense these divisions provided the capacity to brief the prime minister on policy, allowing him to initiate where he regarded it necessary or to challenge and question the details of other policies being brought to cabinet. The advent of the Labor government brought more changes to reflect different priorities. In particular a division concerned with women's affairs was created as an indication of the importance the new government gave that topic. Within this general structure, organisational review is continuous.

The growth in the policy capacity of PMC has been comparatively recent. Throughout the 1950s and 1960s the department filled a role similar to that of the Cabinet Office in Britain. It serviced cabinet and its committees, circulated the minutes and was primarily a post-box. Then for a time the two main functions were separated. From 1968 to 1971 the Cabinet Office had a separate existence from the department of the Prime Minister. The reasons were political, not organisational. The incoming prime minister, John Gorton, wanted his own policy adviser and chose the abrasive Lenox Hewitt to head the department; but he also had to find a position for the then secretary of PMC, Sir John Bunting, who had been head of department since 1958. Therefore the cabinet-servicing function was divided from that of advising the prime minister. The split did not work well, partly because of the personalities involved, but primarily because the prime minister's principal adviser was not in cabinet and therefore less able to understand all that was going on, while the secretary to cabinet did not have a large advisory role. The two halves were reunited under Bunting after Gorton's fall.

Later, under Whitlam and even more under Fraser, the department developed a greater policy capacity. In 1974 Whitlam replaced Bunting with John Menadue, once Whitlam's private secretary and more recently an executive in the Murdoch newspaper empire. Whitlam wanted an active department that could give him policy advice on a wide range of issues. As a result the department increased its ability to advise on particular functional problems, particularly in the economic arena, because both Whitlam and Fraser were suspicious of the Treasury and argued that they needed a second opinion on economic questions. Given the monolithic nature of the Treasury and its recognised obstinacy, it was a reasonable position.

Policy advisers were not intended to initiate alternative solutions, or to provide unexpected information with which the prime minister could gain the upper hand in cabinet. 'It is not our business to have ministers surprised in the Cabinet Room with questions they have not anticipated, or be faced in the Cabinet Room with propositions they have not considered' said a secretary of the department (Yeend 1979: 143). Nevertheless on a range of issues PMC is far more than a simple co-ordinator of government initiatives. It plays an active role and is prepared to acknowledge it: 'We do not feel inhibited in what some might interpret as the role of second opinion. Our branches have built up an understanding of policy issues and an expertise in coordination; our officers are sought out for their advice and assistance. We have scope for probing and proposing' (Yeend 1979: 143). On occasions, such as the publication of a Green Paper on energy, PMC did much of the drafting because the relevant department had been unable to deliver at the right time and there were political pressures for quick action. At other times taxation proposals and alternative emphases in economic policy have also emerged from the department.

Yeend (1979: 146) has commented: 'A Prime Minister's Department is a tool of government that can be used in a very direct and telling way in ensuring that government policies are got underway, that changes in direction are made, that there is a responsiveness by the public service as a whole to new instructions and changes of style'. He acknowledged that these powers had to be used sensitively to ensure the department's co-ordinating capacity was not threatened, but saw no contradiction between the two functions.

How active PMC is in policy areas depends on how much policy advice the prime minister wants. Fraser was an activist prime minister who wanted to be kept informed about everything that went on, at least in part, so that he could maintain a check on his ministers' proposals. Hawke, initially at least, has been less concerned to initiate ideas, nor does he want the same amount of detail. He absorbs briefs quickly but is less concerned to do his ministers' job for them. As a result, the policy divisions have seen a reduction in the pressure of demands. Whether that will last depends on the degree to which Hawke is prepared to remain uninvolved in the detailed initiation of policy.

Two other public service departments report to the prime minister. The Office of National Assessments provides an independent intelligence assessment. The Public Service Board, responsible for the recruitment, staffing and efficiency of the public service, is an independent statutory authority within the prime minister's jurisdiction. On important matters, such as the level of staff ceilings, the chairman has direct access to the prime minister. On other matters, including public service reform, it works to a minister assisting the prime minister in public service matters.

The prime minister receives further support from a private office. One or two of its members are on secondment from PMC; the others are political appointments. The growth of the office has substantially been a development of the last decade. When Whitlam gained office in 1972, he relied at first on his personal staff for alternative advice to that provided by the public service; it was made particularly necessary by the limited capacity of PMC. The office was highly partisan, concerned to ensure that the party's platform was implemented and that the Labor government had a good chance of being re-elected. The involvement was varied and hectic, although the office remained small. At times members of the office had a considerable impact on details of policy, even though those policies were not always successful. Gradually, however, the importance of the office declined as the role of PMC expanded under John Menadue. By November 1975, when Whitlam was dismissed by the governor-general, its policy impact had lessened; its leading figures had moved on.

Under Fraser the private office went through several forms. Several people headed it, the most notable being David Kemp, a professor of political science. By 1981 it consisted of about 30 people. In part it is responsible for ministering to the prime minister's needs, making appointments and so on, but it has also developed the capacity to provide advice on policy questions. Afterthe 1980 election it included four senior academics on secondment, with ready access to a fifth who was nominally attached to the department of Foreign Affairs. Its influence reached its height under Kemp whose position in Fraser's confidence was secure enough for his comments to be regarded as authoritative. When he left, the leading members of the office lacked his weight and the office declined in importance.

The business of the private office is the business of the prime minister, including everything that goes across his desk—foreign affairs, economics and particular interests of the moment. The members of the office may sit in on official committees to inform themselves or to suggest political factors that may need consideration; they do not attend meetings of cabinet. Their purpose is to aid the prime minister and the cabinet (in that order) to maintain coherence; to help integrate the philosophy and policy of the government; and to assist the prime minister by adding an alternative voice to that of the bureaucrats. Their briefings are totally confidential—for the prime minister alone. In other words the office is responsible for a 'political input', a role that can be played far more readily there than in PMC, even if it is extraordinarily difficult to determine exactly what that political component is. The office can, by asking the right questions, ensure that all the political implications of proposals are worked out. The members of the office are aware of the need to avoid upsetting ministers, who want to be assured that the office is always working constructively. Usually contact between PMC and the office is close; ideas initiated in the office will be tested with PMC, and often with other departments. But the functions and institutional interests of the office are different from those of PMC and all other departments. It is the one group whose institutional interests are identical to those of the office-holder. That is possibly why it is better that the prime minister's office is staffed primarily from outside the public service. It is the place where party and bureaucracy intersect. Even so, its capacity to provide advice must be limited by the sheer range of the prime minister's responsibilities. The office has always kept out of the public gaze in Australia; with the exception of some rather overwrought performances by the press staff, its activities have seldom been noted. There is not a single press interview given by a member of the office since 1975.

Hawke's PMO is of a similar size; it includes political advisers (one being the successful former secretary of a state branch), academic economists, press secretaries and links with the party. The office is loyal to him and entirely appointed by him.

CANADA

The Canadian prime minister is supported by the Privy Council Office (PCO), the Federal-Provincial Relations Office (FPRO) and the Prime Minister's Office (PMO). The first two are staffed by career civil servants, the third by political appointees.

The most important sections of the PCO are the Operations and Plans Divisions. They have about 70 operational and 70 support staff. The Operations Division corresponds to the highly formalised cabinet committee structure. Each cabinet committee is serviced by a small secretariat, organised by subject matter. The PCO also has sections dealing with the co-ordination and scheduling of cabinet business and the distribution of cabinet documents. The Plans Division contains secretariats for those committees which the prime minister chairs, or is heavily involved in. As an official PCO submission (1979: 4–12) has stated: 'To a degree it is helpful to think of the operations division in terms of support to Cabinet and the Plans division in terms of support to the Prime Minister.'

PCO officials are always likely to be involved in the preparaton of cabinet memoranda; they will ask whether the proposals are timely, coherent, comprehensive and accurate, how they relate to other proposals and whether they give genuine choices to ministers. The basic belief is that the prime minister should be protected from receiving advice from only one institutionalised source (PCO 1979: 4–30). The PCO ensures that adequate analysis and co-ordination of policies and policy proposals are carried out (Doern 1979: 44). As it has increased its control over the rules of cabinet, so it has added to its capacity to monitor the content of policy (Mallory 1977: 15). Again in these secretarial and co-ordinating functions, the PCO supports cabinet and therefore the prime minister as team leader.

The PCO has also developed a capacity to support the prime minister's attempts to introduce more rational decision-making procedures.

Under Trudeau it developed a highly sophisticated planning system, drawing on many theories of organisational behaviour. It tried to develop coherence in government programming. 'The unique contribution of the PCO as a central agency is through the process of policy consideration—in terms of relationships between new proposals, existing policies and the government's overall objectives' (PCO 1979: 4–32). It tends to be 'the main source of overall governmental and strategic organisational advice' (Doern 1979: 43–4). The PCO therefore developed a planning system that was concerned first with priority-setting, second with priority problems and third with policy review. The policy problems were often those broad topics which did not fall easily into any single portfolio.

The process of priority-setting at times was highly ambitious. In 1974 and 1975, following the return of the Trudeau government with a newly regained majority, the PCO undertook a massive exercise to determine the priorities the government should adopt. Departments were asked to express their own priorities so that all could be related. The idea was that the final list of five to ten priorities would guide the speech from the throne in the autumn of 1975. In practice the completed document was too late, too long and too general to be useful; economic circumstances already dictated priorities, even though 'the veneer of technocratic sophistication seemed almost to deny their essential and overriding realities' (French 1980: 79). Indeed the whole exercise illustrated the tremendous difficulties faced by any policy co-ordinating unit. Priorities in government are often so broad as to be meaningless, or so narrow as to be highly debateable. What the exercise illustrated above all was that the PCO saw itself taking a very active role in its service to cabinet as a whole and in shaping the directions which the government chose to take.

The FPRO, established in 1974, has the responsibility for maintaining a general review of the government's relations with the provinces and for intervening in some areas of policy where relations with provincial premiers play a key role. Its first head, Gordon Robertson, had previously been the clerk of the PCO; while he remained in the FPRO he retained responsibility for senior civil service appointments. He and his successor always had direct access to the prime minister. The staff of the FPRO was always small, but it provided advice from a perspective of considerable importance to the prime minister. As long as it existed it ensured that there was a second senior official to whom the prime minister could turn.

In Canada the PMO is large. It is entirely politically appointed, serving during the pleasure of the prime minister. The loyalty of its members is directed to the prime minister personally. It organises the prime minister's schedule, answers his correspondence, links him to the party apparatus, interacts with the media and briefs him for his appearances in Question Time. It also gives advice on both policy and personnel matters. Its members provide advice on senior appointments, and on major issues of policy and priorities (French 1979: 385).

The actual role has changed at times with the interests of the principal private secretary. Lalonde and Austin were deeply interested in policy, more recently Coutts (1975–81) stressed the switchboard role. In part this may be because the bond between Trudeau and Pitfield, head of the PCO until 1983, meant that a counterweight to the bureaucracy was not regarded as necessary. The PMO has also adapted its functions to suit political demands. When the government was in a minority—as in 1972–74—immediate political tactics were more important than many of the technocratic programming debates that had been undertaken beforehand. Members of the PMO, in the Canadian tradition, can attend both official meetings and cabinet committees, even though one adviser thought it wrong for a member of the PMO to go to a committee and then have the last word with the prime minister. But the active role of PMO officers was often very public and openly acknowledged, both because of the size of the office and the range of its functions.

Before Joe Clark became prime minister in 1979, he had attacked the size of the PMO. Although he reduced its budget, he actually increased its staff. They were divided into five units: Personal Services, Communications, Administration (including all correspondence), Human Resources (advice on all appointments) and Policy (a group of four close advisers). The policy group concentrated on a few key items like energy and budgetary changes. The easy transfer of essentially unaltered structure from Trudeau to Clark suggests that the enlarged PMO has now become established and that the large politically sensitive body is seen as an integral part of the Canadian prime ministerial structure.

Nevertheless there are limits on what·the PMO can do. For a time its staff carried responsibilities for overseeing party progress in individual provinces, a function which had previously been undertaken by the senior ministers from each province. This function was seen as usurping ministerial prerogatives and partly returned to ministers although the Cabinet Committee on Western Canada, responsible for oversight of the government's impact there, was still serviced by the PMO. Three or four times a year it also services the strictly political meetings of ministers that are held to review strategy. Much of the time it does not have the capacity to undertake deep policy analysis. One adviser in foreign policy occasionally acted as Trudeau's emissary. That was exceptional. On the whole there was too much to do solving immediate problems for the PMO to usurp the role of departments. It was concerned with intelligence, not expertise. On the other hand, by dealing with correspondence and appointments, it undertook the more blatantly political functions that civil servants are somewhat loath to be seen to be doing. Opponents claimed that the influential role played by senior PMO officials meant that the prime minister was 'isolated from uncongenial advice' (*Globe and Mail* 10 February 1981). PMO officials deny this, pointing out that not only is it undesirable, it is also impossible.

There is no clear difference of function between the PMO and the PCO in most policy debates. The rearrangement that occurred in 1980 required the head of the PCO, Michael Pitfield, to provide support for the prime minister's 'interests', to be his principal adviser in those areas of government with which the prime minister was personally concerned. His deputy was reponsible for the areas covered by the prime minister's prerogatives. The main difference, according to one account, was that the PCO was non-partisan, operationally active and politically sensitive, while the PMO was partisan, politically active and operationally sensitive (Lalonde 1971). In practice, they work closely together. Each morning there is a meeting in which the prime minister canvasses the main problems of the day and his likely time-table with his main advisers from both the PCO and the PMO. Their main functions, in serving the prime minister, are very similar.

BRITAIN

In Britain the 'team leader' part of the prime minister's job gets the greater amount of support. This comes primarily from the Cabinet Office. Although there are around 400 members in the Cabinet Office, the important sections consist of some twenty people, plus their support staff. They are divided into four sections: Economic Affairs; Europe; Overseas and Defence; Home Affairs, Social Affairs and Parliament. Each is staffed by four or five high flyers, on rotation from other departments. The Cabinet Office has the duty of servicing cabinet committees, chairing the official committees that process many of the submissions to cabinet. The cabinet committee structure and the cabinet agenda are determined by the prime minister on the advice of the Cabinet Office. Its main concern is to ensure the smooth running of government machinery, achieved primarily through its superb intelligence network. Better than any other department except the Treasury, it knows what is going on throughout the government and it knows best where the political problems may develop. In this role the Cabinet Office serves the cabinet as a whole.

For thirteen years the Cabinet Office also had an analytic capacity nominally at the service of all ministers. The Central Policy Review Staff (CPRS) was founded by Heath in 1970. Then headed by Rothschild, it had a small talented staff (some civil servants, others partisan) and was designed to serve several functions—to provide strategic assessments of the government's programme, to undertake studies of special projects and to provide advice to cabinet on any items coming to it. Originally created as a means of providing an alternative source of advice, it had easy access to Heath but later became absorbed within the Cabinet Office. Its success has been challenged. Some of its reports, on subjects like the foreign service, were controversial (and described disparagingly by a senior official as being of the standard of sixth-form essays). Tony Benn (1981: 60) claims that it was sometimes used to undercut ministers and had 'in practice become a powerful lobby for the Cabinet Secretary himself'. The CPRS retained the capacity to advise all cabinet members; the 'Chequers weekends' where ministers meet to discuss progress was one of its forums. Its activities remained selective, but increasingly it seemed to be working more to the prime minister as an individual. It was abolished by Thatcher in 1983.

What does advice to a 'team leader' entail? Primarily it is procedural. Each submission to cabinet is accompanied by a note to the prime minister (or to the chairman of the cabinet committee) giving details of likely points of dispute, pointing out potential hazards—'you may wish to press the minister on paragraph 7'—and suggesting ways in which solutions might be reached. The brief may touch on preferable strategies and possible solutions. Such advice will always have some implications for policy; the position of chairman when no votes are taken is always powerful. Touching on possible outcomes means that the procedural brief may well become a policy brief, even if its main stated objective is the smooth running or the machinery. It is necessary to avoid understating the amount of policy advice the prime minister receives. According to one prime minister, the secretary of the office is secretary *of* cabinet but *to* the prime minister. The Cabinet Office spends much of its time working for the prime minister. There is no doubt, according to participants, that it will inevitably move towards more policy advice in future years; at present it has no capacity for *sustained* policy advice. Indeed Lord Armstrong claimed that the prime minister is unlikely to know as much detail about any topic as the relevant minister should.

In Britain the prime minister was sometimes served personally by the CPRS when asked for notes on particular items. So too the Cabinet Office always works partly for the prime minister, anticipating demands, providing information, consulting with permanent secretaries. Within No. 10 the prime minister has a small personal staff. Most are civil servants, high flyers who spend a short stint in the prime minister's office. The task of principal private secretary is usually regarded as a quick route (strenuous if interesting) to the top of the civil service. Private secretaries are responsible for areas of government activity.

The partisan political component of No. 10 is very small and its very existence has been erratic. Lloyd George developed his 'garden suburb' but it was disestablished after his fall. Churchill was aided by Lord Cherwell. Macmillan was assisted, on a personal basis, by Wyndham. In his first government Wilson was surrounded at different times by a group of personal staff who played an important advisory role on a wide range of topics, both political and in terms of policy. Heath had one political secretary, Douglas Hurd, who played a more minor policy role. Only when Wilson returned to No. 10 in 1974 did he deliberately create a policy unit, headed by Dr Bernard Donoghue. It was always small, never more than seven or eight people. It had regular and immediate access to the prime minister and to papers all over the place (although from choice it stayed out of Treasury affairs). Its purpose was to give the prime minister his *own* capacity to question items being presented by his ministers. It could feed in ideas, particularly on politically sensitive issues; its members attended cabinet committee and officials' meetings, occasionally in place of the prime minister. They worked closely with other officials, like the press secretary, Joe Haines.

Callaghan maintained the unit but after the Conservative victory it was abolished. A new unit was headed by John Hoskyns, with only one or two assistants at different times. Initially this looked at the government's medium or long-term strategy, being regarded almost as a 'surrogate think tank' (*Economist* 27 December 1980, 47). Inevitably it became more involved in day-to-day matters and, with the departure of Hoskyns, the very role of the unit under its new head, Ferdinand Mount, came under review (*Times* 4 May 1982). Thatcher has at various times had other non-official staff, such as David Wolfson, but her partisan advisers were initially few, probably 'far too few to enable a policy unit to achieve even minimal monitoring ... required to ensure that a strategy is being followed' (Stephenson 1980: 33). The Labour experiment was thus barely continued, and even that limited policy support for the prime minister has been severely reduced. Indeed the weakness at the centre has been the subject of considerable comment (Stephenson 1980; *Economist* 27 December 1980, 7 February 1981; *Times* 4 May 1982). In 1983 Thatcher was obviously dissatisfied with the lack of advice available to her; she seconded to No. 10 the former ambassador to the United Nations, whom she had come to trust during the Falklands crisis, and a leading economist. She also re-floated the idea of an enlarged department with the capacity to advise on policy. By the end of 1982, *Economist* (25 September 1982) could argue 'A partial consensus exists about [the need for a prime minister's department] among the permanent secretaries and the would-be remoulders of the Whitehall machine. They recognise that the demands of the job and Mrs Thatcher's personal style of brisk interventions in other minister's business mean that she could do with more back-up'. The Franks report on the Falkland crisis showed how inadequate co-ordination of information at the very top could be.

Yet, even after her 1983 victory, Thatcher has still not established her own department or greatly strengthened her own staff. She certainly uses her civil servants effectively and is not captive of the machine (Burch 1983: 408), but the system has not changed much since the *Economist* (30 May 1981) wrote:

> Mrs Thatcher has quite deliberately loaded the dice against herself in her supposed bid for presidentialisation. Not for her the Wilsonian kitchen cabinet. She has kept her Downing St. staff small and relatively weak on the explicit grounds that 'my cabinet are my political advisers'.

The effectiveness of personal staff has always been much disputed. Certainly for some it has been used as a path to political office; Kaufman, Hurd and McNally are all MPs. The Policy Unit, together with the introduction of ministerial advisers, has been described as 'the most significant, though as yet relatively small, institutional change in the political direction of government in Britain since 1945' (Rose 1980: 45). Yet its value is questioned even by participants. Some members thought it had achieved rather more than was anticipated; they had feared it would be frozen out by officials. Others argued that it had had little impact, that there were no specific occasions where its existence made a major difference. Anyway, one argued, the prime minister could only run with a few issues and the Policy Unit could make little difference to that.

The British prime minister is also formally First Lord of the Treasury and between 1969 and 1981, while it existed, head of the Civil Service department. These positions also allow the prime minister to seek advice officially from those departments. The Treasury often works as much to the prime minister in crucial areas as to the chancellor.

NEW ZEALAND

In New Zealand the small size of the political system is reflected in the provision of political support to the prime minister. Before 1975 prime ministers usually held the Foreign Affairs portfolio. For a time in the 1950s Holland was also minister of finance and John Marshall, prime minister in 1972 for ten months, chose to hold no other portfolio; but these were exceptions. As a result the department of Foreign Affairs included an embryonic Prime Minister's department and the Cabinet Office; the permanent secretary of Foreign Affairs also served as head of the Prime Minister's department.

When Marshall became premier in 1972, a deputy secretary, aided by one member of staff, was given the job of servicing Marshall's needs. But there were too many divisions of responsibility and the need for greater support was recognised. Kirk and Rowling reverted to the traditional combination of holding the premiership and the Foreign Affairs portfolio. Nevertheless there was a growing appreciation, among senior officials and among party leaders on both sides, that greater policy support was needed for the head of government. It was accepted that with the growing weight of government prime ministers could not operate without substantial staff advice. After the National party's electoral victory in 1975, the head of Foreign Affairs resigned his second hat and a separate Prime Minister's department was established.

The department was small. It included the Cabinet Office, consisting of ten people, which was responsible for the smooth running of cabinet, that is the form of submissions, the taking of minutes and the circulation of decisions. That is the traditional role of the Cabinet Office which does not require any policy, as contrasted to procedural, input. The new component was the Advisory Group. It has never composed more than eight people and has variously been called a 'think-tank' and a 'liaison' group. Its members are drawn from both inside and outside the public service and their appointment is temporary. They come from a variety of backgrounds. The group does not have a strategic role. Its responsibility is to act as the eyes and ears of the prime minister, to fix problems, collect data, chase, hustle, follow up, facilitate and monitor proposals. It can ensure in interdepartmental meetings that, where the prime minister's views are explicit, they are taken into account and that recommendations are consistent with government policy. It keeps the prime minister informed of proposals that are likely to surface and what tensions surround them. Because some of its members come from the business world it keeps open lines there too, but in itself it has no institutional memory. There is no hierarchy for reporting; it has only one steno-secretary as support staff and no files are kept. If information is required, it is obtained from the department. These practices were established in part to *prevent* it becoming a department in the accepted sense.

Access to the prime minister is frequent. The head of the department will see him several times a day when both are in Wellington. The whole group works on the floor below the prime minister in the Beehive executive buildings; once a week, on Friday afternoons, all the members meet the prime minister in a session which is useful for both the exchange of information, discussing policy ideas and providing instructions. That one-and-a-half hour session is a sacrosanct part of the prime minister's timetable.

The Advisory Group is widely seen as significant but, despite fears to the contrary, the public service does not see it as unduly intrusive. If the prime minister were to change, there might need to be an alteration of the staffing; if the prime minister was not also minister of finance, another economist might be employed. But it is perceived necessary to keep it small, flexible and integrated. Members may present policy proposals or start off new lines of thought, but they do not try to administer policies. Whenever time allows, they keep departments informed about what advice they are giving the prime minister (for details see particularly Boston 1980; also Jackson 1980).

The Prime Minister's department has never been the sole source of advice. As minister of finance since 1975, Muldoon receives support from the Treasury. He is therefore the *one* person in cabinet to be briefed on the broad policy and economic consequences of particular items. He also has access to senior public servants through cabinet committees. His personal staff is small; the Press Office is part of the Cabinet Office and has only four people. One member of the government Policy Unit assists in providing material for parliamentary business, such as question time. The other advice and contacts he receives from outside the bureaucratic or political machine. However ministers have regular access and contacts between prime minister and minister are direct. The head of the Prime Minister's department will not relay messages from one to the other, or allow ministers to lobby the Advisory Group. Outside cabinet committees, they deal primarily with officials.

COMPARISONS AND CRITICISMS

This brief survey of the activities of prime ministerial bureaux illustrates that institutions follow different lines of development, even when meeting similar demands. Some of the distinctions between Canadian, British and Australian answers can be explained in part by constitutional factors. In Australia and Canada prime ministers have to deal with state and provincial premiers and, from the very beginnings of the PMO in Australia in 1901, the centralising and routing of correspondence to the states was one of its primary functions (PMC 1979: 29). In Canada the importance of this function is illustrated by the creation of the FPRO. The development of prime ministerial diplomacy has shown how necessary it is to draw together the threads of office in a central agency in all three countries.

In part differences can be explained by the distribution of portfolios. With a few brief exceptions, all Australian prime ministers before 1949 held other substantial portfolios, often being attorney-general or minister for external affairs and, in wartime, minister for defence. When Liberal–Country party coalitions were in power between 1922 and 1958 the Country party monopolised Treasury but at least one Labor prime minister was also treasurer. In 1949 Menzies became the first prime minister to hold no other ministerial position. In Canada prior to 1957 some prime ministers held other portfolios too (Matheson 1976: 53); they relied on the departments supporting those portfolios for advice on any problems that emerged. A few held only the official position of president of the Privy Council. The institutional links which the British prime minister developed as First Lord of the Treasury were replaced by ties to the portfolios held by the prime ministers; when they were discarded, they needed to create a new bureaucratic structure to provide them with briefing on the broad questions of concern. The continued connection in New Zealand between the prime minister and the Foreign Affairs portfolio explains the delay in the emergence of the department there.

The development of PMC and PCO as forceful bodies was slow. Before 1939 the Australian PMC fulfilled a varying range of functions and provided only the rudiments of a cabinet support system (PMC 1979: 29–35); the Canadian PCO was primarily a registry for decisions (Hodgetts 1973: 93). Both increased their capacity as the need for greater formalisation of cabinet proceedings became more obvious under the pressures of war and the growth of government functions. Their origins as important co-ordinating agencies can therefore be traced back to the bureaucratic leadership of Strahan in Australia and Heeney in Canada in the early 1940s. The development of a policy-analysing capacity came later still. Therefore although PMC and PCO have had a long formal existence, bolstered at times by constitutional requirements, their influence as co-ordinating and policy instruments does not predate that of Britain's Cabinet Office. Indeed changes in central management were mutually reinforcing. The Australians looked to British and Canadian developments as possible precedents.

In Britain a prime minister's department has never been developed, although it has occasionally been mooted, mostly recently by Thatcher in late 1982 when she was disatisfied with advice from the civil service. Those engaged in this argument come in three categories: those who see the need for such a department, those who see benefits in the idea but are cautious about its implementation, and those who believe the present system is adequate.

The first group, many of whom have worked closely with No. 10, argue for an increased capacity for giving the prime minister policy advice. Lord Armstrong emphasised the need for a group of people who could examine policy problems from the prime minister's perspective, so that they understood the peculiar pressure that prime ministers face. Joe Haines (1977: 39) has written of the need for ministers to have several sources of expert advice, at least one of which should be non-official. Sir Kenneth Berrill has stated:

> The more fundamental question is not whether the volume of advice presented to a Prime Minister is adequate but *the depth of work and knowledge behind that advice*... What in my view is at issue is whether a Prime Minister should have a support system with time to work on problems *in some depth across the width of government activities*. At present the advice is given and very presentably too, but the depth is invariably patchy. (1980: 3, 14— emphasis added)

The points emphasised are central to the argument about whether the prime minister needs advice about policy as well as procedure.

More recently Sir John Hoskyns, Thatcher's personal adviser, has argued:

> There is a need for a small department, responsible for the development and overseeing of the government's total strategy, across all departments, integrating policy and politics into a single whole. This department could be quite small—perhaps one hundred to two hundred people. It would certainly incorporate the CPRS and might, as some have suggested, emerge as a 'Re-constructed Cabinet Office'. It would be headed and partly staffed from outside, though it would also include a substantial number of high-flying career officials. (1983: 147)

Obviously such a department would serve the prime minister.

Other arguments used by ministers and officials to make the case for increased prime ministerial support point out that they are not well-served by the lack of early warning systems, that it is surprising how much they do not know, that it is difficult for them to share in policy-making in an *informed* way, and that it is difficult for them to know what advice they need. But much of the argument comes back to one crucial point. Should prime ministers play additional roles? Should they act as the central link in policy formulation and hence do they need support for analysing policy and making partisan political judgements?

The proposal for the creation of a prime minister's department has received qualified support from the Association of First Division Civil Servants. A report claimed that a department built around the staff of No. 10 'would, subject to suitable safeguards, appear to be quite compatible with the Civil Service as we know it in this country' (*Times* 24 January 1983).

Others agree that the prime minister needs greater support but are uneasy about the creation of a prime minister's department. If nothing else, one person argued, it would bring the reality rather close to the public image. In his incisive paper on collective responsibility Edmund Dell (1980: 44) argued for strengthening the prime minister's position, yet baulked at the prospect of creating a prime minister's department. Others believe that, even though the prime minister needs greater support, the bureaucratic and political costs—in terms of civil service opposition and ministerial suspicion—would outweigh the immediate advantages. Or, as another put it, 'Of course Britain needs a prime minister's department—as long as it is called the Cabinet Office'.

Some like G.W. Jones consider the existing arrangements are working smoothly, primarily because of the flexibility they contain. Jones has argued: 'there is a prime minister's department, and it operates effectively—largely because it is not cast in a bureaucratic mould' (1978: 121). Offices like the Policy Unit, the European Unit and the CPRS can be moved in and out to suit the personality of the incumbent. Jones's opinions represent the orthodox vision in Whitehall and reflect the views of many ministers and senior officials. They have received an explicit seal of approval from Harold Wilson (1976: 106–7), even though he had earlier stated the need for a strong but small prime minister's department (Jones 1973: 375). They are therefore analysed in detail here.

At times it is difficult to understand precisely what is included in the prime minister's department that Jones criticises, for he discusses approvingly the flexible interaction of the partisan and non-partisan components of the staff at No. 10 (Jones 1978, 1979). Presumably such a department would included the former CPRS, the Cabinet Office, the private secretaries in No. 10 and such bodies as the European Unit. Whether the partisan components like the Policy Unit are inside or outside is not stated, although it seems probable that the distinction between the political and non-political would remain.

Jones has suggested six reasons for opposition to the creation of a prime minister's department in Britain:

1 'A prime minister cannot help cabinet colleagues arrive at a unified decision if he is the protagonist of a particular line' (1981: 219). 'A department might, especially if large, develop a view and momentum of its own' (1976: 37) and 'put up to the Prime Minister a certain line' (1979: 20).

2 The prime minister's 'role is to help forge politically acceptable solutions and to relate policies together in an order of priorities by providing a coherent theme, tone or philosophy. His contribution is not to be a substitute for his ministers, but a supplement' (1981: 220).

3 A prime minister's department 'can never be as informed about any policy and its consequences as the department with responsibility for its implementation... Its intervention will be regarded as naive and meddlesome and its policy prescriptions as ignorant and damaging' (1981: 220).

4 A department 'will generate a large amount of paper, which the Prime Minister will find difficult to master' (1979: 20); 'his gaze will be distracted away from considering the problems of government as a whole towards what worries his department' (1981: 220).

5 'The establishment of a Prime Minister's department, formal, structured, bureaucratized, might diminish the personal power of a Prime Minister to draw help from many sources and in many ways ... a disorderly, ad hoc, personalized system serves only him' (1973: 375; see also 1976: 37; 1978: 121, 123). Also a prime minister 'might have to acquire a further set of private secretaries and political aides' to control such a department (1978: 123).

6 'There is a danger in having a single head... Everything might be channelled through that one person. The present system enables the Prime Minister to be in charge, not a single subordinate' (1979: 20).

These arguments raise important questions not only about the way the support can be organised but about the roles that prime ministers should play. By examining the problems that Jones posits against the practice in Australia, New Zealand and Canada, it is possible to gain useful insights into the activities of prime ministers' departments. If those problems do not occur elsewhere, then perhaps the organisations that support British prime ministers can be reviewed in a fresh light.

1   *Prime ministers will become protagonists of their department's*
    line; this will hinder the process of getting a consensus.

It is difficult to get evidence for an argument of this kind one way or
the other. Whether a prime minister supports the recommendation his
or her department proposes *because* it is their recommendation, because it has already taken account of his or her predilection or because
cabinet agrees with it, is likely to become a circular question. In
cabinet it is difficult to trace the source of many ideas. However some
general impressions are possible.

In Australia PMC provides an exclusive brief to the prime minister
on every item that comes before cabinet. The brief will include a recommendation on the course of action the department regards as desirable. In cabinet, ministers acknowledge that the prime minister is fully
briefed, both on likely divisions of opinion and on the implications of
possible amendments. Far from making it difficult to help cabinet
reach a unified decision, it makes ministers aware of the need to master their own portfolios properly and thereby improves the standard
of information available to cabinet. PMC's officers are also involved
in the interdepartmental committees which may be required to thrash
out the problem in a proposal. In those committees they may initially
be cautious in expressing views, but they do play two roles. First, they
become aware of the alternative views that are discussed and, second,
they have the capacity to suggest that individual questions should be
seen in the broad perspective of government strategy. Officials in
PMC argue that they do not often attempt to initiate proposals or
present total alternatives. They are also cautious about invoking the
prime minister's name, but they will point out the contradictory
policy implications.

It is seldom that the prime minister's views are sought while proposals are being formulated; he is far too busy. In practice many of the
questions raised by PMC may lead to a proposal being sent back for
further consideration. Whether the prime minister then accepts their
recommendation is obviously a matter for him. There is no evidence
from interviews with ministers to suggest that Australian prime
ministers have felt constrained to support the department, or obliged
to accept a line of argument presented. But ministers agree that for
him to be conscious of the implications of likely amendments is important. Nor does the department feel obliged to press its views if
ignored.

When PMC officials head task forces they are acting to general instructions and providing advice—usually on expenditure cuts—to
cabinet committees. In this their behaviour is similar to that of the

PCO in Canada. There the PCO is intent on opening out options; departments are warned of likely objections. On some occasions prime ministers may accept a compromise thrashed out by the PCO, if they have no strong views, for in Canada most routine items are directed through the cabinet committee system. Prime ministers are briefed mainly on those items of particular interest to them; their views are well-known and it seems unlikely that they will be limited by what their officials propose.

In New Zealand, the prime minister has always had alternative sources of advice and there is no indication that Muldoon has felt bound to support his Advisory Group's line. Indeed interaction is so continuous that he has probably had some discussion of all important items before they come to cabinet.

It seems strange to suggest that prime ministers would not be able easily to ignore departmental advice for they, more than their colleagues, have a broad view. The available evidence, admittedly qualitative, suggests that prime ministers are not so constrained. Also their departments are generally careful not to pre-empt decisions by suggesting it is 'the prime minister's view', except in those cases where that view has been clearly expressed. Whatever the bureaucratic framework, any central network is likely to be good enough to get those messages across.

> 2 *Prime ministers should be a supplement to,*
> *not a substitute for, their ministers.*

The sentiment is unexceptionable; but it is difficult to understand how the existence of prime minister's departments may frustrate that objective. Indeed both Australian and Canadian prime ministers might well ask how they could be expected to undertake those tasks without their existing bureaucratic support.

The PCO is explicit in its desire to set priorities; the 1974–75 priorities exercise and the set of procedures called the 'Cabinet Planning System' (French 1980: 41–58) are evidence of that desire. It attempted to draw together the threads of policy, to identify those sensitive areas that might fall between two departments and to create some coherence. The difficulties it had as a department illustrate the immense complexity of the process. The PMO is concerned with the politically acceptable. Acting as link between the party and the bureaucracy, it can raise thorny problems without fear of straying its proper jurisdiction. Both the PCO and PMO are concerned with political solutions; they work for and with the prime minister to achieve them.

PMC has never undertaken as grandiose a task as the PCO's priorities exercise of 1974–75. In part this may be because Australian central agencies have always been sceptical of management techniques. It may also be because PMC started to develop its broader capacities only after 1974—a time when, as the PCO discovered, economic conditions forced priorities on to governments. To a large extent it has been concerned with setting negative priorities, and with determining where cost-cutting can be most efficiently applied in line with the government's stated objectives.

In New Zealand Muldoon has combined the ministry of finance with the prime ministerial role. Economic strategy comes more from the first function than the second; no other broad strategy seems to be followed. However the Advisory Group does maintain a watching brief on government policy to ensure that proposals inconsistent with government policy are recognised early.

Indeed PMC, PCO and the Advisory Group have a capacity to question and evaluate policy, to raise doubts about the consequences (and they all do have politically sensitive antennae), and to protect the general cause. Further, because their perspective is largely that of the head of government, they can assist the partisan appointees in the PMO to see the links between administrative methods and political priorities. They are after all the only bureaucrats whose main perspective is the prime minister's; they are uniquely placed to assist the prime minister in the function of priority-setting.

In modern government the interrelatedness of so many issues has increased the burden of the prime minister. The Trudeau response was in part to increase the collegiality of ministers so that they were involved in decisions on a wider range of topics through the system of cabinet committees. Awareness of the broad implications of proposals has thus grown, while P&P has been able to consider the most important issues. The existence of the PCO has added to, not limited, that collegiality. Whitlam and Fraser both increased the burden on cabinet itself while adding to the policy capacity of their department to assist in their judgement. In neither case did the existence of those departments reduce their capacity to consider the broader view or dull their capacity to ensure politically viable solutions; indeed the reverse seems likely.

3 *The department will be regarded as naive and meddlesome and its policy prescriptions ignorant and damaging*

In both Canada and Australia the increasing authority of PCO and PMC is regarded with some dislike by departments. Since the central agencies do get involved in policy issues (Campbell and Szablowski 1979: 82) in which departments claim to have the expertise, that is not surprising. Their interference is often regarded as ill-informed, particularly where it appears to frustrate cherished plans. The process by which PMC ensures that the proper procedures are accepted is seen by some departmental heads as squeezing the life out of proposals and reducing the number of alternatives, although that is a criticism of the whole process of central co-ordination, not just of PMC.

Ministers too have complained of the excessive centralisation that the cabinet procedures required. In Canada these complaints were as often directed at the emphasis on collegiality as at the PCO itself. In Australia some ministers argued they would be concerned if prime ministers listened too much to their own officials and too little to ministers (Weller and Grattan 1981: 195). When the minister for industrial relations resigned in protest at Fraser's style he argued: 'The role now given to the Department of the Prime Minister and Cabinet challenges the authority given ministers under section 64 of the Constitution' (*Sydney Morning Herald* 20 April 1981). The argument is muddled, but the sentiment was not uncommon among ministers who were consistently unable to carry their proposals through cabinet.

Of course the capacity of PMC and PCO is limited. There are likely to be only a few people working in areas covered by whole departments. They can seldom provide clear alternatives and usually do not try. At times their contribution may seem insubstantial, naive or irrelevant to departments submerged in the importance of their own proposals. But whether they are meddlesome is a matter of opinion. The PCO is concerned to ensure that all options are revealed, to ensure that several channels are also available to the prime minister. An Australian prime minister put it explicitly: 'Specialist departments are not always right; they may have an axe to grind in a particular area and there is nothing wrong with that; but to have people with knowledge on a subject to ask questions—just to make sure that everything comes out in cabinet—is very useful' (Interview 1980). In these circumstances the value of a policy counterweight is accepted. If PMC does not play that role, who else can? What if departments are loath to provide alternatives or slow to provide recommendations and the cabinet wants speedy action? On these occasions PMC officials have to fill the gap. Nevertheless in general both PMC and PCO still have to rely on departments for much of their work. Van Loon and Whittington (1976: 348) have concluded that 'most of the time the substantive information [PCO officials] are dealing with originates elsewhere, either "above" them in the political world or "below" them in the technical one'.

Trudeau was always conscious of the need not to pre-empt powerful ministers. When in 1974 his principal private secretary sought to establish a panel of economists to advise Trudeau, the finance minister, John Turner, objected strongly and the proposal was dropped. It was the formalisation that Turner objected to; he regarded himself as the government's main adviser on economic matters.

In New Zealand the Advisory Group has never been faced with this criticism. The sensitivity of its original head and the determination of the group to maintain harmonious relations have ensured comparatively smooth working relations. Muldoon too was careful to 'keep the reins on' his department.

Co-ordination may slow down proposals and at times it may appear excessive to departments. Central agencies are never likely to be popular, but the role they play in Canada, New Zealand and Australia is regarded as essential for the prime minister's welfare and for the general strategy of the government.

4   The department will distract the prime minister from problems of government as a whole.

Both the PCO and PMC are partly concerned with serving cabinet. In so doing they act on the prime minister's behalf as guardians of the cabinet process, enforcing the regulations set down in various cabinet handbooks. When they service prime ministers as individuals, it is probably true that they account for much of the material going to them. According to one estimate, 65 per cent of the paper going to Trudeau came from the PCO. At the same time, like the officials in No. 10, they act as a sieve for much of the material, drawing attention to those factors they consider most important. Like every other organisation including the Cabinet Office they have their bureaucratic interests to protect in the sense that they are concerned to protect their influence. But the security of existence that they have means that these do not loom too large. One observer of the Policy Unit in No. 10 argued that the politics of sheer survival were often paramount and time-consuming. When the policy analysts are secure, departmental problems may indeed take less of the prime minister's time.

Beyond that, to suggest that the activities and interests of the prime ministers' departments determine the agenda of the prime minister is to misunderstand the way that these bodies work. Most of the time they react. The PCO is so organised that it can react quickly to meet the demands created by the prime minister's priorities. PMC spends much of its time briefing the prime minister on the implications of other ministers' suggestions or on any event that has occurred. If the prime minister wants more detail he will ask for it. Usually the briefs are constructed in consultation with the operating department, but if the department is slow in responding the brief goes ahead regardless. The Advisory Group meets weekly with the prime minister, discusses its projects with him and then goes where *he* wants. The initiative is the prime minister's.

Thus the existing departments, working in places with a partisan PMO, ensure that the prime ministers can spend their time on items of importance to them. There is no evidence that their success in this area is any less than those of the civil servants in No. 10. In Australia both Fraser and Whitlam have been hard-working with wide-ranging interests. Their support has been organised to meet those needs.

5 *A hierarchical bureaucratic structure would be too inflexible to satisfy the different styles of prime ministers.*

There are few organisational problems in re-orienting the PCO or PMC in new directions. PMC provides a suitable example. It has been constantly reorganised to meet the changing interests of the prime minister (see Mediansky and Nockels 1981). When Fraser wanted improved advice on industrial relations, the department recruited the necessary staff and created a new branch. New organisation charts are issued regularly to keep up with changes. Other divisions are formed and reconstructed to suit new interests. Its staff are also used to providing high-level support for major task-forces, particularly in economic areas. When a large group of PMC officials was seconded to organise the Commonwealth Heads of Government Meeting in Melbourne in 1981, they were easily integrated back into the department. In PMC flexibility of organisation is accepted as crucial. PMC has been used at times to nurture new functions into which the federal government is choosing to expand. Federal involvement in education and Aboriginal affairs both began under the control of a branch in PMC; now both are the main focus of complete departments. Women's affairs and support for the arts both started there too, before being hived off elsewhere. In 1983 women's affairs returned with added status. It is explicitly accepted that, while the support of prime ministers may be necessary to get such projects off the ground, it is not advisable for a co-ordinating department to run a programme for too long (Yeend 1979: 142).

In Canada, changes to the PCO's functions can also be easily made. When Trudeau created co-ordinating ministries for Social Services and Economic Affairs, the sections of PCO that had served cabinet committees in these areas were ceded to the new departments. Those departments now serve the cabinet committees and, in the same manner as the PCO, assess the proposals presented there. In New Zealand the Advisory Group determinedly has refused to grow or become organised in any hierarchical way; it has no files, no staff and no hierarchy.

Indeed the clear distinction in Canada and Australia between a partisan PMO and a non-partisan department probably increases the latter's flexibility. Jones (1973: 364) mentions the tensions that can exist in No. 10 when the principal private secretary has to draw distinctions between political and official roles. When the obviously political functions, along with the general time-table, are organised by the PMO, such problems do not often arise. Obviously the practical distinctions between official and political are always blurred for advice comes from everywhere, but they are organisationally distinct and within those organisations flexibility is easy to achieve.

Jones (1976: 38) argues that the private secretaries in No. 10 are doing essentially the same job as a century ago, but the staff and organisation of PMOs in Australia and Canada have changed regularly to meet new demands. The PMO in Canada has undergone several transformations under Trudeau as his style changed (Campbell 1980). In both countries the prime ministers' public service organisations have been easily adapted to the inclusion and then hiving off of functions, and to different styles. The departmental form has not been a hindrance; rather it has allowed the departments to adjust substantial resources to meet new demands.

6   There is a danger of having a single head of department through which everything might be channelled.

The secretary of PMC is the Australian prime minister's main bureaucratic adviser; the same is true of the clerk of the Privy Council in Canada. The two share that role with the secretary of the Cabinet Office in Britain. In New Zealand the head of the Prime Minister's department shares the role with the head of Treasury. While they are obviously powerful officials, possibly the most powerful, none is or ever could become the only conduit through whom advice to the prime minister is channelled.

There are four obvious reasons. First, PMC, PCO and the Advisory Group are not organised so that all advice is channelled through the head of department. The limitations of time and pressure of work prevent that from happening. Indeed, as suggested earlier, the PCO has an explicit belief that the prime minister should be protected from receiving advice from one source. Two or three officials attend the briefing every morning and several officers have direct access to the prime minister. In PMC all eight division heads have regular access as well as the secretary, the undersecretary (effectively a second permanent head) and the three deputy secretaries. Branch heads will sign off notes to the prime minister in areas of their expertise and the prime minister will ring them direct for information. All this occurs at a hectic pace. In New Zealand every member of the Advisory Group has regular access. Working arrangements in these departments are fairly flexible. The departmental form does not prevent these bodies acting in a manner similar to the flexible Cabinet Office and the staff of No. 10. Even if Australia and New Zealand do not spell out explicitly a belief in multiple access, their practice ensures it happens.

Second, prime ministers in both Australia and Canada have partisan PMOs to whom they can, and often do, turn for advice. Third, the prime ministers have other official sources of advice in specialist areas; in Australia the Public Service Board and the Office of National Assessments (an intelligence analysis organisation, attached nominally to PMC) can report direct to the prime minister. In Canada the FPRO (for much of its existence headed by a former clerk of the PCO) has direct access to the prime minister. In New Zealand there is the Treasury. Bureaucratically therefore the heads of the Prime Minister's departments do not sit astride the access to the prime minister. Nor could they if they wanted to.

Finally, and most important, the existence of a Prime Minister's department does not make any less true the fact that in Australia, New Zealand and Canada the prime minister's main advisers are ministers. All the forces mentioned by Jones as forces of cohesion in Britain (Jones 1976: 37) are as strong there too. It is collective and party government. Of course there are complaints about the role of PMC and PCO; there have been plenty of complaints by Crossman, Benn and others of the role of the Cabinet Office too. But their existence cannot invalidate the basic truth that all prime ministers rely heavily on their ministerial colleagues for advice. That has not changed since the policy capacity of PMC and PCO has been increased. Nor will it.

The comparatively open access to Canadian, New Zealand and Australian prime ministers is also illustrated by the simple facts of geography. In Britain the office and residence of the prime minister are part of an interconnected set of offices which give easy access for the staff of No. 10 and the Cabinet Office. In Australia the prime minister and private staff always work from a suite of offices in Parliament House. That suite includes the Cabinet Room. All ministers work in Parliament House too. PMC by contrast is some 300 metres away. In Canada both the PCO and the PMO have their offices in the

Langevin Building, again some distance from the office of the prime minister in Parliament House. In New Zealand all ministers work in the Beehive; so does the prime minister. As a result of their continuous presence in the same building, access for ministers and backbenchers is perhaps easier in Australia, New Zealand and Canada than in Britain, and prime ministers are probably *less* cocooned by their officials.

WHAT LESSONS CAN BE DRAWN?

It is not useful to ask which is the best method of supporting prime ministers or the best constellation of organisations. What works in one place may not work in another. Even *whether* they work well at all will be disputed. Campbell and Szablowski (1979: 323–33), for example, would like to see British institutions moulded on to the Canadian centre. However it is possible to draw two main conclusions from the empirical evidence that is available.

First, of the specific criticisms launched against Prime Minister's departments none is fully sustained by an examiniation of other systems. Indeed of the six main dangers posed by Jones only one—the view of the meddlesome department—has any validity and even that depends on the perspective of the commentator. Whether these dangers would occur in Britain is a matter of speculation, but it can be stated categorically that they are not the inevitable consequence of the creation of a Prime Minister's department in a parliamentary system.

Second, Jones ends one set of arguments against a Prime Minister's department with a general proposition: 'In any case a prime minister's department would be a revolution in the constitution, a move from a ministerial and cabinet system to prime ministerial government' (1979: 20). That is sheer nonsense. It would mean that, because of the existence of the Prime Minister's department, Australia and Canada *ipso facto* have prime ministerial government. It is difficult to sustain a comprehensive argument that British prime ministers are weaker than their Australian and Canadian counterparts. More fundamentally, such a comment is contrary to Jones's own careful and persuasive argument that prime ministerial power is limited by a whole range of institutional and personal factors (Jones 1969). Since the bureaucratic support is only one—and not a major one—of those factors it would be surprising if a change in the one area could negate the remainder of Jones's argument. In practice it does not; any concept of prime ministerial government needs to rely on far more than bureaucratic support. A Prime Minister's department certainly increases the policy advice available; it cannot and does not replace ministerial colleagues or remove other party and parliamentary constraints.

IMPLICATIONS FOR THE CENTRE

To assess the impact of the supporting structures on the prime minister's influence, three of the necessary functions of a prime minister can be considered: horizontal or administrative co-ordination; vertical or central co-ordination; and individual policy advice.

Horizontal or administrative co-ordination is concerned with 'alleviating inconsistencies that result from involuntary overlaps which often lead to duplication or gaps or to working at cross-purposes. Efficiency and economy are the principal aims' (Mediansky and Nockels 1981: 398). Supporting the team leader is a central concern, ensuring that the machinery of cabinet works smoothly, that all necessary consultations take place, and that the submissions to cabinet are adequately prepared. All countries have that type of bureaucratic support. It is necessary for the proper functioning of government.

Central or vertical co-ordination seeks to impose coherence on government policy, ensuring that the many parts interlock with one another and that they are consistent with the government's stated priorities and fit together into a strategy. At times the PCO has sought to determine broad priorities for government, particularly in the priorities exercise of 1974–75. Much of the language used by the PCO emphasises the need for rational policy-making. The machinery is still in place for another attempt if required. In Britain strategic planning was one of the proposed roles of the CPRS where Chequers weekends were to be a forum for discussing the government's general directions. In practice this function was one of the first to fall into disuse as the CPRS became more concerned with the collective briefing of ministers and task-force investigations into sensitive topics, and as ministers became more concerned to consider problems of immediate importance within their portfolio. In Australia the attempt to determine priorities was never made, despite the existence of the Priorities Review Staff under the Whitlam government. Like the overseas model on which it was based, the PRS soon became involved in day-to-day problems. In relation to the strategic function there seems little difference in the lack of effective systems everywhere. In New Zealand a planning council was established, but it was not integrated into government decision-making. Perhaps the argument should be for the strengthening, not the weakening, of the prime minister's support— as Hoskyns (1983: 147) Berrill (1980: 14) and Dell (1980: 43) have proposed in their different ways and supported by their personal experience.

The most important distinction is in the degree of individual briefing that prime ministers receive from their departments on particular policy items. There is no doubt that prime ministers everywhere become deeply involved in particular areas: Muldoon in broadcasting; Callaghan in aircraft, education and wages policy; Trudeau in bilingualism and the constitution; all of them in economic policy. There is no way they will be prevented from effectively running some policy areas if they choose. That is a matter of record. If they choose to 'interfere', will they merely irritate ministers, as Eden did (Sampson 1967: 128; Carlton 1981: 376) because of his unfamiliarity with the subjects, or will they be effective or constructive? Sometimes, one prime minister agreed, prime ministers must initiate policy ideas, because ministers become bogged down in detail. Given their involvement, what support do they get? In Australia and Canada the policy advice is often exclusive to prime ministers and may allow them to challenge the minister's submissions. The PCO and PMC have the capacity to develop advice rapidly on almost any policy question and they are designed to satisfy the prime minister's needs in policy matters. In New Zealand the Advisory Group is designed to keep the prime minister aware and informed. In Britain, even with the CPRS and the Policy Unit, and with the growing policy involvement of the Cabinet Office, the number of people concerned is still small and there is no systematic coverage of all areas of policy in depth. As the comments of Hoskyns et al quoted earlier indicate, the support for the prime minister may be inadequate here too. Thatcher's appointments to the No. 10 staff seem to support this view.

What is important is this: if prime ministers choose to become heavily concerned with the details of specific policies, do they have adequate resources to intervene effectively, particularly where they may disagree with the line supported by the functional minister? As one Australian minister commented: 'Prime ministers tend to be superheated individuals and they can't leave things alone, particularly things that interest them and their tastes are usually pretty eclectic'. Media and international pressures will force prime ministers to answer questions on a wider range of issues. If they also choose to extend their own role, then the new circumstances may make impossible demands on the old style at the centre. Wider briefing, more detailed analysis and more widely co-ordinated advice, arranged from their own perspective, may be required.

In those circumstances the Canadian, New Zealand and Australian responses have been to increase the policy-analysing capacity and staffing of the Prime Minister's departments and office. Those departments appear to have a greater capacity than that of the centre in Britain. Yet it seems possible the new functions undertaken by Callaghan and Thatcher in pursuing the detailed direction of some policies might lead to new forms, if only to keep up with the new demands. A Canadian participant argued: 'Every Prime Minister should have the benefit of a broadly experienced, mature and politically sensitive staff which is honest in its approach to its tasks and respectful of the democratic process' (D'Aquino 1974: 77). That is what some systems have provided; in the process they have shown that, despite British fears to the contrary, a Prime Minister's department is quite compatible with collective solidarity and cabinet government.

7

Prime Ministers and Parliament

Parliament is the formal arena in which all prime ministers must publicly peform. They have no choice. As long as parliament is in session, there are official occasions in which they are expected to be on display; their performance there is consistently being assessed. British observers believe that all prime ministers exert their dominance over the House of Commons: Churchill and Macmillan were both regarded as great 'Commons men'. In Canada John Diefenbaker claimed: 'He who doesn't know Parliament cannot be a good Prime Minister' (Hockin 1977: 248).

The continuous debate throughout the century on the degree to which parliament can have an influence on the executive is unlikely to be conclusive. But to what extent does parliament have an impact on a prime minister's position? There are several factors: the degree to which parliament is used as a training ground, the participation of the prime minister in parliament, the degree to which opponents (both in the opposition parties and within the prime minister's own party) can delay or alter executive actions, and the parliament's impact on the prime minister's standing, that is, reputation among political peers.

PARLIAMENT AS TRAINING

In Westminister systems parliament is traditionally regarded as a training ground. By the time anyone rises to the position of prime minister, he or she is well-grounded in all the elements of politics; prime ministers are likely to have been in parliament for several years and to be proven performers there. Since they are usually drawn from parliament, they will have held various ministerial positions, and usually senior cabinet jobs. Whereas American presidents may emerge with little administrative experience or knowledge of how Washington works, parliamentary leaders have had their mettle tested in precisely those areas in which they are required to perform as prime ministers.

In Britain that set of assumptions has largely been borne out by past examples. All prime ministers have been in parliament for at least fifteen years; some, like Churchill, Macmillan or Callaghan, had over 30 years of parliamentary experience. They all had ministerial experience at cabinet rank, often including senior positions such as chancellor or foreign secretary. Heath and Thatcher had less than others, and Attlee's was gained mainly in the wartime coalition; but all knew something of the pressures of cabinet and the realities of existing in a parliamentary forum. Performance in parliament was regarded as important; Thatcher's ability in the economic debates after the Conservative loss of office in 1974 is given as one of the explanations for her rise to leadership (Cosgrove 1979).

Not all these factors are true of other systems. Length of parliamentary service had generally been required for the prime ministership in New Zealand: Holland, Holyoake and Marshall all served long apprenticeships; Muldoon had been in parliament for fourteen years. In Australia Whitlam and Fraser had been MPs for twenty years. However, since changes of government are less common, ministerial experience is limited to those in the conservative parties. Neither Whitlam nor Kirk had even been a minister; Whitlam had not even been a backbencher when Labor was previously in power. Nevertheless each in his way was regarded as a good parliamentarian. Whitlam was a superb parliamentary performer, dominating the house for a decade. So did Menzies. Fraser was a stolid performer, rough, hard and aggressive though seldom witty or subtle, but he could not be dominated. The elusive Holyoake and the barnstorming Muldoon were each able to use parliament to their ends; Muldoon, in particular, used the advantages of the privileged forum to destroy political opponents with a ruthless viciousness unprecedented in the usually gentle environment of New Zealand politics (Muldoon 1977: 184–5; Zavos 1978: 192–203).

This situation appears to be changing in both countries. In New Zealand David Lange was elected deputy leader of the Labour party two years after coming to parliament in 1977 and became leader a mere three years later, in 1982. His deputy had been in parliament only two years. Media performance, rather than long parliamentary experience, was regarded as the more important quality. In Australia Hawke was elected leader in 1983 after only two undistinguished years as an MHR. Three weeks later he became prime minister; his performance as a parliamentarian was regarded as mediocre before his promotion and he has yet to appear comfortable in the parliamentary environment, or to care much for the institution. He believes that his audience is the electorate. Parliament seems to be regarded as an unfortunate necessity. Besides it does not suit his political style. 'Hawke's way is to conquest by inclusion; parliament ritualises disagreement' (Little 1983: 438). It is likely therefore that Hawke will continue to bypass parliament when it suits his purposes.

The traditional model of parliament as a training ground for leaders is being replaced by the more utilitarian Canadian approach which gives less emphasis to the value of parliamentary experience. St Laurent and Pearson were both persuaded to enter parliament as a means of taking over important ministerial posts; St Laurent immediately became Mackenzie King's Quebec lieutenant. Trudeau had only three years in parliament, and only one of those as a backbencher, before being elected leader. Yet that year on the backbenches was the only one spent there by *any* of the Liberal leaders this century! Of the PC leaders, Stanfield had been a provincial premier, Clark had four years in parliament and Mulroney had never been elected to any public position. Further, continued membership of parliament is not considered necessary for those with leadership ambitions. John Turner left parliament in 1975, yet almost a decade later he was still regarded as the heir apparent to Trudeau's Liberal crown—and he duly won the leadership in 1984 with considerable support from the incumbent ministers.

In Britain parliament is a career; maintaining a presence there is a condition of political ambition. To leave parliament (voluntarily) is virtually to leave politics. In Australia and New Zealand it remains a means towards that end: a parliamentary seat is regarded as necessary, even if long experience no longer is. For Canadian leaders parliament is regarded as part of a career pattern, to be entered and left as circumstances demand. In this respect Canadian leaders reflect the political society. The turnover among MPs is high. Insecurity of tenure among politicians leads to a lack of knowledge of how the system can best be worked. For instance, after the 1968 and 1972 elections, respectively 83 per cent and 75 per cent of the elected MPs had *less* than seven years previous parliamentary service (Lovink 1979: 164).

The result in Canada is an impatience for parliamentary debate and proceedings:

> As for Parliament, you can't really establish leadership there as Prime Minister unless—I don't want to be too dogmatic about this—you have a deep and genuine feeling for Parliamentary institutions. For this, it is a great help to have had a long parliamentary experience; to have risen from the ranks in Parliament where you can acquire, if you have not had it instinctively, a feeling for Parliament, of its importance and its traditions. I always had a feeling of deep respect for Parliament (after all I had been a constitutional historian!), but I entered at the top, on the front benches. I

had been in civil service for many years before being elected and I had never done any Parliament apprenticeship. And I confess I never had any great love for parliamentary battle and rows. I could get worried up about issues as much as anybody else, as a competitive human being, but I always thought debates which were repetitive and prolonged and too violent wasted too much time. I used to get impatient because you couldn't get things done quickly enough because of those struggles in Parliament that other people may have loved. (Pearson 1977: 258)

Trudeau's contempt for some of the procedures in parliament was evident in his attack on members of the opposition who were filibustering his attempt to revise the rules over time-limits. He claimed that 'When they get home, when they are out of Parliament, when they are fifty yards from Parliament Hill, they are no longer honourable members—they are just nobodies' (quoted in Radwanski 1978: 219). According to his biographer, Trudeau

finds the raucous, often juvenile heckling and point-scoring deeply offen-sive, both because of the personal insults levelled against him and because it violates his view of politics as a rather solemn activity. As he puts it: 'When I say I don't like the Commons, it's because it's a place where men are shouting, where people yell at each other—yell as one wouldn't dare in a classroom. I find that vulgar. It offends me'. (Radwanski 1978: 219)

Both Pearson and Trudeau wanted to speed up the processes of parliamentary debate, to make the process more efficient. Their impatience was attacked by their critics. For instance, the *Globe and Mail* (3 July 1980), always willing to condemn Trudeau, argued that statements which 'belong in Canada's parliament' were being made abroad; 'Trudeau administrations over the past twelve years have tended to treat parliament as a cross that the government must bear'. In comparative terms, there is some justification for the statement.

PRIME MINISTERS IN PARLIAMENT

Parliament is always time-consuming and, however extensively the executive may maintain control over its proceedings, likely to create difficulties for a government. Prime ministers cannot ignore par-liamentary proceedings. Even if they are no longer leaders of the gov-ernment in the house, they maintain a close interest. Therefore the frequency of parliamentary sittings is an important indicator of the amount of attention that must be given. On that basis, parliament plays a larger role in Britain and Canada than in Australia (see Table 7.1).

Table 7.1   Sitting days of parliament by year

Britain		Canada		Australia		New Zealand	
1977	160	1971	192	1971	74	1971	111
1978	170	1972	93*	1972	60*	1972*	76
1979	147*	1973	197	1973	81	1973	111
1980	174	1974	117*	1974	62*	1974	118
		1975	172	1975	69*	1975*	97
				1976	79	1976	96

Note: *Election year.
Sources: Stewart (1977: 204); Coaldrake (1980: 111); NZPD (vol. 436, Appendix Schedule of Business: 5).

In Britain the House of Commons usually sits for 160–200 days a year; in Canada the figure is similar, except for election years when the days of sitting are likely to be nearer 110. In New Zealand the figures rise to just over 110 or slip to 75 in election years. In Australia even in its busiest years the House of Representatives is unlikely to sit for more than 80 days and may sit for as few as 60—one-third as many as the British and Canadian parliaments. If it is accepted that to have parliament in recess reduces some of the pressure on prime ministers by removing an arena in which criticism can most easily be invoked, then that difference must make life easier for Australian leaders.

Within parliament the most challenging period that prime ministers must face on a regular basis is question time. There the requirements differ in the various parliaments. In Britain 'Prime Minister's Questions' are taken from 3.15 to 3.30 p.m. on Tuesdays and Thursdays. All prime ministers are likely to prepare extensively for that period because the sting is in the supplementaries rather than in the original question. Further the link between the two questions is often tenuous (Wilson 1976: 164–70). To a large extent the questions are therefore without notice and the prime minister must be able to reply on any item. Further the occasion is likely to be partisan and receive considerable public attention. Kaufman's advice to new ministers was to 'instruct your Diary Secretary to put the Prime Minister's Question Time as a permanent engagement in your diary. You should also do your best to attend all the major debates in which the Prime Minister speaks' (1980: 77).

British prime ministers are always the centre of parliamentary attention. They answer around 1000 questions in a session. Among those questions, international affairs will always figure prominently, general matters on machinery of government slightly less so. During the 1970s questions on economic affairs increased until they became the most frequent topic (Rose 1980: 13–16). 'Question-time consumes a significant portion of the Prime Minister's time whenever parliament is sitting, which is most of the year' (Rose 1980: 13). At other times prime ministers speak in parliament only on important occasions. For instance, in 1972–73 the prime minister gave six speeches, in 1974–75 four and in 1976–77 six again. That is less often than their principal ministers (Rose 1980: 17). However parliamentary business remains a standing item on the agenda of the cabinet; the leader of the House of Commons and the chief whip are senior members of the party and will maintain a close liaison with prime ministers, who remain vitally interested in their party's progress there.

Elsewhere the prime minister's position is less exclusive. Although direct comparisons between parliaments are difficult because of the discrepancies in sitting days, Table 7.2 gives some indications of the contributions that prime ministers make in the different parliaments.

In Canada, New Zealand and Australia prime ministers attend question time every day; questions without notice may be directed at them on any occasion. In Canada they may be followed by a number of supplementaries; in Australia standing orders require that questions be asked alternately by government and opposition members, and no supplementaries are allowed. Australian prime ministers are therefore protected to an extent from a barrage of consecutive and related questions, and may also end question time by asking that all future questions be put on notice. In each country prime ministers may either answer the questions themselves or deflect them to the responsible minister. At different times Fraser used both tactics, particularly on economic matters. Because the period is not exclusively for attacks on the prime minister, the concentration on them, although still considerable, is less complete than in Britain.

The result is that much less attention may be directed at the prime minister. In the two parliamentary sessions for which figures were calculated Trudeau answered respectively only 7 per cent and 8.2 per cent of the questions, less than those answered by the ministers of transport and labour in the first session or by the minister of finance in the second. Yet even so he was criticised for answering too many questions himself. In the first Australian session the prime minister answered 14.5 per cent, almost twice as many questions as the treasurer and nearly three times as many as any other minister; in 1979 he answered 10.4 per cent more than anyone except the minister of transport. In New Zealand the range was much greater; Rowling's 11 per cent was exceeded only by those asked to the minister of finance. Muldoon answered fewer questions than almost any of his ministers; in that session, as in almost every other year, he was absent from parliament during four overseas trips. Clearly he does not see parliament as a vital forum. The differences may depend in part on the

Table 7.2 Prime ministerial participation in parliament

	Question time		Legislation	Other contributions		
	No. answered	% of total questions asked		Censure[a]	Statements	Other
Canada						
Trudeau (Jan.–April 73)	105	7.0	0	1	1	7
Trudeau (Feb.–May 78)	125	8.2	0	0	0	4
Australia						
Whitlam (Feb.–July 75)	203	14.5	12	2	3	30
Fraser (Feb.–June 79)	256	10.4	1	2	10	15
New Zealand[b]						
Rowling (May–Oct. 75)	116	11	25	1	1	56
Muldoon (May–Dec. 79)[c]	18	1	30	1	2	14

Notes: [a] Includes address in reply.
[b] In New Zealand questions to the prime minister have been kept separate from questions to the minister for foreign affairs (in Rowling's case) or to the minister for finance (in Muldoon's). They would add 11 (1%) to Rowling's figure and 57 (3.2%) to Muldoon's.
[c] Muldoon was overseas for much of the session: 7–17 June, 6–13 July, 28 July–15 Aug., 17 Sept.–15 Oct.
Sources: House of Commons Debates (Canada); *Parliamentary Debates* (New Zealand); *House of Representatives Debates* (Australia).

inclination of the prime ministers. While the questions asked them are likely to be the most political, the most sensitive and the most noticed, they have some choice in answering. Whitlam, for instance, revelled in question time; Fraser sometimes passed to other ministers the majority of questions aimed at him. For all prime ministers the briefing is an important daily ritual when parliament is sitting; they meet advisers who have tried to anticipate likely questions and propose possible answers.

The subjects on which questions are asked have changed gradually. In Canada economic affairs generally accounted for about 30 per cent of the questions, foreign affairs for 6–15 per cent, machinery of government for 12–30 per cent while federal-provincial relations are at times significant. In Australia Whitlam's questions were evenly divided between general machinery matters, foreign affairs and, to a slightly lesser extent, economic matters. For Fraser in 1979 foreign affairs was less important and a quarter of the questions concerned economic matters. Half of the questions addressed to Rowling and Muldoon as prime ministers related to foreign affairs, with the others distributed over the field. The choice of questions related to both current problems and prime ministerial interests.

Outside question time the distinctions between countries are far more clear. For instance, in neither session under review did Trudeau speak on any bill; he made only one ministerial statement and one contribution to the speech from the throne. His participation was minimal. By contrast Whitlam spoke on twelve pieces of legislation, made three statements and spoke on two major censure motions; Fraser replied to two censure motions in each session, joined in three other debates and in one session made ten ministerial statements. In New Zealand prime ministers are involved regularly in legislative debate and far more frequently at other times. With a small house they must participate to a much greater extent. Their appearances are less formalised and unusual than the set-piece contributions of British prime ministers. The expectations thus differ, and that must have an impact on the way that prime ministers prepare for, and spend time in, parliament. In all countries participation was likely on the items of greatest importance, although, as Trudeau showed, that participation can be kept to a minimum.

CONTROLLING PARLIAMENT

Every prime minister must face the problem of getting legislation through parliament. How long does it take? How difficult is it? It is worth quoting again the conclusion of Denis Smith when Trudeau was revising the means of applying the guillotine: 'The provision meant that if necessary a determined Government could guide a piece of controversial legislation through the House in a minimum of *four* days of debate over a period of *ten* sitting days, against the protests of the minority' (1977: 322—emphasis added). The emphasis indicates what seems to Canadians the minimum requirement for reasonable parliamentary discussion of a proposal.

Both closure and the guillotine may be applied by the Canadian government if standing orders are strictly applied, but their use is often clumsy and protracted. Notice of closure has to be given at a previous sitting, to be followed by a day's debate on the closure motion itself. It has to be moved at each stage of the bill. Its application is controversial and rare; the passing of the pipeline bill in 1956 in a mere fifteen days is still discussed as an outrage:

> Closure at Ottawa is a major rite. The entire operation—from the moment when a minister, standing in his place, gives notice to an excited House, through the moving of the closure motion at the next sitting and the immediate vote on that motion, through the tense day-long debate to the final vote before packed galleries well after midnight—resembles so much a death sentence and a public execution that ministers shrink from using it; and when they do, the opposition, regardless of their true sentiments, feels obliged to lament the end of a thousand years of freedom and democracy. (Stewart 1977: 244)

In 1969 the government introduced a standing order to provide a formal basis for the negotiated settlement of time disputes in the house. Yet it was complicated to apply, including 'a notice of motion, a debate on the motion, a provision for amendments, separate motions for each stage, and at least a day's debate at each stage before the motion can be presented to the House' (Jackson and Atkinson 1980: 118). This was the change that to Smith was an indication of Trudeau's 'unerring presidential instincts' (1977: 322) because he chose not to seek compromise with opposing parties.

How accurate is that version? First, it is notable that in the same parliament it was only used twice, in one case to end a debate which had already gone on for 27 days (Stewart 1977: 256–7). Second, even in the late 1970s the government appeared unable to get its legislation through. Said one observer:

> Another sign of the growing inefficiency of the government was the difficulty it was experiencing in getting legislation through Parliament. The number of bills successfully piloted through the legislature declined, and the number of important pieces of legislation that died on the Order Paper before the end of the Parliament rose. (Meisel 1981: 38)

That is not the image of a dominant executive. Opposition spokesmen still have the ability to use standing orders to delay or impede government legislation and to filibuster. Use of closure and the guillotine are comparatively rare. In October 1980 they were used to bring the motion on patriation to a vote, but only after ten days debate. When the government ended the debate on the mail strike in July 1981, it was accused of misusing closure. Jackson and Atkinson's conclusion 'that opposition criticism has not been stifled in the House by procedural innovations' (1980: 119) seems fair.

In the Antipodean parliaments the Canadian tolerance of opposition is unknown. In Australia governments use the guillotine and the gag (closure) regularly. Complaints that the democratic process is being abused are routine and rhetorical; they are not meant to be taken seriously. Standing orders can be suspended by an absolute majority of either house to push items through. Censure motions or grievance debates are ended without notice after two or three speakers from each side have made their contribution. The pressure on time becomes particularly strong in the last weeks of each session, when the government wants to clear the legislative decks. The motion for the guillotine requires a debate for twenty minutes, but it may refer to more than one bill. 'The most extraordinary recent use of the guillotine was in 1977, when the Fraser government had nineteen bills guillotined through the Senate in just four hours' (Solomon 1978: 68). Those bills went through all stages in that time.

In New Zealand one observer wrote of 'the fastest law in the west' (Palmer 1979: 77–94), arguing that in 1978 the unicameral house passed on average of 1.6 statutes per day. A government can claim 'urgency in the public interest' on any bill, so that the house remains in session until business is completed. It can use closure, so that the question is put immediately without further debate. In 1978 urgency was taken on seven successive days and in one 8½-hour sitting 15 bills were taken from the second reading through all stages and 22 were put through the third reading, 37 bills in all (Palmer 1979: 92). The contrast to Canada is complete. What one parliamentary system regards as untoward domination of opposition rights to another would be unbelievable richness of opportunity.

In Australia, however, one vital caveat must be remembered: the Senate. In the last twelve years, the government has controlled the Senate for only six—from 1975 to 1981. Between 1972 and 1975 it was controlled by the opposition; since 1981 a minor third party, the Democrats, has held the balance of power. The Australian Senate is no mere house of review. While the House of Lords or the Canadian Senate may be able to delay legislation, they cannot stop it for long.

The Australian Senate has no such problems. Apart from the prohibition on initiating money bills, it can do in practice everything the lower house can. In 1974 and 1975 it stopped supply and effectively caused an election, in the latter case against the government's will. It can and quite often has destroyed government legislation, even that based on specific electoral promises. As an elected body, senators claim to have their own mandate. The prime minister's only means of coercion is a threat of a double dissolution; if the Senate twice rejects a piece of legislation, with a three-month gap between the two votes, then all the senators may be forced to face the electors at the same time as the members of the house. That is a final step. In the meantime prime ministers who do not control the Senate—and for the foreseeable future that will be *all* prime ministers—must live with, and negotiate with, those Democrats who hold the balance of power. The Australian parliament may be as easy as any to control if the government has a majority in both houses, but it may be the least amenable to coercion if the government does not control the Senate.

PARTY DISCIPLINE

Even if prime ministers have the means at their disposal to run legislation through parliament, that assumes that they lead a cohesive party on which they can rely. In most cases that is true. In Canada, New Zealand and Australia, the parties have usually voted solidly. In late 1983 the New Zealand government lost two divisions when two different groups of MPs crossed the floor. That was exceptional, and also unusual in that the government had a majority of only one. According to a backbencher who was one of the rebels, that is the *only* factor giving backbenchers clout in the party room. But it is not often used.

In Australia Liberal senators occasionally have crossed the floor, but that has not led to a defeat of any piece of legislation important to the government. Labor MPs have almost never split. Members sign a pledge before they stand for preselection in which they agree to vote in parliament as a majority have decided in caucus. To break that pledge is tantamount to expelling oneself from caucus. In Canada party cohesion has been accepted as overriding an individual's opinion on particular questions.

The one divergent case is Britain. In the 1970s party discipline declined, first under Heath, then under the Wilson and Callaghan minority government. Under the Heath government 20 per cent of all divisions saw some members voting against their party; in 1974–79, 28 per cent of all divisions fitted this category. All six of the Heath government's defeats were caused by party dissent. Of the 42 defeats the government met in 1974–79, 23 were caused by their own members. Further they took place on important issues—on the dock work regulation bill, on the guillotine motion on the Scotland and Wales bill and on amendments to the bill itself. There was of course no question of bringing the government down. When the government was first defeated, it immediately put down a vote of confidence and the rebels flocked back to save it. Later they did not even bother to follow that device. Labour members also brought about a further 64 defeats in standing committees (figures from Norton 1981: 227–31). No longer could British leaders take their supporters for granted. Even with her moderate majority after 1979 Thatcher was defeated over new immigration rules. In January 1984 Heath and several ex-ministers of the Thatcher government voted against the government's rates capping bill. That type of defection by senior party members is unknown in the other countries. That is not to suggest that parties have lost control of MPs or that they no longer dictate the terms. But it does show that the leadership must take account of the wishes of its backbenches to a greater extent than in the past; if it does not, they are prepared to use their votes to embarrass or defeat particular bits of government legislation. It is unlikely the House of Commons will go back to the cohesion and discipline that existed before 1970 (Norton 1981: 234).

To Richard Rose, however, 'the iron cage of party discipline' is still strong in Britain. He points to the fact that the proportion of government bills passed is higher in Britain than in the other three countries and suggests that there 'a government is less certain of carrying out its wishes' (1983: 293). He implies that this result is due to less party discipline. His conclusions are misleading, in part because the years he cites, a five-year period up to the early 1970s, predated the main period of cross-voting in Britain. More importantly the reasons for the failure to pass legislation in Canada, Australia and New Zealand were not party rebellion. Cohesion there was and remains almost total. In Australia, for instance, no piece of government legislation has been defeated in the House of Representatives in the last 40 years. The lower proportion of bills passed can be explained by the ability of the Canadian opposition to delay legislation, by minority governments and by hostile Senates, as well as by bills cut off by dissolution. The discipline of governments MPs is a problem for British prime ministers that is not faced by the leaders elsewhere.

When a government is in a minority, parliament can cause real uncertainty. Even the Lib-Lab pact in Britain could not guarantee the safety of the Callaghan government because the Liberals had constantly to be persuaded to abstain or to vote with the government (Barnett

1982: 147–8). Parliament became a permanent electoral college, as it does with all minority governments. But the frequency of defeats did lead to the 'convention' that the government would only resign if defeated on a motion that it had explicitly chosen to make one of confidence.

In this it followed precedents created by Canadian minority governments. In 1968, while several ministers were crossing the country seeking votes before the leadership convention, the government was defeated on the floor of the house. Pearson went on television to explain it was an accident; he refused to resign and set down a formal confidence motion the next day which he duly won. In 1972–74 Trudeau announced that he would not resign after a mere defeat; rather, he would go the the polls only after a vote which he had in advance declared to be one of confidence. Conventions were flexible. Yet both Pearson and Trudeau were backed by solid parties.

As suggested earlier, perhaps the different levels of cohesion can be explained in part by the role of the parliamentary parties (see Chapter 2). Where members are, however nominally, given an opportunity to debate legislation and criticise ministers in private, where their influence can be seen to be effective (even if only occasionally), they may be more prepared to vote with their party on those issues in which they were overruled in the party room. A greater sense of private participation may lead to greater public discipline. Significantly Rose has argued that, even in Britain, debate within the parties is replacing inter-party debate as the main mechanism for influencing government (1983: 287).

The smaller size of parliament—and the occasional narrow majority—makes the need for cohesion even greater. Four of the last ten Australian majorities were less than ten. Since 1962, four out of seven Canadian elections have returned minority governments. Accustomed to small majorites and greater participation, the energies of MPs have been channelled to activities in different parts of the parliamentary scene.

CONCLUSIONS

For prime ministers, time is a valuable commodity. What they spend on activities which they cannot avoid, they do not have spare for those areas where they want to get involved. In the parliamentary arena, British prime ministers must work within the confines of a parliament that requires reverential treatment, which they must face (and for which they must brief themselves) twice a week, which sits for almost

200 days each year, in which the more brutal use of guillotine and gag are not used too readily, and in which backbench members of their own party appear unresponsive to party discipline.

The difficulties can of course be exaggerated. The Canadian parliament, for instance, has fewer resources for ramming legislation through. The cabinet still determines what parliament discusses and usually what is passed. But each problem takes up some prime ministerial time and attention. Whether or not Thatcher herself gets involved, her contacts with the chief whip are continuous; and parliamentary business is one of the standing items on the cabinet agenda. Parliament looms large on the British political scene.

Not so Australia or New Zealand. As long as the Senate is friendly, passing legislation quickly is no problem. Question time may be less taxing; cohesion is maintained through the party room. Since in Canada, Australia and New Zealand the prime minister's offices are either in or attached to the parliament building, access is easy to and for backbenchers.

The points are of course relative. It would be dangerous to overemphasise the role of British backbenchers, or to underplay the part played by New Zealand or Australian party rooms. All require *some* attention. But the evidence suggests that greater efforts need to be made in Britain.

In one respect, political standing with their peers, parliament is important for all prime ministers and party leaders (see King 1975). Reputations can be made, or at least maintained, in parliament. Backbenchers want the team leader to do well, and to be seen to be doing well. Parliamentary performance may be one of the first indications that a prime minister is slipping. Some opposition leaders (Snedden in Australia, Marshall in New Zealand, both in 1974) have been undermined because they could not match rampant prime ministers. For prime ministers, who have so many more advantages, the correlation is less direct, but if they cannot deliver or perform well that intangible standing is likely to slip. Above all, in the arena of parliament the glare of publicity is on the prime minister; they must perform at least adequately to maintain their position.

8

Prime Ministers as Public Figures

Prime ministers are very public people. Whatever they say is newsworthy and liable to detailed scrutiny. Whatever they do is publicly assessed for wisdom and consistency. Domestically and internationally they speak for their nation, their government and their party. They appear frequently on the media, explaining and defending their actions, attacking their opponents and appealing to the voters for support. They must be articulate and effective public performers.

Prime ministers perform in three main public arenas. First, they usually play a distinctive role in foreign affairs, whether at bilateral meetings or international conferences. They must be able to speak authoritatively, in the certain knowledge that their views will be supported when they return home. Second, they dominate election campaigns. The timing of these is largely in their hands and the media concentrate on their activities; whatever they say is taken to be party policy or a direct challenge to established policy. Comments are likely to be quoted back to them in government, often as a means of indicating broken promises. They are held primarily responsible for their party's electoral performance, receiving credit when elections are won and blame when they are lost. Third, prime ministers must constantly interact with the media. Politicians try to use the media; journalists try to explain and explore political decisions. The two feed off one another, often uncomfortably. Prime ministers try to manipulate the media for their own ends, whether these concern the internal politics of the government or the greater—or more selective—education of the electorate.

Thus the public image of prime ministers is regarded as vital to their performance, but that leaves another question: how important is the public image or public performance of prime ministers as a means of giving them power? Prime ministerial power has been defined as the ability of prime ministers to have an impact on the intended actions of governments. To what extent do public performances affect their internal position? How is the rhetoric of publicity turned into an ability to initiate changes in policy? This chapter will discuss briefly each of the three arenas, and then analyse the different ways in which each might have an impact.

FOREIGN AFFAIRS

Most prime ministers are addicted to the world stage and to the field of foreign policy, but here the role of head of government can be desperately demanding. Wilson(1976: 150–1) records that in 1974–75 he attended fifteen multilateral meetings and six meetings with the president of the US; took thirteen trips for bilateral meetings; hosted 59 meetings with heads of government in London, most of which involved two days of discussion and entertainment; and held a mass of other meetings with other overseas visitors. Muldoon had five overseas trips in 1980, two of which lasted three and seven weeks respectively, another five in 1981 and six in 1982. In 1983, Hawke's first year in office, it was expected that he would be talking to 60 state leaders at home and away, the majority at international conferences like CHOGM. So even leaders from isolated countries like Australia and New Zealand can, with the advantages of modern technology, be active on the international stage.

Yet there is a need to show that involvement in international affairs is the same as influencing them. In Britain Attlee declared: 'Foreign affairs are the province of the Foreign Secretary and it is, in my view, a mistake for a prime minister—save in exceptional circumstances—to intervene personally' (1954: 169). Other British leaders, like Eden, were heavily involved in running foreign affairs, often at the expense of domestic matters. Heath led his party into the EEC. Thatcher's hard line on the Falklands crisis ran directly counter to the advice being provided by the Foreign Office.

On what does influence depend? First is the calibre of the foreign secretary. In each country, the office has been filled both with political heavyweights and potential ciphers. In Britain, the Foreign Office is regarded as one of the great offices of state. When leading figures are appointed as foreign secretary, the prime minister is likely to rely on them. Bevin under Attlee, Eden under Churchill, Callaghan under Wilson or Carrington under Thatcher: all were strong, independent and persuasive. In the cases of Selwyn Lloyd under Eden, Owen under Callaghan or Howe under Thatcher, it seems that, whatever their abilities, they were given less freedom of maneouvre by their prime ministers because they had less experience and less political stature.

In Canada St Laurent gave Pearson a fairly free hand; after all, Pearson had been deputy minister of external affairs before he entered parliament and was an established international figure. When Pearson became prime minister, he left the running of detailed policy to his external affairs minister, but he maintained a close interest and ensured that he made the big decisions on issues like that of nuclear arms. Few foreign policy issues came to cabinet. Under Trudeau there were strong political figures like Mitchell Sharp and MacEachen, and far more junior ones like MacGuigan. Trudeau was always deeply concerned with foreign affairs; his was the impetus that led to the wide-ranging review of Canadian foreign relations in 1967–70 (Thordarson 1972); his involvement in areas like nucelar policy was consistent. For a long time he used his adviser, Ivan Head, as personal emissary to other international leaders and he always maintained an advisory capacity in the PCO. However his advisory structures did not cut the department of external affairs out. External affairs ministers were constantly kept informed of what was going on and the department was nearly always consulted. Indeed, it was argued that it was to its advantage to 'have an inside man at the skunk works' who had access to the prime minister. Trudeau also played a leading, and often independently constructive, role in international conferences. One observer commented that, while cabinet often discussed foreign affairs, Trudeau made the policy. When supported by ministers with the weight of Sharp, he left them with considerable independence in the areas where he had less direct interests, such as trade negotiations.

In Australia the ministry of foreign affairs has often been used as a position in which to isolate rivals. After McMahon challenged Gorton for the prime ministership in 1969, he was shifted against his will from the Treasury to Foreign Affairs. Fraser left Peacock there from 1976 to 1980. One of the conditions Hayden imposed for standing down from the leadership in 1983 was that he became minister for foreign affairs. On the other hand Gorton's choice of Freeth in 1969, Whitlam's transfer of the portfolio to Willesee in 1973 and Fraser's promotion of Street in 1980 were all instances where the prime minister preferred a more malleable colleague.

Appointing rivals to the post has the advantage that they are often absent from crucial economic cabinet meetings and are therefore less able to build a power base from which to challenge the leaders. At the same time there is no doubt that, when prime ministers choose to become involved, they have seniority and can impose their will. The two most distinctive policies under Fraser—hard-line hostility towards Russia and consistent support for black Africa, particularly

Zimbabwe, against South Africa—were very much Fraser's personal crusade. In fact, Peacock supported Fraser's African policy, even if most of his party did not. In other instances, when policy differences did occur, as over the derecognition of the Pol Pot regime before the 1980 election, the foreign minister could often win.

In New Zealand the prime minister was usually foreign affairs minister, thus removing any potential tension. Since the two offices were separated under Muldoon, the foreign affairs minister has been both a leading rival, deputy prime minister Brian Talboys, and a person with no experience in international affairs, Warren Cooper. After Talboys's challenge, Muldoon has been clearly determined to maintain control of foreign affairs.

This process has become more marked in all countries with the growth of 'summitry'. National leaders now meet more frequently, in economic summits, Commonwealth Heads of Government Meetings or other forums. Foreign ministers often do not accompany their leaders and, when they do, it is in a clearly subordinate role. Such summits are of course not new—Munich and Yalta provide early examples—but their frequency is, and that requires prime ministerial involvement in foreign affairs on a regular basis.

Second, prime ministerial influence on foreign policy depends on the ability of cabinet to become involved in discussions. In Britain foreign affairs are regularly at the top of each cabinet agenda. The foreign secretary has to report each time, even if not always fully. At times of crisis—Suez or the Falklands—the item may be delegated to a cabinet committee that keeps the full cabinet occasionally informed. On other occasions, the prime minister may be able to postpone or limit discussion, but at least some formal opportunity, however constrained, is there.

In other countries foreign affairs may not be discussed in cabinet at all. Under the Whitlam government only one cabinet debate on foreign affairs was held in three years. For the first year, Whitlam himself was foreign secretary and had no intention of bringing his decisions to cabinet for approval. Later matters were generally settled by Whitlam and the foreign minister. Hawke's decision to ignore the Labor party platform on Timor was not debated in cabinet; the first most Labor members heard of it was when reports of the discussions between Hawke and Soeharto were filed in the Australian press. Nevertheless, because of the existence of the party platform, Hawke will be required to face internal criticism at the next party conference. There are, of course, no sanctions with which the party can force action or require the prime minister to renege on international commitments, but the process of explanation could prove embarrassing. Fraser's attitude

towards the black African states directed his government's policies
without open opposition, but without wide support either. In New
Zealand Muldoon keeps foreign affairs far more to himself.

This distinction is not to suggest that British prime ministers cannot dominate foreign policy. At particular times they obviously do, and
at the very least they set the framework for action. But the Foreign
Office in Britain, with its long traditions, its bureaucratic strength and
its institutional stature, is far more influential than the equivalent
organisations in the other countries. In Canberra, for instance, the
department of Foreign Affairs is seldom considered bureaucratically
significant; indeed, it loses most of its official fights (see Hawker *et al.*
1979: 204–31). Thatcher's discontent with the Foreign Office (*Economist* 27 November 1982) is notable because both are seen as powerful in
their own right.

Further there is a tradition in the commonwealth countries for
prime ministers to run a personal foreign policy. In Canada Mackenzie
King held the Foreign Affairs portfolio for much of his long premiership; in New Zealand that tradition continued until 1975. In
Australia prime ministers have generally dominated foreign policy
(Edwards 1982; Harries 1968). In all three countries the structure of
commonwealth relations meant that the Colonial Office in London
wanted one spokesman and naturally expected this to be the prime
minister. Since external relations, particularly in Australia and New
Zealand, initially meant the links with Britain, that gave most
prime ministers almost complete independence of action. Peter Edwards has skilfully traced administrative and political developments in
Australia and concludes:

> the Australian political culture not only accepts but expects a far more
> prominent role for the Prime Minister. ... this prominence was not based
> merely on personalities or other historical accidents, although these factors
> played their part. Changing ideas on the proper role for Australia in world
> affairs and the development of what one might call 'the imperial system'
> had a far more pervasive and enduring effect on policy-making in Australia
> than has generally been realized. Prime Ministers were encouraged to be-
> come not just channels of communication and the principal spokesmen for
> Australian views, both at and between Imperial Conferences, but virtually
> the exclusive formulators of policy. Governments in London consistently
> made it clear that, if they had to take Dominion opinions into account,
> they wanted those opinions to come from one authoritative exponent.
> From Joseph Chamberlain's attempts to exclude State governments from
> any role in external affairs to Churchill's dictum that any minister other
> than the Prime Minister 'would not be a principal but only an envoy', this
> was a constant theme of British policy. In both peace and war, Dominion

Prime Ministers were admitted, more or less reluctantly, into the inner circle of imperial policy-making, but were actively discouraged from consulting or sharing privileged information with their Cabinet colleagues or departmental advisers. (1982: 189–90)

When these pressures are coupled with the smaller size of the polities, a factor which reputedly allows individuals to dominate foreign policy, it can be argued that the greater needs for consultation in Britain perhaps restrict most British prime ministers more than their counterparts elsewhere.

However, involvement in foreign affairs need not be the equivalent of exertion of power. Rhetoric is common, but success depends on the behaviour of others who are certainly outside the prime minister's control. Foreign affairs may have the ability to upset supporters, but amid the economic traumas of the 1970s and 1980s it is less certainly an important electoral issue (for evidence of the almost total unimportance of foreign affairs as an election issue see Rose 1980: 38; for Australia, Beed 1977: 251; Harries 1977: 257; Goot and Beed 1979: 170; for New Zealand, Roberts 1980: 240). Often intense activity leads to no outcome. Prestige abroad is difficult to translate into votes. Trudeau's image outside Canada was of a thoughtful, charismatic internationalist; that image did not help his domestic popularity. Fraser was held in high regard by African nations for his support of Zimbabwe; there is no evidence that it helped him electorally. The Falklands war probably helped Thatcher, just as Suez destroyed Eden, but wars are in a different category.

'What power does the Prime Minister exert through involvement in foreign affairs? the answer is Not much' (Rose 1980: 38). In Australia and New Zealand prime ministers may dominate foreign affairs without it giving them power to affect internal decisions. Their power may be extensive in one area, but it need not carry over into others. However it is likely to be more uninhibited than in Britain. Perhaps the best example was the Lusaka Commonwealth Conference which preceded the Lancaster House agreement on Zimbabwe, an issue which was crucial to British interests. In the proceedings of that conference, Carrington dominated British policy; Fraser Australia's.

ELECTIONS

Of all a prime minister's functions, electioneering appears to be the most presidential. The focus is on the leader, from the time that the calling of an election is contemplated until the results are known. Prime ministerial popularity is continually assessed, prime ministerial statements are examined, prime ministerial composure is analysed. Credit for victory or blame for defeat is given, in part at least, to the leader—after all, leaders are expected to win elections. But how far can campaign statements be turned into internal power, or popularity translated into influence? And to what extent does that impact differ from country to country?

Timing

In his discussion of the factors that determine prime ministerial power, King (1975: 228) lists the power to dissolve the legislature. All prime ministers have that power, but the expectations of its use vary. In Britain and Canada, where parliaments run for five years, it is unusual for the full term to expire. In New Zealand only two early elections have been called this century. In Australia, electoral timing is complicated by the need for half-Senate elections every three years, or by the possibility of a double dissolution of both houses which can be called only when the Senate has twice rejected a piece of legislation. Notionally prime ministers have to give reasons for any request for an early election, a practice now acknowledged to be fairly meaningless. In 1983 Fraser called a double dissolution and, soon afterwards, declared that he would not reintroduce the bills that were the formal excuse for the poll. That was then used against him, as an illustration of the cynicism of the move.

Although the final choice remains with the prime minister, consultations with colleagues are common. In Britain Wilson discussed electoral prospects before the 1966 election, when 'cabinet was summoned and we formally decided the election date' (Crossman 1975: 464), and before the 1970 elections when it was discussed in the Management Committee, but cabinet was merely kept informed (Crossman 1977: 904, 920). Heath was under considerable party pressure to go to the polls in 1974 and the final decision came only after a series of meetings with party and cabinet colleagues (Hurd 1979: 127–33). Thatcher was encouraged from all sections of the party to go in 1983. The decision may have been hers, but the atmosphere was such that an election was expected and accepted.

In Canada Pearson discussed the 1965 election widely. He put it to the vote in cabinet and was eventually persuaded by a group of party colleagues (Wearing 1977: 330). When he failed to win a majority, one of the leading advocates of an election, Walter Gordon, resigned on the grounds that his advice had been wrong. By contrast Trudeau's decision to go to the polls in 1968, directly after his election as prime minister, was his and his alone.

In Australia Fraser called two early elections—in 1977 and 1983. The first, he argued, was to synchronise the half-Senate and House of Representatives election. In 1983, he chose to go eight months early, with a double dissolution, against the advice of cabinet and party organisers. Just as he was calling the election, the Labor party changed its leader and Fraser never regained the initiative (for details, see Weller 1984). The decision was his.

At times, of course, prime ministers have no option. Trudeau in 1974, Clark in 1979, Callaghan in 1979 were all defeated in a House of Commons vote on a budget or censure motion. Diefenbaker was forced into an election in 1963 by internal dissidence (there is no evidence he called it to discipline his ministers). In 1974 and 1975 Labor had its supply stopped in the Senate and Whitlam was forced to the polls. In 1963 in Britain, in 1979 in Canada, the term of parliament expired. Timing related to the best days, rather than best months.

Decisions not to go to the polls are also likely to be the prime ministers alone. Trudeau rejected advice to go to the people in late 1977, when his party's ratings had improved, because he did not feel strong enough to campaign. As a result all decisions made in the next eighteen months were taken, according to one participant, in an electoral context. Callaghan chose not to go in late 1978, despite widespread support for an election in the party.

> At a Cabinet meeting on 7 September, Jim Callaghan told us he was not proposing to have an autumn election. It was a total suprise to all but a handful of his closest colleagues ... The Prime Minister had no objection to our discussing his decision but he said 'I told the Queen of my decision last night'. In those circumstances, and as he had the right to make the decision anyway, there was not much to discuss. (Barnett 1982: 154)

At times prime ministers do not give in to persuasion.

New Zealand appears to be an exception:

> The power of dissolution, a weapon which can bring parties to heel and enhance authority when used with skill to secure an increased majority, means little in a country when elections occur with semi-automatic precision in the November of every third year. That of 1951 has been the only premature election in the present century. (Mitchell 1966: 32)

Despite the increased political temperature of New Zealand politics, elections were still held 'on time' up to 1984. Rowling considered an early election when he became prime minister after Kirk's death, in order to gain a personal mandate. But, in retrospect unwisely, he decided against it. In 1984 Muldoon then called one four months early. But the resignation of one National member had removed his nominal majority of one and that provided a reasonable excuse for the decision.

Is Mitchell right that power over timing can bring parties to heel? It is true that, when caucus is restless, Muldoon drops hints of early polls to quieten it down. In Canada Diefenbaker apparently believed threats of an election kept supporters in line (Wearing 1977: 228);it did not seem to in 1963. Schindeler declares that, while a prime minister can use small ploys like patronage, 'his fundamental weapon is the power of dissolution' (1977: 30). He argues that both ministers and opposition members do not want to risk their seats too often. But as a means of maintaining discipline it has always been an unlikely proposition. As Epstein (1967: 323–4) persuasively argues, the costs of going to the people with a divided party would be electorally too great. Whatever the threats, they have never been carried out. Timing is concerned primarily with maximising the party's advantage. It appears easier to choose a time without criticism in Canada or Britain than in New Zealand. Unlike Australia and New Zealand, the debate there never appears to be about the *propriety* of an early election.

Campaign policy

Shaping party platforms may not always be the prerogative of prime ministers. As the earlier section on party policy illustrated, in the more radical parties the extra-parliamentary wing has considerable influence in determining what the platform is. In Britain combined meetings of cabinet and the NEC determine the party manifesto (see e.g. Castle 1980: 180). In Australia Labor's policy speech is constructed by the prime minister and close advisers, but it is expected to be consistent with the platform. In 1972, for instance, the style was Whitlam's, the choice of emphasis was his, but the main issues were already part of Labor's platform. Non-Labor leaders have fewer problems. In Canada, where the parties are electoral rather than programmatic, there is no binding platform to which they need appeal. In Australia a Liberal prime minister may discuss a policy speech with colleagues, but is not obliged to and does not always do so. In Britain a Conservative leader undoubtedly has the last word.

The existence of the platform is restricting, but it need not be severely so. In 1974 Wilson simply ignored the more radical sections of the party's platform, emphasising a more moderate and managerial image. In 1979 Callaghan reputedly threatened to resign if the combined committee insisted on including in the manifesto too radical proposals; he got his way. Since prime ministers receive the bulk of the media's attention, their influence is likely to be crucial.

What prime ministers emphasise or choose to ignore may construct the political agenda of the campaign, but written platforms do create difficulties. Although Wilson promised not to implement the more radical items of the 1974 Labour platform, it was still there as official policy. Where possible, leaders may be intent on watering policy down to what may be popular electorally. In 1982 the Australian Labor party's national conference assessed the wording of planks on uranium or a capital gains tax on the basis of what the electorate would stand and what could be sold.

Of course the emphasis on what leaders say does allow for change of emphasis, even for promises to be made conditional. In 1983, when Hawke was certain of victory, he effectively retracted all his electoral promises in the last week by declaring they were all conditional on the state of the economy. So leaders can delay even written and published commitments.

Nevertheless, because the press can point to differences between platform and campaign promises, because Labor leaders have to compromise to some extent in drawing up manifestos, they probably have less freedom to manoeuvre than those prime ministers of parties that are electoral machines or which give total deference to their leaders. In these cases what the prime ministers says is policy. To deny it would be to rebuff the leader at a critical time—as differences of opinion between Liberal and National party coalition leaders during the 1972 and 1974 campaigns illustrated, that can be electorally dangerous.

Popularity

Popular leaders are regarded as essential, but the significance of popularity can be exaggerated. Findings in opinion polls which indicate a prime minister is more popular than the leader of the opposition, or is regarded as a better prime minister, do not also mean that the leader's party will succeed. Not only can the poll figures be misleading (see Crewe 1981: 275–6 for Britain; Roberts 1980: 241–3 for New Zealand), but there are many examples of popular leaders losing. Wilson always led Heath in popularity (Rose 1980: 10); Callaghan was more popular than Thatcher in 1979; Trudeau was regarded as likely to be a far better prime minister than Clark, but still lost one election to him. Whitlam received more positive reactions than Gorton in 1969. Among the reasons given for electoral success of parties, leadership is seldom rated highly. In Australia Fraser was never a popular figure; for most of his career he rated well below his party (see *Bulletin* 7 February 1984) and in 1977 all references to party leaders were negative. In 1979 Thatcher's popularity ran far behind that of her party; as did Clark the same year, in Canada. Where party is still, in part at least, based on class, leadership is perhaps given too much publicity.

So in what way does popularity matter? In some cases very little. In Britain the two large parties appear to ignore poll findings in their choice of leaders. When Thatcher and Foot were elected, the polls suggested that Whitelaw and Healey would have been more popular figures. Foot was chosen because he appeared best able to keep the party together, Thatcher because she had had the courage to challenge Heath.

Popularity has been regarded as more important elsewhere. Trudeau was selected in 1968 in part because he best suited the demands of a television age. Muldoon replaced Marshall because his aggressive style was thought better able to defeat Kirk on the hustings. In Australia Hawke ousted Hayden as leader of the ALP, not because Labor members thought he would make a better prime minister (at the time most of them didn't), but because they thought he could win. When Hawke challenged Hayden in July 1982, the main argument used by his supporters was that the polls showed that while Hawke led Fraser in a choice of prime minister, Hayden trailed him.

For an incumbent prime minister popularity, or at least the view that he or she is performing well, is a protection against disaffection. Even if a party could remove an unpopular figure—and of course they cannot always—there is never any discussion of removing a popular one.

Despite the concentration on leaders, there is little evidence that they are the main reason for a party's success. In 1979 policy and party image were vital for the Conservative victory in Britain; the electors preferred Labour ministers but Conservative measures (Crewe 1981: 282). Measures won. In 1975 and 1977 Australian voters did not regard leadership as a cause for voting one way or other. Indeed in 1980 the Liberal campaign was switched away from its emphasis on the value of strong leadership, as represented by Fraser, because it was having little impact. In New Zealand Muldoon may not have been popular, but the voters still preferred National. In Canada, even when leadership was an issue in 1979, it received comparatively little attention (Fletcher 1981: 316). However the evidence suggests that in Canada there is a substantial sub-set of voters whose decision is affected by the leader's image (Winham and Cunningham 1977: 139) and this may be as large as 10 per cent of the voters (*Globe and Mail* 2 March 1983). With little ideological difference between the parties in Canada, that may be unsurprising. Even in 1982, Trudeau was described as the 'single most attractive commodity' the Liberal party had (*Globe and mail* 18 October 1982).

The difficulty of turning popularity into votes is illustrated by the

'Hawke phenomenon'. In 1983 Hawke was the most popular prime minister Australia had had for a long time. A year after his election, polls suggested that 73 per cent of the electorate approved his performance (he even led the leader of the opposition among Liberal voters), but the increase in people prepared to vote Labor had only risen by 5 per cent (*Bulletin* 4 February 1984). That was a substantial figure in Australia's evenly balanced electorate, but it does indicate that many who thought Hawke was doing a good job would still not vote for him. Popularity helps; it can not replace the party image.

Of course what is important is not what happens but what is perceived to happen. Campaigns have become so personalised that everything leaders do is regarded as newsworthy. The first stories each day are likely to report their activities. In 1980 a Canadian PC minister of finance scheduled an important economic statement on the day his leader had a rest from campaigning in order to give it maximum impact, but the first news item on the PC party showed Clark having a haircut on his day off. Even a leader doing nothing is more newsworthy than a senior colleague making an important statement.

Surveys of newspapers show the extent to which this occurs. Prime ministers are invariably given far more attention than opposition leaders, even if it is not always positive (see Fletcher 1981: 308 for Canada in 1979; Rose 1980: 21 for Britain). As a result prime ministers have a far greater capacity to get their message across than anyone else. It is not surprising that they so readily take either the blame or the credit for the result.

THE MEDIA

James Margach, for a long time chief political correspondent of the *Sunday Times*, is in no doubt that British prime ministers have sought to manipulate and control the media:

> Prime Ministers are men who may be in a job one day and out the next. And so, having pursued power and seized it, they proceed to use and abuse it in order to dominate the Press in an apparently paranoid pursuance of survival. Each has his own style. Some are blatantly wooing and anxious to please, others play hard to get ... The reality is that they are manipulating the Press, using all the arts of statecraft. (Margach 1979: 3)

Margach's bitter title, *The Abuse of Power*, emphasises the message. As prime ministers accumulate power, relations with the media deteriorate.

These soured relations are not limited to Britain. Many prime ministers begin their period of office honeymooning with the media:

Trudeau in 1968, Kirk and Whitlam in 1972, Hawke in 1983. Others, like Fraser and Muldoon, never have that advantage. A few, such as McMahon, are ridiculed from the day they take office. Sooner or later however, the honeymoon deteriorates. Trudeau's disdain for the media and his refusal to pander to their pride (Radwanski 1978: 204–9) alienated much of the Canadian lobby. Whitlam remained personally popular with the lobby journalists, but his government lost all support from the press. Hawke has a litigious tendency when anyone challenges his integrity, but his popularity relies so much on the ability to maintain a consensus that if that collapses, and if the media become critical, the love-affair of the first year might be very quickly embittered. Of Australian prime ministers only Menzies, with lofty disdain, retained good relations with the press most of the time. That was much easier for him than for Labor leaders because the Australian press ownership is highly concentrated and usually conservative. Yet since the media are concerned with uncovering problems, and the government with hiding them, their interests must be contradictory. Governments, and particularly prime ministers, want favourable coverage.

As Margach illustrates, there is no doubt that prime ministers have great authority and are prepared to use it. The techniques for manipulation are alike in all democratic countries. The timing and frequency of press conferences, briefing of chosen journalists, favouring of electronic over print media, selective leaking and backgrounding, door-stop appearances—all these resources are available to prime ministers. Since access to prime ministers is limited and they control most of the information, their wishes are likely to be met. They decide what gets out, how it is presented, to whom and in what form. Trudeau, for instance, differentiated between material best presented on the electronic media, and the more detailed arguments that are presented in the print media: constitutional change does not make riveting television. Of course the press is always attempting to reduce this control, and in particular cases may put the prime minister off balance, but the weapons are uneven.

Nevertheless prime ministers not only fear the media, they need them—to get their message across, to educate the voters. They need to understand the technical requirements of timing, the length of clips, the chances for editing and all the new media technology. They need to know what should be presented and how. At times they must respond to events created by the media. Leaks, scandals, crises or exposures create difficulties that prime ministers must face. The media has the capacity to show a government in disarray. Its influence must not be underrated. In these areas all prime ministers are in a similar position; there are no systemic advantages for one over the other.

All prime ministers are supported by a press office. In Canada it has four officers, in New Zealand two or three. In Britain the No. 10 Press Office sometimes contains professional information officers (Macmillan's Evans and Thatcher's Ingham) or political journalists (like Wilson's Haines). It presents a point of contact, provides a means of drawing attention to prime ministerial statements, or putting a particular gloss on occasional items.

How much influence this gives the prime minister depends in part on what facilities are available to other ministers or departments. In Australia Whitlam let each of his ministers appoint a press secretary; the result seemed to be competition for headlines and an impression of incoherence. Fraser limited the appointment of press secretaries to a few senior ministers. That did not stop leaks or kite-flying, but it appeared to introduce more discipline. Most countries have at various times appointed cabinet committees to co-ordinate information, but prime ministerial control seems more distinct in Australia and New Zealand than in Britain. In part this is a function of the size of government. It is easier to keep an eye on sensitive items when there are fewer established links between the media and parts of government.

In Britain departments like Defence have their own momentum. During the Falklands war, for instance, overall public relations were determined by an interdepartmental committee, chaired by the head of the No. 10 Press Office, Bernard Ingham (Harris 1983: 101). Yet Ingham was consistently critical of the ministry of Defence's handling of the media. One journalist claimed: 'We got the distinct impression that Number 10 was more than unhappy at the way the MoD [Ministry of Defence] were handling the war—*more* than unhappy—and there were times when Number 10 were briefing on subjects which the MoD refused to talk about' (quoted in Harris 1983: 116). No. 10 was reduced to counter-briefing because it could not direct the ministry—the established procedures and institutional sensitivities were too great, even in an area of absorbing interest to the prime minister and in which No. 10 was notionally involved. It is likely that a New Zealand or Australian prime minister would have entirely taken over such an exercise.

The regularity with which press conferences are held provides an indication of the methods by which prime ministers may control access to the media. Muldoon held press conferences twice a week, often after cabinet meetings so that he could announce what cabinet had decided, preferably when the news was good. He regularly attacked individual members of the press gallery, particularly when they breached the accepted rules or got facts wrong, and he constantly kept the journalists on the defensive. He was *the* manager of the news. He also wrote a weekly column in *Truth*, allowing him scope to attack his opponents in their own medium. In Canada Trudeau held fortnightly press conferences and always went on the record. In Australia Fraser and Whitlam initially promised frequent conferences, but these became much more rare. When Fraser did meet the media he often restricted the occasions to the electronic media. Their questions were more bland and he could control what was shown to the public more directly. Prime ministers can also decide whether they wish to give 'door-stop' interviews as they arrive at work each morning and on what topic.

A second factor may be the structure of the media. In Britain established correspondents like Margach or David Wood of *The Times* have served for a long period; the newspapers are national and each party gets some support. In Canada and New Zealand all papers are regional, as are all but Murdoch's *Australian* (which has a small readership) in Australia. In Australia at least there has been a regular turnover in leading correspondents; few have been based in the Canberra Press Gallery for ten years, many for much less. They may be educated and critical, but few have depth of experience. Prime ministers may play favourites or, like Fraser, talk to editors and the very few proprietors.

In New Zealand Muldoon has been able to go further. Before 1970 almost no paper supported Labour, even if some were at times neutral (Cleveland 1980: 186–7). Political society is so small that Muldoon dominates access to the media; in 1983 he banned for a time any direct contact between his ministers and the *Dominion*, a daily Wellington paper. Even when papers do campaign against the prime minister, as many Canadian papers have attacked Trudeau, their impact is likely to be regional. A national and prestigious press, with its own traditions, may be harder to manipulate and control than more regionalised ones.

Of course, in a federal system, a regional structure may also create problems. The prime minister's statements are likely to be balanced by those of state or provincial premiers who are considered locally important. In a unitary state prime ministers may only compete for attention with other party leaders, a contest they are certain to win. In a federal state, state and provincial premiers may compete forcefully (Fletcher 1977: 94–7). In the region 'national messages do not always get through. Regional identities are strong ... and in several provinces a significant proportion of the population feels a sense of grievance against the federal government' (Fletcher 1977: 94).

A small system in which there is no rival spokesman and in which some of the media are either government-financed (NZBC) or regionalised is the easiest to dominate. Muldoon does that. He attacks journalists publicly, ridicules their errors, isolates them, keeps them off balance, even while giving them regular access. It is an aggressive performance in which he guarantees headlines whether at home or abroad. But he can only do it because of the unitary governmental structure and the structure of the press. Besides, most press proprietors are scared of attacking the government too strongly because they anticipate being awarded licences if commercial television is introduced.

Presentation on television is now seen as essential by many party supporters. Pearson argues that it is and has become too important: 'one can appear to be a leader on television if he is a good performer, a good actor' (1977: 258). Whether voters make decisions on the basis of image or not, the media 'amplify' this image (Rose 1980: 22). Prime Ministers need the media to get their message across; they need to control it to do that on the most favourable terms. That is why there is a constant struggle, in which the prime ministers of New Zealand start with greater advantages than their counterparts.

DIRECT CONSEQUENCES

Public image may serve several immediate ends, such as winning elections and maintaining personal popularity, but it does not necessarily follow that it has an impact on internal governmental decisions. Messages may not get through; education may be ineffective. Fletcher concluded a study of the Canadian prime minister as public educator with the caveat that the evidence suggested 'severe limitations on the prime minister's persuasive powers. The prime minister appears to be able to raise issues at will but to have more difficulty selling his solutions ... Image-making, too, has its limitations. Personal popularity is not always easily transferred to policies and to programmes' (1977: 110). It is therefore necessary to identify the types of impact that the prime minister may have through public performances and to see if they differs from system to system.

1   They may commit the government to certain actions or attitudes.

Statements in election campaigns or impromptu public comments (not always carefully thought out) fit this category. Policy speeches are the most obvious means of stating what the party will do; this does not mean that everything in the speech will be implemented. But if prime ministers choose to push for a particular plank, they can use their public promise as a method of persuasion. Kirk and Whitlam both argued that if something had been promised, then opposition to it in cabinet was wrong, whatever the consequences. In 1983 Hawke announced a royal commission into allegations about a former ALP national secretary's dealings with a KGB agent without consulting cabinet.

Prime ministers are entitled to speak for their government without consultation, though some, like Muldoon, use that right more than others. To refuse to implement a public statement from the prime minister is an indication of his or her defeat in cabinet. It can and does happen—Thatcher failed to achieve the expenditure cuts she had publicly espoused—but that does not negate the point that a public statement, not previously agreed with cabinet, is a means by which prime ministers may bring pressure on their colleagues to adopt a line. Usually they are effective.

On other occasions prime ministers use their access to the media to put political opponents on the defensive. Trudeau, for instance, used television debates 'to persuade the country that provincial intransigence forced him to make unilateral changes'in the patriation of the constitution (*Globe and Mail* 9 September 1980). The media provide all leaders with the opportunity to make a stand.

However, it would be wrong to assume that because a prime minister announces a policy, that policy was decided without consultation. Cabinet may recognise that the prime minister is the best person to announce it because the initiative will then be guaranteed attention by the media. Barnett (1982: 173) recalls an occasion when cabinet agreed that Callaghan should refer to a new policy in a speech in the house: Callaghan 'was initially reluctant to do so, preferring the responsible minister to make a formal statement, but he gave way jokingly: "In my usual way of 'dominating' cabinet I will announce the £3.50 in the debate"'. Hawke is regarded rightly as the most effective spokesman for his government. Because he can get the message across, he will often announce government policy; that is not the same as saying he decided it alone. Media concentration on a leader's statements may exaggerate their influence.

2   They may make final arrangements and present them as a fait accompli.

In any negotiations with outside bodies, prime ministers have a much greater capacity than anyone else to reach final settlements which can be presented to cabinet for rubber-stamping. In international forums prime ministers can use the excuse that an agreement needs the approval of cabinet as a means of delaying decisions (see Evans 1981:

248 for Macmillan's comment on the need to take a Polaris agreement to cabinet), but equally they can bind their countries. The Lusaka Conference, which led to the Lancaster House agreement over Zimbabwe, was one in which Fraser, Thatcher and Carrington were free to negotiate. On economic affairs the British cabinet effectively had to accept the IMF terms arranged by Callaghan and Healey; they also had to accept the terms of the Lib–Lab alliance.

It is accepted that in foreign affairs some independence is ceded to all prime ministers and their foreign secretaries. It is also true that in domestic matters prime ministers can present final arrangements to cabinet (for some Canadian examples, see Wearing 1977: 332–3; Pearson 1977: 262). Autocratic procedures can work—for a time. But it is still probable that they are only acceptable if cabinet generally approves of the final decision, or at least does not disapprove too strongly too often.

3 They may use public statements to end existing disagreements.

Public statements may be a means of ending deadlocks. When in 1978 Trudeau returned from an economic summit and announced a cut of $2 billion from the federal budget (Clarkson 1981: 157), he had become impatient with the continual wrangling in the cabinet. Callaghan could end discussion on the size of acceptable wage rises by announcing a figure. A public statement, guaranteed attention because of the prime minister's access to the media, can end internal debate. The public image can therefore help to an extent in determining internal policy problems.

INDIRECT CONSEQUENCES

Among the analytical categories that King (1975: 225) regards as important is public prestige. How does that have an impact on prime ministerial influence? It may be possible to chart popularity through the polls but it is more difficult to be precise about its effect.

Public prestige certainly helps prime ministers get their own way. If they are regarded as the only possible leaders, their demands may be brutal. Whitlam's reputed comment, 'The government only has one asset and you are wasting his time', is one such indication. According to Sedgemore, Callaghan was prepared to use similar tactics:

I personally heard James Callaghan threaten resignation (with an implied dissolution threat) on two occasions at meetings of the Parliamentary Labour Party and according to colleagues of mine in the Cabinet he did the same thing there on several occasions; according to other sources he also threatened it in order to get his way once or twice at meetings of the National Executive Committee of the Labour Party. On 2nd April 1979 he threatened to resign over the contents of the election manifesto. One would imagine that such threats would be the subject of diminishing returns but apparently not. (1980: 66)

There are, of course, more positive sides to the advantages of prestige. A leader who is perceived as having been personally responsible for electoral victory can carry that over into cabinet. Fraser's prestige as a political winner was high within the party, even if he was not popular in the electorate; after all, that was the main reason he stayed leader. In Canada Mitchell Sharp, a senior minister under Pearson and Trudeau, explained the difference:

> Trudeau never came into the cabinet and said 'This is what we will do'. But at the same time, we recognised that we were a majority party in 1968 because Trudeau had been the leader. We all had the sort of feeling that we were there because Trudeau was the prime minister. It wasn't as if he laid down any policy approach, but we realized he was the man who had brought us where we were. Pearson was merely one of us, whereas Trudeau was not—he was someone extraordinary. (Radwanski 1978: 155–6)

Pearson was made by the party in his election; in 1968 Trudeau appeared to *be* the campaign. Thatcher's triumph in 1983 may give her similar advantages.

As a government approaches an election, the clout of a popular prime minister may increase. Ministers are aware that they need that leader. Hawke's ministers assume that, as long as he retains his remarkably high level of popularity, the government will probably be returned. They are therefore more likely to indulge his wishes on *particular* items. But as a government lasts longer, it is less certain that the weight of popularity will remain unchanged:

> There may be some incentive to follow the leader when an election victory creates a 'state of grace' or simply the feeling that, without the leader, the party would be lost, but that sentiment soon fades out ... Cabinet government quickly settles for its main decision-making mode, the committee of relatively equal members discussing together the basis for a compromise. (Blondel 1982: 223)

Status and popularity may help provide a general climate of deference; they do not necessarily determine the result of individual submissions unless the prime minister has a clear preference.

Unpopular leaders may have greater difficulty, but that depends in part on their vulnerability. Trudeau's low rating led to dissatisfaction in the late 1970s but not to a challenge. Thatcher's unpopularity before the Falklands war led to press speculation about the firmness of her grip, but again no real threat. Not so when Fraser was regarded as a liability in 1982 or Muldoon in 1980, but there is no direct evidence in either case that their control of government was weakened. Public prestige may be a means to buttress prime ministers; it can be, and at times is, used by prime ministers. In some instances lack of prestige *may* lead to less policy control.

9

Is There a Job Description?

The comparative approach adopted in this book has thrown into relief the strengths and weaknesses, formal and informal, of prime ministers in four countries. Factors often taken for granted in single-country studies have become more apparent when compared to others. For instance, Australian and New Zealand prime ministers are more vulnerable than their British, and far more so than their Canadian, counterparts; this alters the way that they must relate to their back-benchers. Canadian and Australian leaders must take into account the multiple centres of power within the party that are created by the federal structure; the federal structure also effects the distribution of patronage. By contrast New Zealand leaders often involve the party in appointments, while British prime ministers are the least restricted.

Yet British prime ministers are not served by a department with a perceived policy capacity; New Zealand prime ministers have a limited support group; Australian and Canadian leaders have substantial partisan and non-partisan support. The cabinet committees are permanent, public and regulated in Canada and Australia, but seem easier to manipulate in Britain. Parliament can be treated with disdain by prime ministers in Australia and New Zealand, but takes more time, even if it is not taken much more seriously, in Canada and Britain. Cabinets take far more decisions in New Zealand and Australia than in Britain and perhaps act more readily as a collectivity.

The contrasts are legion. Different checks and balances have de-veloped as a means of restricting, to some extent, the power of prime ministers, whether it be the observances of constitutionalism in Bri-tain or the ruthless response to failed leaders in Australia and New Zealand. In each the prime minister's position is strengthened by some forces and weakened by others. Prime ministers may be in a far strong-er position than presidents to undertake some tasks: 'No Canadian', commented one civil servant and minister, 'would want their prime minister to be as weak as the American president'. In other areas their powers may be heavily constrained. Those areas too vary between the four countries.

Of course each country is unique, with its own historical traditions, its own utilitarian conventions to which the prime ministers may appeal. Each system provides opportunities and limitations. The comparisons have shown how differently the prime ministerial position has developed within parliamentary systems that use similar strands of conventional rhetoric, derive from a similar heritage and use similar structures.

Yet, even given the complications and difficulties of comparison, it is possible to derive some views about which country's prime ministers have the greatest capacity to exert independent power. That power can be either created by the positive use of powers or limited by the existence of formal or informal institutional constraints. Table 9.1 presents a set of categories, drawing on the evidence presented in the earlier chapters. Other categories could perhaps be added; the intention is merely to illustrate. The tentative conclusion to be drawn is that British Conservative prime ministers have fewer and weaker limitations on their ability to get their own way than other prime ministers. They are probably followed by National leaders in New Zealand, by Canadian prime ministers and British Labour leaders, by Australian Liberals and finally by the Labor leaders in Australia and New Zealand.

Within each category, of course, there is a tremendous range of opportunities. An effective, charismatic Canadian prime minister may dominate government decision-making more than a compromise prime minister leading the British Conservative party. Yet in doing so the Canadian leader may have still to work within severe limitations and have to consider a range of power centres. The table suggests only that, when prime ministers choose to exert their power, some have to overcome greater institutional problems than others. Nor do the categories imply that prime ministers are not more powerful than their ministerial colleagues. Prime ministers, for instance, are affected by vulnerability only when their reputation is in decline. Firing ministers may be difficult; it is not impossible. The exercise is essentially *comparative*, arguing that prime ministers in some countries have greater difficulty in exercising their powers than others.

When the influence of *particular* prime ministers is considered, in whichever country, then an analyst must be concerned to identify how that individual pulls together the different institutional threads of power. Many prime ministers will stretch their position to the limits of the possible, maintaining a balance between the parts of the political system. What they attempt to do depends on nerve as much as formal

Table 9.1 Comparative power of prime ministers[a]

	Britain		Canada	Australia		New Zealand	
	Conservative	Labour	Liberal	Liberal	Labor	National	Labour
Vulnerability	medium	medium	high	low	low	low	low
Control of party	high	low	medium	low	low	high	low
Cabinet committees	high	high	medium	high	medium	high	medium
Patronage	high	high	medium	medium	low	medium	medium
Hiring/firing ministers	high	high	medium	medium	low	medium	low
Level of policy advice	low	low	high	high	high	high	medium
Control over parliament	medium	medium	low	high/low[b]	high/low	high	high

Notes: [a] 'High' means the situation adds to their power; low means it constrains
[b] Depending on whether the government controls the Senate

authority. Institutional analysis explains what can be done and how the structure may differ.

It is more difficult to explain how prime ministers exert control over other individuals. The personal interaction is hard to identify. Mackintosh (1977a: 20) dismisses one writer for 'a genuinely academic inability to grasp the effects of power in a political system'. But he regrettably does not then explore how one individual, without using formal authority, gains compliance from other powerful people. In his discussion of executives, King (1975) develops ideas raised by Neustadt's study of the American presidency and lists factors which need to be explored if the influence of leaders is to be understood. He distinguishes between their standing in the eyes of cabinet colleagues, their professional reputation (what they are seen to be good at), their political standing (what the power-brokers and influentials think of their capacity to influence others) and their public prestige. Obviously each of these can be regarded as analytically distinct. A leader may be perceived by outsiders to be influential, without being regarded as an efficient administrator. But the concepts are often difficult to analyse; as King acknowledges, some prime ministers may be good at some things, but not others. For instance, Harris (1982: 405) argues that Britain has seldom been better governed in a technical sense than under Attlee, but he still performed poorly at the polls. Skilled chairmanship of cabinet, such as by Hawke, Trudeau or Macmillan, or brutal treatment of inefficient ministers, by Fraser, Muldoon or Callaghan, can ensure that particular ends are reached. Menzies was regarded by his colleagues as the best-informed and best-briefed member of cabinet, but did that have an influence on those ministers who were themselves well-briefed?

Standing and professional reputation will vary; there will often be disagreement among cabinet ministers as to how well the prime minister is performing. To understand what effect standing and reputation have, it is probably necessary to explore the relationship between particular individuals and their colleagues, as Robert Caro (1983) has done so brilliantly for Lyndon Johnson. That book succeeds in understanding the loyalty that leaders, however personally ambitious, may engender. Few biographies of prime ministers have treated that feeling of belonging or analysed the technical exercise of pesonal power (for one attempt, see Radwanski 1978: chs. 10 and 11). Techniques of managing colleagues must be personal and particular rather than systemic. A comparative study of the institutional position provides an understanding of the available levers of power and thus an essential underpinning to individual case studies or biographies. It cannot replace such studies.

LEARNING FROM COMPARISONS

If it is accepted that the influence of prime ministers can be affected by institutional structure, then comparative studies provide indications of how changes to those structures can be achieved, or at least in what alternative ways people have worked. It is not only that observers invariably believe that, when their system is not working well, others are so much smoother. This 'grass is greener' syndrome is usually based on a detailed knowledge of the system that does not appear to be working and a more formal understanding of the other. Ironically, people seem to see fewer constraints on their own prime minister than on others. Campbell (1980: 50–1) argues that 'the Cabinet-dominated government in Britain today differs greatly from that in Canada, especially since the British Prime Minister is subject to more political constraints than the Canadian counterpart'. Perhaps absence makes the observer more tolerant, or nearness make the exercise of marginal power seem more overwhelming.

Comparative studies allow observers to see what has been considered or tried elsewhere, what has worked, and what the possible implications for change might be. Constitutional dogmatism can be replaced by more sensitive analysis. Comparison allows sensible responses to those attempts at institutional engineering that often can be found in the political science literature. Ridley has argued that 'the traditional purpose of political science [has been] the improvement of one's own system of government'; this can best be done by the descriptive comparison of constitutions with 'perhaps some thoughts on transferability' (1975: 102). Some authors end a study of one country's institutions by proposing that a different model be adopted; thus Campbell and Szablowski (1979) want to graft the methods of the British central agencies on to the Canadian government. By contrast many practitioners, like Benn and Sedgmore, want to change the system and recommend a series of proposals *without* looking elsewhere to see how they may have worked. In other cases, such as Jones's opposition to the establishment of a prime minister's department, arguments *against* change are also mounted without seriously examining comparative data; indeed British scholars and practitioners seem particularly loath to see with what effectiveness the parliamentary/cabinet systems have adapted elsewhere, perhaps because they regard themselves as the repository of proper practices.

Comparative analysis does allow some judgements to be made of the advantages of transferability, or at least of some possible outcomes. For instance, Benn (1982: 39–41) argues that seven reforms could reduce the British prime minister's power to more restricted, and therefore preferable, levels. They are:

1 An end to peerages
2 Election of Cabinet ministers and the confirmation of the allocation of portfolios by Labour MPs
3 Development of Commons Select Committee system
4 Institution of a parliamentary confirmation system for major public appointments
5 A freedom of information act
6 Return of the powers of law-making from Brussels to parliament
7 Strengthening the powers of the parliamentary Labour party.

Of these proposals, comparative data can be explored for numbers 1, 2, 4 and 7. For instance, no other prime minister has access to peerages and indeed it makes it easier to bring outsiders into cabinet or to promote people 'upstairs' to the House of Lords. However peerages are only part of an extensive network of patronage and quite possibly not the most important one. The appointment of colleagues to ambassadorships or similar positions is an even more effective way of removing rivals—and is almost as often used.

The election of cabinet ministers, if overseas examples are followed, would make comparatively little difference to the personnel of cabinet. Whether ministers are chosen or elected, factional balance must be taken into account. The last two or three positions may be different, but not many more. Indeed, as the Hawke cabinet illustrates, it may be easier to isolate factional opponents *because* they are elected. For whatever reason—double-cross or poor voting support— the fact that the leading left-wingers balloted poorly allowed them to be given the least significant portfolios. It would be harder for a new prime minister to achieve that effect if he or she had sole responsibility for selection.

What Benn does not mention is that granting the power of election to caucus may restrict the power of prime ministers to sack. If they retain that power, then presumably caucus elects the replacements, but how easily prime ministers can sack those whom they did not appoint and with what implications Benn has not discussed.

Benn (1982: 41) also wants 'the party meeting to have the right, at all its meetings, to discuss all recommendations relating to the handling of Parliamentary business, or proposed amendments of all kinds, which should, in every case, be put to Party meetings for approval'. In a sense this would give the PLP the same rights as parliamentary parties in Australia and Canada: the right to discuss in advance most of the legislation that will be presented to parliament. It certainly does give greater opportunity to backbenchers to discuss proposals, but the limitations are also evident. Caucus remains reactive; time and information are scarce; the pay-roll vote remains substantial. It is not the easy solution that Benn seems to believe. But there is no doubt that it does make the prime minister more conscious, when parliament is sitting, of what caucus will accept.

Another attempt at institutional engineering has been the proposal of the Australian Labor party to adopt a cabinet committee system similar to that of the Trudeau government. The committee structure introduced in 1972 was based on an early Trudeau version; those of the 1980 and 1982 task force reports used the idea of a priorities and planning committee and two other co-ordinating committees, with five functional committees.

However there was one obvious difference. In so far as the Canadian system worked well by decentralising and expediting business, and therefore allowing the prime minister time to concentrate on the most politically sensitive issues or those in which he was particularly interested, it was because Trudeau delegated responsibility to those committees without requiring personal involvement. He acted as chairman of only three committees. Though kept informed, he was not involved in detail. The problem with the Whitlam committee system was that it needed continuous political involvement and commitment by the prime minister to make it work, and it did not get it. The 1982 task force has notionally included the prime minister as chairman of the priorities and planning committee and of all five functional committees. Since prime ministerial time is one of the scarcest resources in government, that arrangement seems unfortunate; the system saves the time of other ministers, but not of Hawke. He may choose to delegate the task of chairman to others, but it seems unlikely that such a scheme will operate expeditiously if the prime minister tries to do everything.

These examples can be extended to most of the areas discussed in this book. The British Labour party has adopted a system of conventions for electing its leaders; did it consider the problems of removing leaders that might follow? Australian prime ministers spend much of their time dealing with dissidence within their party because it is federal in structure; what would happen if the party became confederal? If, as is more likely, two coalition parties were to combine at state level, would it destroy the national structure of the party system and hence the stability of the coalition? Those sorts of changes are constantly discussed, sometimes with explicit comparisons, sometimes as though from first principles. In each case an understanding of how those arrangements have worked elsewhere will illuminate the discussion. The power of prime ministers has been an obvious case because demands for change are so frequent.

CAN PRIME MINISTERS HAVE A JOB DESCRIPTION?

Is there a set of principles that could be codified as a job description for prime ministers in Westminster systems? Drawing on a wide range of views it is possible to distinguish between the roles that prime ministers *must*, *should* and *choose to* play. They *must* chair cabinet, prevent fragmentation, arbitrate; fight fires; meet media and international demands. They *should* be guardian of the strategy; focus priorities. They *choose to* run individual policy areas; keep control of/an eye on individual policies. Each category concerns political, policy and administrative problems.

The first set of roles is seldom challenged. It describes the minimum required to allow the system to work. Cabinets have to reach conclusions about particular conflicts and prime ministers have to ensure that they stick. Prime ministers spend much of their time reacting to, or settling, issues that they cannot avoid. Inevitably these functions take up much of their time. Yet, even so, what receives the greatest emphasis will depend partly on the prime ministers' own leanings.

Criticism is voiced most frequently in relation to those areas where prime ministers *choose* to intervene. Every country has had prime ministers who chose to participate in making decisions that lay within ministers' areas of responsibility (Thatcher, Callaghan, Trudeau, Fraser, Whitlam, Muldoon) and those who were more aloof (Douglas-Home, St Laurent, Holyoake, Hawke). When they do intervene, it is argued either that they pre-empt proper decision-making, undermine the minister or circumvent cabinet in particular areas; or that the result has been a disaster. However it can be asked whether prime ministers always have a choice. Sometimes they must be involved; they are often asked about economic matters and need to have some answer. In other areas they care about the results. To argue that it was wrong for Trudeau to become deeply involved in constitutional or bilingual matters, or for Fraser to play a role in determining African policy is by itself absurd. It *may* have point only if it is shown that, by chasing these hares, prime ministers neglect the routine matters they must fulfil. That is sometimes argued, particularly in discussion of strategy. What is not shown is that the general strategy was ignored because of the interest in detail.

This becomes particularly relevant when it is noted that the functions in the second category—which observers argue prime ministers *should* play—are often performed inadequately, if at all. Attempts at maintaining coherent strategies—except for maintaining political supremacy—are generally regarded as failures. Trudeau's planning policies changed regularly; Heath's U-turns were notorious; Wilson's failure to provide any coherence was one of Crossman's most frequent complaints; Fraser's economic rhetoric, according to critics in his own party, was seldom matched by performance. Thatcher, at least in her first term, was unable to cut expenditure to the extent she wanted. Economic policy is often regarded as ad hoc. Priorities are never set explicitly in any way that is coherent. The British expenditure planning systems have primarily become control mechanisms; only the Canadian system of envelopes still seems to approach a *system* of planning. *All* accounts of cabinet decision-making emphasise that it is sequential and ad hoc and that cabinets have grave problems in determining priorities. Yet prime ministers are supposed to have the responsibility for providing general direction.

The perceived failure in this area may be attributed to at least two causes. First, the problem may be systemic: that is the cabinet and parliamentary system does not have the capacity—for political, economic or institutional reasons—to develop and sustain a coherent set of priorities (see e.g. Brittan 1977; Beer 1983). Blondel has argued that

> Cabinet government is ill-suited to the requirements of modern administration ... because it is better suited for short-term on-the-spot decisions than for long-term planning. It is too egalitarian, at least within the oligarchies that run political parties; it is also too 'political' in its overall conception... The whole decision-making arrangements are based on agreements, arrived at gradually, not on order or command... Cabinet government is government arrived at by discussion.
> ... An even more serious problem results from the fact that cabinet government is in essence too 'political' to be sufficiently concerned with 'administrative' or managerial matters. (1982: 222–3)

This conclusion has some plausibility. It suggests that there is little to be gained from planning or designing strategy because the system, not the individuals working it, is antipathic to such schemes.

An alternative cause is that prime ministers do not have sufficient power to direct cabinet, that the forces and interests ranged against them are too great. Often the argument is made that greater support is needed for decision-making by cabinet as a collectivity. However those solutions that have been tried—the CPRS in Britain, the PRS in Australia—have failed precisely in that collective and strategic role; that may be in part because they are trying to serve both prime minister and cabinet.

Whichever way the prime minister's role is conceptualised, it is clear that there is no simple way to build up a job description. Three points need to be made. First, a job description cannot be derived from the Westminster system; it could have no *constitutional* basis. Westminster principles are essentially general; they provide no detailed prescriptions of what can or should be done. Constitutional authorities tend to derive from those principles rules of behaviour which are of dubious value.

Second, such a job description will have no *political* value. Prime ministers will do whatever they consider necessary at the time; it would be naive to believe otherwise. There is then no point in arguing that they should be forbidden to undertake some functions; or that some functions are proper and others not.

The third point is that parliamentary systems have developed on different lines in the four countries considered in this book. Yet in none of the cases can it be argued that parliamentary government no longer exists or that the Westminster system has been destroyed. Each is legitimate in its own right. Therefore the arguments that Attlee and Morrison used against the practices of the ALP—that they were improper in a parliamentary system—are tenable only if the British system is regarded as the only 'proper' system. It is not.

In all four systems, what prime ministers can do is determined by convention and traditional practice. Those conventions may be observed or not, depending on the political value of maintaining them and the urgency of existing circumstances. Prime ministers may choose to stretch them to their limits. Norms and established practices are of course important, not because they provide cast-iron rules that must be obeyed but because they create expectations that may be disappointed. Prime ministers must calculate the political costs of ignoring what are conceived widely to be constitutional conventions. If those costs are greater than the benefits that are likely to accrue, then action will be postponed. Conventions, however defined, are therefore a factor in the calculations, but not necessarily the decisive one.

The position of prime ministers in each of these parliamentary systems can be changed dramatically without doing any damage to the parliamentary system itself. People may not like the *consequences* of having a prime minister who is vulnerable or of a prime minister's department that initiates policy proposals at the prime minister's direction. But there are not in themselves 'unconstitutional' or 'improper' in a Westminster system.

In constitutional terms 'whatever is, is right' may be correct for a definition of the prime ministers' job in any of the four countries. It does not follow that everyone would also agree that 'whatever is, is desirable'. If there is no job description that is constitutionally valid in parliamentary and Westminster systems, then the criteria to be used must be operational and normative. In those terms the comments of practitioners describing what is acceptable, and of academics describing what is proper, can be considered in a similar light; they are all statements of what the observers want done.

Those normative views have to make fundamental choices between collective and individual action and between directive or consensual behaviour. For instance, if the intention is to increase the strategic competence of a government, assistance can be given to cabinet (or parts of cabinet) or to the prime minister. Blondel wants a collective solution; he believes that cabinet governments need 'a group at the very top which, though in part of some of the ministers, must also include men and women who, together with the leader, are primarily engaged in policy-making and coordination... The group at the top must remain collective' (1982: 233). Other observers have sought to strengthen prime ministers individually. Hoskyns (1983) and Berrill (1980) want increased bureaucratic support to allow prime ministers greater scope for action by giving them advice from their perspective. Dell (1980: 40–4) wants to replace collective responsibility with the concept of collective purpose and to strengthen the centre of government in its relations with the departments. Hoskyns, Dell and Berrill are all practitioners of politics, aware that prime ministers have great difficulty in imposing strategic direction on government, if indeed they want to.

If it is accepted that prime ministers want to participate in decisions in some areas of policy, and if it is believed that these forays often lead to disastrous decisions, then observers should perhaps ask how the systems can be reshaped to allow their intervention to be effective. Inevitably lack of time will force prime ministers to be selective, but perhaps restructuring supporting systems is more useful than regretting that the intervention is taking place.

If observers want the power of prime ministers to be curbed, then, as Benn has suggested, a set of political constraints has to be institutionalised. Self-restraint on its own is unlikely to work; prime ministers are too concerned with results to remain on the sidelines when they are personally interested. But those political weapons have to be carefully designed to counteract the real strengths that prime ministers have, which are as often informal as formal.

If, then, a job description with wide acceptance is unlikely, observers need to be clear what they believe prime ministers should do, make those views explicit and judge particular actions against them. If there has been an accretion of power to prime ministers—and this book contends that they are often more limited than they appear—

reformers also need to be clear about which parts they disapprove of, and which they accept. Too often the debate has been in general terms, with a job description implicitly assumed. Description and normative assumptions have been confused.

CONCLUSIONS

Comparative studies raise questions and point to tendencies rather than clear answers. Nevertheless three points can be made. First, it is necessary to be aware of the actual situation, to understand what prime ministers do, what they can do well, and how they are constrained. Too often that has not happened, partly because the media dazzles us with the image of all-powerful prime ministers, and partly because we take the institutional machinery for granted. This study may have gone some way towards illustrating the different structural factors that have some impact on the prime minister's power.

Second, it is necessary to acknowledge that, if there is a desire to limit, restrain or even reduce prime ministerial influence—their actual influence, not their media image—then there are often overseas examples to which we can turn, not for immediate transfer, but for indications of how those examples worked, what problems they met and what advantages they brought.

Third, when prime ministers choose to act in different arenas which constitutionalists argue may be stretching their power, we need to ask not *whether* they should be doing it but, since they have chosen to, are the available systems adequate to allow them to do it properly? If not, then there is a need to limit prime ministers, either for political reasons or because the job is becoming too hard for one person, or to change the supporting systems, administrative and political, so that these can ensure greater success. There is no constitutional job description for prime ministers, though there may be a range of legitimate views on how best that job should be done and on what prime ministers should spend their time. Form should then be redesigned to follow function.

The late twentieth century has changed the structure of political power. Within the political machine, prime ministers remain the most powerful individuals, perhaps to an even greater degree than in the past. We need to come to terms with the reality of their position—extra-constitutional, undefinable and based on the expedient and the possible. If we cannot declare what they should do, let us at least understand what they do do. If we find it excessive, constraints can be sought. If we find it desirable, procedures can be created to ensure it is done effectively. Constitutional myths about cabinet government serve their own purposes inside government, but they need to be replaced by a proper understanding of prime ministerial power, its sources of strength and its constraints. Then we can re-fashion those myths or principles so that they better reflect reality in each of the parliamentary systems.

Appendix
Prime Ministers since 1945

Britain

Attlee (Lab)	1945–51
Churchill (Con)	1951–55
Eden (Con)	1955–56
Macmillan (Con)	1956–63
Home (Con)	1963–64
Wilson (Lab)	1964–70
Heath (Con)	1970–74
Wilson (Lab)	1974–76
Callaghan (Lab)	1976–79
Thatcher (Con)	1979–

Canada

Mackenzie King (Lib)	1935–48
St Laurent (Lib)	1948–57
Diefenbaker (PC)	1957–63
Pearson (Lib)	1963–68
Trudeau (Lib)	1968–79
Clark (PC)	1979–80
Trudeau (Lib)	1980–84
Turner (Lib)	1984–

New Zealand

Fraser (Lab)	1941–49
Holland (Nat)	1949–57
Holyoake (Nat)	1957
Nash (Lab)	1957–60
Holyoake (Nat)	1960–72
Marshall (Nat)	1972
Kirk (Lab)	1972–74
Rowling (Lab)	1974–75
Muldoon (Nat)	1975–

Australia

Chifley (Lab)	1945–49
Menzies (Lib)	1949–66
Holt (Lib)	1966–67
McEwen (CP)	1967–68
Gorton (Lib)	1968–71
McMahon (Lib)	1971–72
Whitlam (Lab)	1972–75
Fraser (Lib)	1975–83
Hawke (Lab)	1983–

Select bibliography

Aitken, Judith (1980) 'Women in New Zealand Politics' in Penniman (1980)

Aitkin, Don (1982) *Stability and Change in Australian Politics* 2nd edn, Canberra: Australian National University Press

Alderman, R.K. (1976) 'The Prime Minister and the Appointment of Ministers: An Exercise in Political Bargaining' *Parliamentary Affairs* 29, pp. 101–34

Alley, Roderic M. (1978) 'Parliamentary Parties in Office: Government-Backbench Relations' in Levine (1978)

Attlee, C.A. (1954) *As It Happened* London: Heinemann

Bailey, Peter (1974) The department of Prime Minister and Cabinet: an inevitable case of schizophrenia, seminar paper, Australian National University

Barnett, Joel (1982) *Inside the Treasury* London: Andre Deutsch

Bassett, Michael (1976) *The Third Labour Government: a personal history* Auckland: Dunmore Press

Beed, Terence W. (1977) 'Opinion Polling and the Elections' in Pennniman (1977)

Beer, Samuel (1983) *Britain against itself: The Political Contradictions of Collectivism* London: Faber & Faber

Benn, Tony (1981) *Arguments for Democracy* London: Cape

Berrill, Sir Kenneth (1980) *Strength at the Centre: The Case for a Prime Minister's Department* London: University of London

Blondel, Jean (1982) *The Organization of Governments: A Comparative Analysis of Governmental Structures* London: Sage

Borins, Sandford F. (1982) 'Ottawa's Expenditure "Envelopes": Workable Rationality at last?' in Doern (1982)

Boston, Jonathan (1980) High Level Advisory Groups in Central Government, MA thesis, University of Canterbury

—— (1980a) 'High Level Advisory Groups: The case of the Priorities Review Staff' in Weller and Jaensch (1980)

Boyle, Edward and Crosland, Anthony (1971) *The Politics of Education* Harmondsworth: Penguin

Brittan, Samuel (1977) *The Economic Consequences of Democracy* London: Temple Smith

Brown, A.H. (1969) 'Prime Ministerial Power' *Public Law* 1, pp. 28–51; 2, pp. 96–118

Brown, George (1971) *In My Way, Memoirs* London: Gollancz

Burch, Martin (1983) 'Mrs Thatcher's Approach to Leadership in Government: 1979–June 1983' *Parliamentary Affairs* 36, 3, pp. 399–416

Burns, J.F. (1978) *Leadership* New York: Harper Colophon Books

Butler, David (1973) *The Canberra Model: Essays on Australian Government* Melbourne: Cheshire

Butt, Ronald (1969) *The Power of Parliament* London: Constable

Cabinet Handbook (1983) *Cabinet Handbook* Canberra: AGPS

Campbell, Colin (1980) 'Political Leadership in Canada: Pierre Elliott Trudeau and the Ottawa Model' in Rose and Suleiman (1980)

Campbell, Colin and Szablowski, George (1979) *The Superbureaucrats: Structure and behaviour in central agencies* Toronto: Macmillan

Carlton, David (1981) *Anthony Eden: A Biography* London: Allen Lane

Caro, Robert (1983) *Lyndon Johnson: The Path to Power* London: Collins

Castle, Barbara (1980) *The Castle Diaries, 1974–76* London: Weidenfeld & Nicolson

Chapman, George (1980) *The Years of Lightning* Wellington: Reed

Clarkson, Stephen (1979) 'Democracy in the Liberal Party' in Thorburn (1979)

—— (1981) 'The Defeat of the Government, the Decline of the Liberal Party, and the (Temporary) Fall of Pierre Trudeau' in Penniman (1981)

Cleveland, Les (1980) 'The Mass Media' in Penniman (1980)

Coaldrake, Peter (1980) 'Party and Government Dominance of Parliament in Queensland' in Weller and Jaensch (1980)

Cosgrove, Patrick (1979) *Margaret Thatcher, Prime Minister* London: Arrow

Courtney, J.C. (1973) *The Selection of National Party Leaders in Canada* Toronto: Macmillan

Crewe, Ivor (1981) 'Why the Conservatives Won' in Penniman (1981a)

Crisp, L.F. (1955) *The Australian Federal Labour Party, 1901–1951* Melbourne: Longmans

—— (1961) *Ben Chifley: A Biography* Melbourne: Longmans

Crossman, R.H.S. (1963) Introduction to Walter Bagehot *The English Constitution* (first printed 1867) London: Fontana

—— (1972) *Inside View: Three Lectures on Prime Ministerial Government* London: Cape

—— (1975, 1976, 1977) *The Diaries of a Cabinet Minister* 3 volumes, London: Hamilton & Cape

Daalder, Hans (1964) *Cabinet Reform in Britain, 1914–1963* Stanford: Stanford University Press

D'Aquino, T. (1974) 'The Prime Minister's Office, Catalyst or Cabal: Aspects of the development of the Office in Canada and some thoughts about its future' *Canadian Public Administration* 17, 1, pp. 55–84

Dell, Edmund (1980) 'Collective Responsibility: Fact, Fiction or Facade?' in *Policy and Practice: the experience of government* London: RIPA

Diefenbaker, John (1977) *One Canada: The Tumultuous Years, 1962–1967* Scarborough: Signet

Doern, G. Bruce (1979) '*The Cabinet and Central Agencies*' in Doern and Aucoin (1979)

—— ed. (1982) *How Ottawa Spends Your Tax Dollars: National Policy and Economic Development* Toronto: Lorimer

Doern,G. Bruce and Aucoin, Peter eds (1971) *The Structure of Policy-Making in Canada* Toronto: Macmillan
—— and —— eds (1979) *Public Policy in Canada* Toronto: Macmillan
Donoghue, Bernard and Jones, G.W. (1973) *Herbert Morrison: A Portrait of a Politician* London: Weidenfeld & Nicolson
Eagles, Jim and James, Colin (1973) *The Making of a New Zealand Prime Minister* Wellington: Cheshire
Edwards, P.G. (1982) *Prime Ministers and Diplomats: The Making of Australian Foreign Policy, 1901–1949* Melbourne: Oxford University Press
Egremont, Lord (1968) *Wyndham and Children First* London: Macmillan
Engelmann, F.C. and Schwartz, M.A. (1976) *Canadian Political Parties: Origin, Character, Impact* Toronto: Prentice-Hall
Epstein, Leon D. (1967) *Political Parties in Western Democracies* New York: Praeger
Evans, Harold (1981) *Downing Street Diary: The Macmillan years, 1957–1963* London: Hodder & Stoughton
Finer, S.E. (1980) *The Changing British Party System, 1945–1979* Washington: American Enterprise Institute
Fletcher, Frederick J. (1977) 'The Prime Minister as Public Persuader' in Hockin (1977)
—— (1981) 'Playing the Game: The Mass Media and the 1979 Campaign' in Penniman (1981)
French, Richard (1979) 'The Privy Council Office: Support for Cabinet decision making' in Schultz *et al.* (1979)
—— (1980) *How Ottawa decides: Planning & Industrial Policy 1968–1980* Toronto: Lorimer
Freudenberg, Graham (1977) *A Certain Grandeur: Gough Whitlam in Politics* Sydney: Macmillan
Fry, Greg (1983) 'Succession of Government in the Post-Colonial States of the South Pacific: New Support for Constitutionalism?' *Politics* 18, 1, pp. 48–60
Goot, Murray and Beed, Terence W. (1979) 'The Polls, the Public, and the Re-election of the Fraser Government' in Penniman (1979)
Gordon Walker, Patrick (1972) *The Cabinet* London: Cape
Gilmour, Ian (1969) *The Body Politic* London: Radius/Hutchinson
Haines, Joe (1977) *The Politics of Power* London: Cape
Harries, Owen (1968) 'Menzies and the Suez Crisis' *Politics* 3, 2, pp. 193–204
—— (1977) 'Australia's Foreign Policy and the Elections of 1972 and 1975' in Penniman (1977)
Harris, Kenneth (1982) *Attlee* London: Weidenfeld & Nicolson
Harris, Robert (1983) *Gotcha: The Media, The Government and the Falklands Crisis* London: Faber & Faber
Hasluck, Paul (1952) *The Government and the People, 1939–1941* Canberra: Australian War Memorial
—— (1980) *Sir Robert Menzies* Melbourne: Melbourne University Press
Hawker, Geoffrey Smith, R.F.I. and Weller, Patrick (1979)*Politics and Policy in Australia* St Lucia: University of Queensland Press

Haupt, Robert with Grattan, Michelle (1983) *31 Days to Power: Hawke's Victory* Sydney: Allen & Unwin

Headey, Bruce (1974) *British Cabinet Ministers: The Roles of Politicians in Executive Office* London: Allen & Unwin

Heclo, Hugh and Wildavsky, Aaron (1974) *The Private Government of Public Money: Community and Policy inside British Politics* London: Macmillan

Herman, Valentine and Alt, James E. eds (1975) *Cabinet Studies: A Reader* London: Macmillan

Hockin, Thomas A. ed. (1971) *Apex of Power: The Prime Minister and Political Leadership in Canada* Scarborough: Prentice-Hall

—— ed. (1977) *Apex of Power: The Prime Minister and Political Leadership in Canada* 2nd edn, Scarborough: Prentice-Hall

Hodgetts, J.E. (1973) *The Canadian Public Service: A Physiology of Government, 1867–1970* Toronto: University of Toronto Press

Horne, Donald (1980) *Time of Hope: Australia 1966–72* Sydney: Angus & Robertson

Hoskyns, Sir John (1983) 'Whitehall & Westminster: An Outsider's View' *Parliamentary Affairs* 36, 2, (Spring) pp. 137–47

Hughes, Colin A. (1977) *A Handbook of Australian Government and Politics, 1965–1974* Canberra: Australian University Press

—— (1981) *1977–81 Supplement to A Handbook of Australian Government and Politics, 1965–1974* Canberra: Working Papers in Political Science

Hurd, Douglas (1979) *An End to Promises: Sketch of a Government 1970–74* London: Collins

Jackson, Keith (1973) *New Zealand: Politics of Change* Wellington: Reed

—— (1978) 'Government Succession in New Zealand' in Levine (1978)

—— (1978a) 'Cabinet and the Prime Minister' in Levine (1978)

—— (1978b) 'Political Leadership and Succession in the National Party' in Levine (1978)

—— (1980) 'Candidate Selection and the 1978 General Election' in Penniman (1980)

Jackson, Robert J. and Atkinson, Michael M. (1980) *The Canadian Legislative System* 2nd rev. edn, Toronto: Macmillan

Jenkins, Robert (1980) *Tony Benn: A Political Biography* London: Writers and Readers Publishing Cooperative

Jones, G.W. (1969) 'The prime minister's power' reprinted in King (1969)

—— (1973) 'The prime minister's advisers' *Political Studies* 21, 3, pp. 365–75

—— (1975) 'Development of the Cabinet' in Thornhill (1975)

—— (1976) 'The prime minister's secretaries' in J.A.G. Griffith (ed) *From Policy to Administration* London: Allen & Unwin

—— (1978) 'The prime minister's men' *New Society* (19 January) pp. 121–3

—— (1979) 'The prime minister's aides', *Hull Papers in Politics* 6

—— (1981) Review of Rose and Suleiman (1980) *Public Administration* 57, 2, pp. 219–20

—— (1983) 'Prime Ministers' Departments Really Create Problems: A Rejoinder to Patrick Weller' *Public Administration* 61, 1, pp. 79–84

Jordan, Grant (1978) 'Central Co-ordination, Crossman and the Inner

Cabinet' *Political Quarterly* 49, pp. 171–80

Kaufman, G. (1980) *How to be a Minister* London: Sidgwick & Jackson

Kavanagh, Dennis ed. (1982) *The Politics of the Labour Party* London: Allen & Unwin

—— (1982a) 'Representation in the Labour Party' in Kavanagh (1982)

Kellner, Peter and Crowther-Hunt, Lord (1980) *The Civil Servants: An Inquiry into Britain's Ruling Class* London: Macdonald

Kellner, Peter and Hutchens, Christopher (1976) *Callaghan: The Road to Number Ten* London: Cassell

Kelly, Paul (1976) *The Unmaking of Gough* Sydney: Angus & Robertson

Kemp, D.A. (1983) 'PM's private office supports "political" role' *Monash Reporter* 6 (August)

King, Anthony ed. (1969) *The British Prime Minister: A Reader* London: Macmillan

—— (1975) 'Executives' in Polsby and Greenstein (1975)

—— (1979) 'The Rise of the Career Politician in Britain—and its Consequences' *British Journal of Political Science* 11, 3, pp. 249–85

Lalonde, Marc (1971) 'The Changing Role of the Prime Minister's Office' *Canadian Public Administration* 14, 4, pp. 509–37

Levine, Stephen ed. (1975) *New Zealand Politics: A Reader* Melbourne: Cheshire

—— ed. (1978) *Politics in New Zealand* Sydney: Allen & Unwin Australia

—— (1980) 'New Zealand's Political System' in Penniman (1980)

Little, G. (1982) 'Fraser and Fraserism' *Meanjin* 41, 3, pp. 291–307

—— (1983) 'Hawke in Place: Evaluating Narcissism' *Meanjin* 42, 4, pp. 431–44

Lovink, J.A.A. (1979) 'Is Canadian Politics Too Competitive?' in Schultz *et al.* (1979)

McKenzie, Robert (1963) *British Political Parties* 2nd rev. edn, London: Mercury

—— (1982) 'Power in the Labour Party: the Issue of "Intra-Party Democracy"' in Kavanagh (1982)

Mackie, Thomas T. and Hogwood, Brian.W. (1983) *Cabinet Committees in Executive Decision-Making: a Comparative Perspective* Studies in Public Policy III, Centre for Study of Public Policy, University of Strathclyde

Mackintosh, John P. (1962) *The British Cabinet* London: Stevens

—— (1968) *The British Cabinet* 2nd edn, London: Stevens

—— (1974) *The Government and Politics of Britain*, 3rd rev. edn, London: Hutchinson

—— (1977) *The British Cabinet*: 3rd edn, London: Stevens

—— ed. (1977a) *British Prime Ministers in the Twentieth Century* London: Weidenfeld & Nicolson

Mallory, J.R. (1971) *The Structure of Canadian government* Toronto: Macmillan

—— (1977) 'The two clerks: parliamentary discussion of the role of the Privy Council Office' *Canadian Journal of Political Science* 10, 1

Margach, James (1979) *The Abuse of Power: the War between Downing Street and the Media from Lloyd George to James Callaghan* London: Star

—— (1981) *The Anatomy of Power: An Enquiry into the Personality of Leadership* London: Star

Marsh, Richard (1978) *Off the Rails: An Autobiography* London: Weidenfeld & Nicolson

Matheson, W.A. (1976) *The Prime Minister and Cabinet* Toronto: Methuen

Mediansky, F.A. and Nockels, J.A. (1975) 'The Prime Minister's Bureaucracy' *Public Administration* 34, 3, pp. 202–17

—— (1981) 'Mr Fraser's Bureaucracy' *Australian Quarterly* 53, 4, pp. 394–418

Meisel, John (1981) 'The Larger Context: The Period Preceding the 1979 Election' in Penniman (1981)

Mitchell, Austin (1966) *Government by Party: Parliament and Politics in New Zealand* Christchurch: Whitcombe & Tombs

—— (1969) *Politics and People in New Zealand* Christchurch: Whitcombe & Tombs

Morrison, Herbert (1964) *Government and Parliament* 3rd edn, London: Oxford University Press

Muldoon, Robert (1977) *Muldoon* Wellington: Reed

—— (1981) *My Way* Wellington: Reed

Neustadt, Richard E. (1970) *Presidential Power: The Politics of Leadership with Reflections on Johnson and Nixon* New York: John Wiley

Newman, Peter C. (1973) *Renegade in Power: The Diefenbaker Years* Toronto: McClelland & Stewart

Norton, Philip (1978) *Conservative Dissidents: Dissent within the Parliamentary Conservative Party, 1970–74* London: Temple Smith

—— (1981) *The Commons in Perspective* Oxford: Martin Robertson

Norton, Philip and Aughey, Arthur (1981) *Conservatives and Conservatism* London: Temple Smith

Oakes, Laurie (1973) *Whitlam PM* Sydney: Angus & Robertson

PCO (1979) *Submission to the Royal Commission on financial management and accountability* Ottawa, Ministry of Supply and Services

PMC (1979, 1980, 1981, 1982) *Annual Reports of the Department of Prime Minister and Cabinet* Canberra: AGPS

Palmer, Geoffrey (1979) *Unbridled Power? An Interpretation of New Zealand's Constitution and Government* Wellington: Oxford University Press

Parkinson, C.N. (1957) *Parkinson' Law* Harmondsworth: Penguin

Pearson, Lester (1975) *Mike: The Memoirs of the Right Honourable Lester B. Pearson, Volume 3, 1957–68* Toronto: University of Toronto Press

—— (1977)—'Canadian Prime Ministers Discuss the Office' in Hockin (1977)

Penniman, Howard R. ed. (1977) *Australia at the Polls: The National Elections of 1975* Washington: American Enterprise Institute

—— ed. (1979) *The Australian National Elections of 1977* Washington: American Enterprise Institute

—— ed. (1980) *New Zealand at the Polls: The General Election of 1978* Washington: American Enterprise Institute

—— ed. (1981) *Canada at the Polls 1979 and 1980: A Study of the General Elections* Washington: American Enterprise Institute

—— ed. (1981a) *Britain at the Polls 1979: A Study of the General Election*

Washington: American Enterprise Institute

—— ed. (1984) *The Australian National Elections of 1980 and 1983* Sydney & Washington: Allen & Unwin Australia and American Enterprise institute

Perlin, George C. (1980) *The Tory Syndrome: Leadership Politics in the Progressive Conservative Party* Montreal: McGill-Queens University Press

Pickersgill, J.W. (1975) *My Years with Louis St. Laurent* Toronto: University of Toronto Press

Pliatsky, Leo (1982) *Getting and Spending: Public Expenditure, Employment and Inflation* Oxford: Basil Blackwell

Plowden, William (1981) 'The British Central Policy Review Staff' in P. Baehr & B. Wittrock (eds) *Policy Analysis and Policy Innovation* London: Sage

Pollitt, C. (1974) 'The Central Policy Review Staff; 1970–74' *Public Administration* 52, pp. 375–92

Polsby, N. and Greenstein, F. eds (1975) *A Handbook of Political Science* vol. 5, Reading, Mass.: Addison Wesley

Porter, John (1956) *The Vertical Mosaic: An Analysis of Social Class and Power in Canada* Toronto: University of Toronto Press

Punnett, R.M. (1977) *The Prime Minister in Canadian Government and Politics* Toronto: Macmillan

Radwanski, George (1978) *Trudeau* Toronto: Signet

Reid, Alan (1969) *The Power Struggle* Sydney: Shakespeare Head

—— (1971) *The Gorton Experiment* Sydney: Shakespeare Head

—— (1976) *The Whitlam Venture* Melbourne: Hill of Content

Riddell, Peter (1983) *The Thatcher Government* Oxford: Martin Robertson

Ridley, F.F. (1975) *The Study of Government: Political Science and Public Administration* London: Allen & Unwin

Roberts, John and Aitken, Judith (1980) The role and influence of Cabinet Committees in the New Zealand Political Executive Process, paper presented to the New Zealand Political Studies Conference

Roberts, Nigel (1980) 'The Outcome' in Penniman (1980)

Robertson, Gordon (1971) 'The changing role of the Privy Council Office *Canadian Public Administration* 14, 4, pp. 487–508

Robertson, John (1974) *J.H. Scullin: A Political Biography* Nedlands: University of Western Australia Press

Rose Richard (1974) *The Problem of Party Government* London: Macmillan

—— (1980) 'British Government: The Job at the Top' in Rose and Suleiman (1980)

—— (1980a) 'Government against Sub-Governments: A European Perspective on Washington' in Rose and Suleiman (1980)

—— (1983) 'Still the Era of Party Government' *Parliamentary Affairs* 36, 3, pp. 282–99

Rose, Richard and Suleiman, Ezra eds. (1980) *Presidents and Prime Ministers* Washington: American Enterprise Institute

Ross, Lloyd (1977) *John Curtin: A Biography* Sydney: Macmillan

Sampson, Anthony (1967) *Macmillan: A Study in Ambiguity* London: Allen Lane

Sawer, Marian (1983) 'From the Ethical to the Minimal State: State Ideology in Australia' *Politics* 18, 1, pp. 26–53

Schindeler, Fred (1977) 'The Prime Minister and Cabinet: History and Development' in Hockin (1977)

Schneider, Russell (1980) *War without blood: Malcolm Fraser in power* Sydney: Angus & Robertson

Schultz, Richard, Kruhlak, Orest M. and Terry, John eds. (1979) *The Canadian Political Process* 3rd edn, Toronto: Holt Rhinehart & Winston

Sedgemore, Brian (1980) *The Secret Constitution: An Analysis of the Political Establishment* London: Hodder & Stoughton

Seldon, A. (1981) *Churchill's Indian Summer: The Conservative Government, 1951–55* London, Hodder and Stoughton

Sexton, Michael (1979) *Illusions of power: The fate of a reform government* Sydney: Allen & Unwin

Seymour-Ure, Colin (1982) 'Rumour and Politics' *Politics* 17, 2, pp. 1–9

Sharp, Mitchell (1977) 'Decision-Making in the Federal Cabinet' in Hockin (1977)

Sharpe, L.J. (1982) 'The Labour Party and the Geography of Inequality: A Puzzle' in Kavanagh (1982)

Sinclair, Keith (1976) *Walter Nash* Auckland: Oxford University Press

Smiley, D.V. (1980) *Canada in Question: Federalism in the Eighties* 3rd edn, Toronto: McGraw-Hill Ryerson

Smith, Denis (1977) 'President and Parliament: The Transformation of Parliamentary Government in Canada' in Hockin (1977)

Solomon, David (1978) *Inside the Australian Parliament* Sydney: Allen & Unwin

Stephenson, Hugh (1980) *Mrs Thatcher's First Year* London: Jill Norman

Stewart, John B. (1977) *The Canadian House of Commons: Procedure and Reform* Montreal: McGill-Queens University Press

Summers, Anne (1983) *Gamble for Power* Melbourne: Nelson

Talboys, Brian (1970) 'The Cabinet Committee System' *The New Zealand Journal of Public Administration* 33, 1, pp. 1–7

Thorburn, Hugh ed. (1979) *Party Politics in Canada* 4th edn, Scarborough: Prentice-Hall

Thordarson, Bruce (1972) *Trudeau and Foreign Policy: A Study in Decision-Making* Toronto: Oxford University Press

Thornhill, W. ed. (1975) *The Modernization of British Government* London: Pitman

Troyer, Warner (1980) *200 Days: Joe Clark in Power* Toronto: Personal Library

Trudeau, Pierre (1977) 'The Prime Minister's Relations with Policy-making Institutions and with his Party' in Hockin (1977)

Van Loon, Richard J. and Whittington, Michael S. (1976) *The Canadian Political System: Environment, Structure and Process* 2nd edn, Toronto: McGraw-Hill Ryerson

Van Thal, Herbert ed. (1974) *The Prime Ministers: From Sir Robert Walpole to Edward Heath* London: Allen & Unwin

Walter, James (1980) *The Leader: a political biography of Gough Whitlam* St

Lucia: University of Queensland Press

Waring, Marilyn (1978) 'Power and the New Zealand MP: Selected Myths About Parliamentary Democracy' in Levine (1978)

Wearing, Joseph (1977) 'President or Prime Minister' in Hockin (1977)

—— (1981) *The L-Shaped Party: The Liberal Party of Canada 1958–1980* Toronto: McGraw-Hill Ryerson

Weller, Patrick ed. (1975) *Caucus Minutes: Minutes of the Meetings of the Federal Parliamentary Labor Party 1901–1949* 3 vols, Melbourne: Melbourne University Press

—— (1980) 'Inner Cabinets and Outer Ministers: Lessons from Australia and Britain' *Canadian Public Administration* 23, 4, pp. 598–615

—— (1983) 'Do Prime Ministers' Departments Really Create Problems?' *Public Administration* 61, 1, pp. 59–78

—— (1983a) 'The Vulnerability of Prime Ministers: A Comparative Perspective' *Parliamentary Affairs* 36, 1, pp. 96–117

—— (1983b) 'Transition: Taking over Power 1983' *Australian Journal of Public Administration* 42, 3, pp. 303–19

—— (1984) 'The Anatomy of a Grievous Miscalculation: 3 February 1983' in Penniman (1984)

Weller, Patrick and Cutt, James (1976) *Treasury Control in Australia: A Study in Bureaucratic Politics* Sydney: Novak

Weller, Patrick and Grattan, Michelle (1981) *Can Ministers Cope? Australian Federal Ministers at Work* Melbourne: Hutchinson

Weller, Patrick and Jaensch, Dean eds (1980) *Responsible Government in Australia* Melbourne: Drummond

Whitaker, Reginald (1977) *The Government Party: Organizing and Financing the Liberal Party of Canada 1930–58* Toronto: University of Toronto Press

Williams, Phillip M. (1979) *Hugh Gaitskell, A Political Biography* London: Cape

Wilson Harold (1971) *The Labour Government 1964–70* London: Weidenfeld & Nicolson

—— (1976) *The Governance of Britain* London: Sphere

Winham, Gilbert R. and Cunningham, Robert B. (1977) 'Party Leader Images in the 1968 Federal Election' in Hockin (1977)

Wright, Gerald C.V. (1976) 'Mackenzie King: Power over the Political Executive' in Hockin (1977)

Yeend, G.J. (1979) 'The department of Prime Minister and Cabinet in perspective' *Australian Journal of Public Administration* 38, 2, pp. 133–50

Zavos, Spiro (1978) *The Real Muldoon* Wellington: Fourth Estate Books

Index